Struggle for the Street

Struggle for the Street

Social Networks and the Struggle for Civil Rights in Pittsburgh

Jessica D. Klanderud

The University of North Carolina Press CHAPEL HILL

Library of Congress Cataloging-in-Publication Data
Names: Klanderud, Jessica D., author.
Title: Struggle for the street : social networks and the struggle for civil rights
    in Pittsburgh / Jessica D. Klanderud.
Other titles: Justice, power, and politics.
Description: Chapel Hill : The University of North Carolina Press, [2023] |
    Series: Justice, power, and politics | Includes bibliographical references
    and index.
Identifiers: LCCN 2022036484 | ISBN 9781469673714 (cloth ; alk. paper) |
    ISBN 9781469673721 (paperback ; alk. paper) | ISBN 9781469673738 (ebook)
Subjects: LCSH: African American neighborhoods—Pennsylvania—Pittsburgh—History—
    20th century. | African Americans—Pennsylvania—Pittsburgh—History—20th century. |
    African Americans—Civil rights—Pennsylvania—Pittsburgh—History—20th century. |
    Civil rights movements—Pennsylvania—Pittsburgh—History—20th century. |
    Pittsburgh (Pa.)—Social conditions—20th century. | Hill District (Pittsburgh, Pa.)—
    History—20th century.
Classification: LCC F159.P69 B53 2023 | DDC 974.8/8600496073—dc23/eng/20220805
LC record available at https://lccn.loc.gov/2022036484

Cover photograph: Charles "Teenie" Harris (American, 1908–1998), *Women, Men, and Children,
Some Holding Signs Reading "Andy Jackson Need Not Have Died" and "Detour, Speedway Closed for
Lack of Lights and Police Protection," Blocking Bread Truck on Webster Avenue, Hill District* (August
1951, Kodak safety film, 4" x 5"), Carnegie Museum of Art, Pittsburgh, Heinz Family Fund,
© 2021 Carnegie Museum of Art, Charles "Teenie" Harris Archive.

Contents

List of Illustrations and Maps vii

Introduction 1

CHAPTER ONE
Wylie Avenue 20
Crossroads of the World, Hill District, 1918–1930

CHAPTER TWO
Bedford Avenue 38
Street Reformers and Social Mothering, 1917–1940

CHAPTER THREE
Deep Wylie 57
The Struggle for Working-Class Social World, 1930–1950

CHAPTER FOUR
Webster Avenue 76
Blight, Renewal, or Negro Removal, 1945–1960

CHAPTER FIVE
Dinwiddie Street 106
Street Capitalists and Policing of the Hill, 1950–1960

CHAPTER SIX
Centre Avenue 128
*Freedom Corner and the Modern Black Freedom Movement,
1945–1968*

CHAPTER SEVEN
Crawford Street 148
*Street Democracy, Violence, and Retreat from the Streets,
1965–1970*

Epilogue 176
Whose Streets? Our Streets!

Acknowledgments 185
Notes 187
Index 215

Illustrations and Maps

ILLUSTRATIONS

1.1 Men and women gathered at Lovuola's Farm for Junior Mothers night picnic during FROGS week, July 1959 28

3.1 Dolores Stanton and Eleanor Hughes Griffin standing in front of George Harris's confectionery store, July 1937 62

4.1 Soldiers from 372nd Infantry marching in parade, July 1942 79

5.1 Funeral procession for Leon "Pigmeat" Clark, April 19, 1950 107

6.1 Women protesting outside of Woolworth's, 1960 130

6.2 Protest march with women and men holding signs for equal rights and CORE, c. 1960–1968 137

6.3 Men and women boarding the 85 Bedford trolley, October 1946 144

7.1 Police officers in riot gear pursuing individuals in crowd near Perry High School, 1968 159

MAPS

1.1 Location of the Hill District in Pittsburgh 2

1.1 Upper and Lower Hill District in Pittsburgh 24

3.1 Prostitution locations in the Lower Hill District before urban renewal 73

4.1 Streets of the Lower Hill District, before the Civic Arena 87

4.2 Highest concentration of Black neighborhood population in Pittsburgh 89

4.3 Streets of the Lower Hill District, after the Civic Arena 93

5.1 Prostitution shift in the Hill District following urban renewal 122

5.2 5th Avenue High School and Dinwiddie Street 124

Struggle for the Street

Introduction

The streets of the Hill District of Pittsburgh, Pennsylvania, and other neighborhoods where African Americans lived and worked were not fixed lines of geography that divided the residents of the city, white from Black. Instead, they formed the arteries that moved goods, people, and importantly, ideas in and out of the neighborhood. Street spaces within the Hill District allowed residents to create Black-controlled public spaces to build and work through their political, economic, cultural, and gendered ideas of proper usage and to push back against the forces that created ghettos and instead allowed them to create a neighborhood. African Americans faced particular problems accessing the avenues of formal power within the structure of northern American cities. Still, they formed their own social networks of information and ideas in segregated neighborhoods as they created their own city within the larger urban space. The streets provided a public space for the formation and transmission of ideas throughout the African American community of Pittsburgh. These streets were sites of struggle and cultural development. It was through those struggles and across class lines that African Americans in Pittsburgh formed a neighborhood and a movement. August Wilson opens his Pulitzer prizewinning play, *Fences*, with a description of the migration of "the destitute of Europe" who "sprang on the city with tenacious claws and an honest and solid dream." Such a newcomer to the city would be offered a "partnership limited only by his talent, his guile, and his willingness for hard work." Wilson counters this vision of the swelling city with a different vision of the migration of the "decedents of African slaves [who] were offered no such welcome or participation." Instead, those who came from Georgia, Alabama, the Carolinas, and the Virginias "settled along the riverbanks and under bridges in shallow, ramshackle houses made of sticks and tar paper. They collected rags and wood. They sold the use of their muscles and their bodies. They cleaned houses and washed clothes, they shined shoes, and in quiet desperation and vengeful pride, they stole, and lived in pursuit of their own dream. That they could breathe free, finally, and stand to meet life with the force of dignity and whatever eloquence the heart could call upon."[1] They built a neighborhood and a home carved out of the hills that rose from the convergence of the Monongahela and Allegheny Rivers as

1

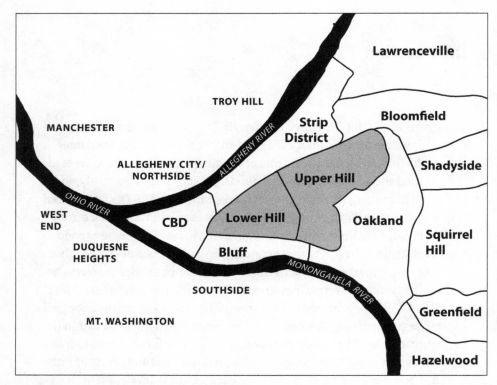

MAP 1.1 Location of the Hill District in Pittsburgh, Pennsylvania.
Jason Klanderud, Altair Media Design, Designer.

they form the mouth of the mighty Ohio River. The Hill District formed on a section of farmland uphill from the point of the rivers but became a neighborhood where newcomers to the city could find affordable rental housing. This space was not originally desirable land. It was waste space on the edge of the city.[2] In map 1.1, you can see the location of the Hill District, between the rivers and wedged between the industrial space of what would become the downtown business district and the residential space reserved for white middle managers and owners. The space of the Hill District, which was both urban and not yet incorporated into the fabric of the developing city, was the home of the "waste people," those who had potential but whose potential came from their ability to work and the sweat of their bodies rather than ties to old families or more importantly, old money.

European immigrants first made the Hill District their home. They were outsiders from foreign nations engaged in the process of *becoming* white. In the early twentieth century, these immigrants soon gained access to the higher-paying jobs of the steel industry and moved into other neighborhoods like Lawrenceville and Bloomfield. As immigrant residents gained access to other areas of the city, early African American Pittsburghers developed a small residential foothold in the eastern section of the city. Work drew African Americans to Pittsburgh from the coal-rich mountains of Appalachia to work in the steel industry. In the early twentieth century, many African Americans participated as strikebreakers in the labor conflicts between workers and industrialists. Although African American steel workers often entered the workforce as strikebreakers, they also worked to form African American steelworkers' unions. The Hill District contained Pittsburgh's relatively small African American population through World War I. During the Great Migration, incoming African American migrants flooded into the Hill District as one of the few African American residential neighborhoods available for them to make a home.

The home they created was formed from the social interactions on the streets of their neighborhood. In urban neighborhoods where African Americans lived and worked, the streets formed the arteries that moved goods and people in and out. The streets were not simply a feature of geography. Street spaces within African American neighborhoods allowed the residents of those neighborhoods Black-controlled public spaces to build their political, economic, cultural, and gendered ideas of equality through the creation of social networks. Street spaces connected disparate African American neighborhoods and provided a public space for forming and transmitting ideas throughout the African American community. These streets were sites of struggle and cultural development. Through those struggles, African Americans in Pittsburgh formed a contested public space where they could define their own freedom.

Though many historians of the African American urban experience have studied the role of space in African American urban history, *Struggle for the Street* argues that within their communities, African Americans used the street in class and culturally specific ways to create and define social networks. Moreover, these struggles over the street transformed African American views on equality in Pittsburgh from 1918–70. Intraracial negotiations occurred over the meaning of the street as a space for cultural development. Consequently, perceived rules for using street spaces changed over time in gendered and class sensitive ways. African Americans in Pittsburgh used the street as a public space, where street culture was formed out of a social struggle between all social networks of African Americans and within the context of regional and local regulations as well as interactions with their white neighbors.

The streets of this study are not boundaries but rather spaces in themselves. Many historians have addressed the ways that streets delineated urban spaces and how urban renewal projects transformed the boundaries of urban and African American neighborhoods in the mid- to late twentieth century. *Struggle for the Street* addresses how African Americans in the twentieth century defined their streets and how those definitions changed over time as well as how the streets functioned as a space for cultural contestation within African American neighborhoods. African Americans also had to share the streets of their neighborhood with the few white residents and residents that were *becoming* white that lived in the neighborhood. In Robin D. G. Kelley's chapter "Congested Terrain: Resistance on Public Transportation" from his essay collection *Race Rebels: Culture, Politics, and the Black Working Class*, he argued that public transportation acted as a "moving theater" where African Americans could contest the public space of public transit. African Americans participated in conflicts on the bus that redefined interracial relations in the city. African Americans used the public transit system as an extension of street spaces as well as a theater to display their discontent with interracial relations within the city. The concept of a theater in two senses, both as a performance space and a field of battle, illustrates how African Americans struggled with other residents of the neighborhood over the creation of social networks and the meanings of public space. Public spaces can be the site of performances designed to illustrate injustice and discrimination and create visions of equality and political activism for those without access to formal networks of power.[3]

Pittsburgh, Pennsylvania offers a unique set of circumstances that make it an ideal location to study how African Americans used street spaces to develop and sustain their own social networks within their neighborhood. Pittsburgh boasts a storied history as an industrial city where immigrants from all over the world met and mingled in the steel mills, railroads, factories, and furnaces of America's industrial engine. Pittsburgh had a small African American population at the turn of the twentieth century, but that population grew alongside the steel industry along with incoming African American migrants from the South in what came to be known as the Great Migration. African American migrants and central and eastern European immigrants often clashed over space and jobs, and many social scientists looked to Pittsburgh to reveal how these contestations would play out as both groups struggled to assimilate to a larger American culture. Pittsburgh's resident African American community developed a closely knit "city within the city," where a small but influential, elite class developed. The center of African

American Pittsburgh developed in a neighborhood called the Hill District. This neighborhood saw the growth of jazz greats like Roy Eldridge and Lena Horne, sports stars like Jackie Robinson and Roberto Clemente, and cultural icons like August Wilson and Charles "Teenie" Harris, who contributed to African American culture throughout the nation.

Additionally, Pittsburgh was the home of one of the country's most influential African American newspapers, the *Pittsburgh Courier*. This newspaper, under the leadership of Robert L. Vann, reported on the highs and lows of African American life in Pittsburgh, the nation, and the world. At its peak, the *Pittsburgh Courier* was at least as widely read as the *Chicago Defender* and the *Baltimore Afro-American*, if not more so. Nationwide circulation allowed African Americans across the United States to read about the lives of African Americans in Pittsburgh, including the society pages and exploits of the African American elite as well as the goings-on of those in the underclass and the denizens of the streets and alleys of African American neighborhoods. The coverage of both elite and working-class visions of African American Pittsburgh allows a unique view of the conflict and consensus among African Americans on the streets of their neighborhoods. Additionally, the pages of the *Pittsburgh Courier* featured many of the photographs taken by Charles "Teenie" Harris of the daily life of African Americans on the streets of Pittsburgh. Harris photographed men, women, youth, and children of all classes in the process of living their lives on the streets of the Hill District. These photographs present an incomparable source to visualize the multifaceted nature of the streets. Pittsburgh offers a unique and rich location to view many of the features of African American urban life present in many of the Rust Belt cities across the urban North and provides an excellent source base to investigate how African Americans use the streets of their neighborhoods as public space.

Pittsburgh, and the Hill District as a neighborhood, make an ideal space to investigate the creation of Black-controlled public space within the boundaries of a neighborhood in transition from primarily immigrant residents in the process of *becoming* white to Black residents navigating cultural shifts through migration. Robin D. G. Kelley argues that public spaces like streets were a "kind of democratic space" for white workers, but for Black people, "white-dominated public space was vigilantly undemocratic and potentially dangerous."[4] The streets of the neighborhood were ethnically mixed but, importantly, not fully white dominated. The immigrant residents of the Hill District were in the process of *becoming* white. Their religious or immigrant status kept them on the margins of cultural whiteness and created a neighborhood that was more in flux than the traditional idea of a ghetto. Contestation within the space of the Hill District could lead to change, at least within the boundaries of their city within a city. These neighborhood streets were theaters in two senses, both sites of performance and in the sense of a military conflict. The streets of the Hill District were essential sites of Black resistance to the dominance of white culture and where the members of the neighborhood created and maintained their own Black-focused public space where they could create a Black-focused vision of equality through the process of resistance and performance. The streets of the Hill District were a site of struggle, a struggle for equality and a struggle for inclusion. Through a shifting performance of respectability within the Hill District, African Americans defined their own spaces where they participated in the everyday conflicts and negotiations that created the conditions for the success of an organized collective movement for the equality of all.

Class plays an important role in *Struggle for the Street*. In the pages that follow, middle-class African Americans will be identified as such by their tendencies to profess upwardly mobile ideals, to express disdain or disaffection with those of lower social status, or to use formal or institutional power to promote their vision for African American social mobility. St. Clair Drake and Horace Cayton discussed these convergences and divergences within the middle class. They defined a number of different subgroups within the middle class. Some members of the middle class affiliated with church organizations while other members eschewed religious organizations.[5] Middle-class African Americans in Pittsburgh showed both characteristics, and this study will flesh out this interpretation of middle-class African American ideals.

While economic mobility is an important aspect of class definitions, it is also important to elucidate the values that permeate class distinctions. Too often scholars equate reform-minded institutions with middle-class values. This is not always the case. African Americans faced economic barriers that other ethnic groups did not face to the same degree. Additionally, some important actions of the middle class coincide with economic exclusivity in the street spaces of African American neighborhoods. These barriers make it possible for African Americans traditionally seen as a part of the working class to be associated with the middle class. To focus on the values behind class designations, this study investigates the shifting strategies of street use implemented by middle-class and working-class organizations and individuals. These differences developed out of social values more than economic status, but the role of economic opportunity played an important role in the manifestation of those values.

Struggle for the Street focuses on the struggles around the creation, maintenance, and shifting expression of social networks on the streets of the Hill District and primarily within the African American working class. Working-class African Americans expressed different ideas of social mobility from their middle-class counterparts, and their connections to each other developed through interactions on the streets of their neighborhood. They focused on social cohesion, often through church affiliation or through work, that reinforced feelings of community. The emphasis on belonging was more important. Maintaining a social network was a survival tool in a dominant culture that limited power. The power of collective belonging was a distinct asset to marginalized communities. Mobility that separated an individual or family from the community was not an advantage. While other scholars discuss the development of an African American working class, and that discussion is relevant and important, *Struggle for the Street* emphasizes the role of legal laborers, those in the traditional working class, as well as those working in quasilegal and illegal industries, in addition to the working (or nonworking) poor. For a population like the African American community, it is critical to address the shifting boundaries between types of labor within a broad definition of working class. These shifting boundaries reveal alliances and tensions within the working classes that labor history otherwise obscures with a strict focus on organized and legal laborers. *Struggle for the Street* expands the definition of the working class by addressing the shifting boundaries between the working class, the working poor, and illegal laborers to reveal how the creation and maintenance of social networks within the African American community included laborers of all kinds in a constructed vision of what equality could mean for *all* African Americans. In his book *Race Rebels*, Kelley includes a footnote that states: "a fine-tuned analysis of the meaning of the street in the everyday lives of black migrants, of the role played by the streets in shaping the contours of community life, of the ways that community institutions were framed by contested meanings of the neighborhood street-scape, and of the ways that the various definitions of respectability were played out daily along neighborhood thoroughfares — such a study would be a tremendous contribution to the literature on black urbanization, community formation, urban politics, and black urban culture."[6] *Struggle for the Street* addresses not only the meaning of the street in the lives of Black migrants, but how the street transforms the neighborhood and the social networks therein. The streets were the place where community formed, where politics happened, where respectability was performed, all were a part of the struggle for the street.

Class divisions within the African American community developed through the processes of migration and industrialization and solidified as the city moved toward deindustrialization. The push and pull factors that caused African Americans to migrate to northern industrial cities came at a social cost. The reasons that someone would choose to migrate often included push factors, such as escaping racial terror and oppressive segregation in the South. Adding to the push out of African Americans, northern cities, and urban areas as a whole, often offered new access to industrial work and developing Black enclaves with opportunity for entrepreneurship and social mobility.[7] While literature on the Great Migration has strongly indicated the presence of chain migration from southern rural areas to southern urban areas, and then to northern and western cities, this movement of African Americans to areas where a family member or social connection already resided does not attend to the social loss associated with the severing of large numbers of social ties in the act of migrating to a new region.[8] The relatively small African American community in Pittsburgh prior to the Great Migration came primarily from Virginia. For these old Pittsburghers, who were already deeply interconnected in social networks, the influx of migrants from Alabama, Georgia, and other areas of the Deep South caused significant social upheaval.[9]

Many of the migrants to Pittsburgh came to the Steel City for work in industrial jobs. This migration swelled the ranks of the working class as Black workers filled positions left vacant by the stagnation of European immigration that industrial employers relied on for their labor force. For the migrants who followed labor recruiters into industrial sector jobs, their migration to the Steel City came from the rural-industrial coal fields in central and southern Appalachia and the seasonal work in southern industry to industrial labor that looked like their previous work but was recently opened to Black labor and offered increased opportunity.[10] In many ways, African American migrants to Pittsburgh were already in the process of developing an identity within the industrial working class. Their social network revolved around other industrial sector laborers and the rhythms of industrial work.

Labor recruiters and the Black press played a critical role in drawing migrants to Pittsburgh, but as Peter Gottlieb suggests, "The welling migration streams were fed by myriad kinship and community networks that channeled individuals and small groups toward specific destinations, northern employers, urban residential districts, and even particular boarding houses and private homes."[11] Migrants passed information on job availability, housing conditions, and racial tensions through their social networks in order to *scout* a potential move. Personal connections were always preferred, but migrants did write to the major Black newspapers, including the *Pittsburgh Courier*, to inquire about conditions in Pittsburgh and other northern destinations. The *Courier* worked to advocate for migrants and support their move to Pittsburgh. This tactic was in opposition to the early stance of the *Chicago Defender*, a rival publication, which attempted to keep migrants in the South.[12]

Migrants maintained their social networks in the South and many had to reform them when they reached Pittsburgh. Peter Gottlieb documents the frequent seasonal migration and migrants' return trips to the South to reconnect with their established social networks maintaining that, "visits down home for some southerners in Pittsburgh became a regular part of the calendar, scheduled to coincide with the Christmas holidays or the lay-by period in cotton cultivation, when rural blacks held church revivals, barbecues, and homecoming celebrations for former residents."[13] The act of reforming social networks following permanent migration involved the presence of social gatekeepers. For new migrants to Pittsburgh, this meant navigating the social world of old Pittsburghers.

In his study of Black migration to Pittsburgh, Gottlieb recounts the development of three social classes within Pittsburgh's Black community. The elite members of the community were "mostly old Pittsburgh families headed by well-educated professional businessmen."[14] Migration transformed these social networks and the class divisions within the Hill District. Membership in the elite was reserved for those within the old Pittsburgh families and who were connected to them through their social networks. The middle class was made up of primarily professional, college-educated African Americans and those who filled the small ranks of skilled labor. Professional organizations relied on mobile college-educated professionals to fill the ranks of their administrative staff and as community-engaged social workers. The Urban League of Pittsburgh (ULP) partnered with the University of Pittsburgh to develop a program to train Black social workers, and these social workers were then suggested to firms who employed large numbers of Black workers to serve as "welfare workers" within industrial employment.[15] This proliferation of college-educated social workers within the ranks of the ULP "allowed the organization to focus on expanding the black professional middle class at a time when few employers hired blacks for white-collar jobs."[16] The working class, on the other hand, was made up primarily of Black workers who were in domestic service, unskilled labor, and other intermittent and informal types of work. As the Great Migration swelled the ranks of the working class and the lower-middle class, the distance between the elite, professional class and the working class of Pittsburgh's African American community grew. Much of this distance stemmed from their lack of any social interaction with each other to a large degree. Elite Black Pittsburghers socialized, married, and went to church primarily with one another.

New African American arrivals to the Steel City also faced additional discrimination based on their ruralness as well as their southernness which set them apart from other skilled and unskilled wage earners as well as from the elite. The lack of available housing outside of the Hill District also pushed migrants into living in the same neighborhoods and streets as those who had more tenuous work. Social organizations like the National Association for the Advancement of Colored People (NAACP) and the ULP tried to meet the needs of incoming migrants but did so from the perspective of the professionalizing middle class. Through the ULP's industrial relations department, the Pittsburgh branch placed primarily Black workers into industrial positions, eventually becoming the home of the state's Department of Labor "Colored Branch" in Pittsburgh. The ULP battled against the common practice of hiring Black men in unskilled positions by focusing efforts on upgrading employment for Black workers, promoting jobs for college-educated Black students, and keeping lists of Black men fit to move into supervisory or clerical positions. Joe William Trotter Jr. argues that "from its inception, and following the lead of the national office, the ULP underscored its commitment to improve the lives of poor and working-class black residents, while simultaneously advancing the interests of educated, middle-class, and elite blacks."[17] Often, the efforts of the ULP to improve the lives of poor and working-class southern migrants displayed a distinct preference for the cultural values of the old Pittsburghers, older-stock African American residents of the Hill District, and other Black neighborhoods. Trotter argues that old Pittsburghers "resented the Urban League for developing programs on behalf of the newcomers."[18] The ULP distributed cards that provided a very particular understanding of appropriate behavior and cultural values to working-class migrants, saying:

1. Get a regular job and work every day.
2. Send for *your family* they need you.
3. Keep your home and person clean. Dirt breeds germs and disease.
4. Send your children to school clean and tidy.
5. Send for a doctor when sick, don't use patent medicines.

6. Join some church, attend regularly.
7. Open a bank account.
8. Don't buy on installment plan.
9. Be quiet on street cars, in the theaters and in crowds *always* appear clean and help *keep down prejudice*.
10. Do this and win the respect of your community and make the community better for Yourself Your Race and Your Country.[19]

Trotter also revealed how the ULP described newcomers as ignorant, irresponsible, and "families of the lower type." Through applied social science, old Pittsburghers emphasized personal responsibility while also targeting single young men as contributing to many of the social ills they saw in Black neighborhoods. Their programming through the housewives' leagues and girls' clubs also encouraged women to *civilize* their men and to cultivate a two-parent nuclear household to help create a more stable workforce. The ULP also promoted specific cultural values often described as middle class, emphasizing fiscal responsibility, cleanliness, and religious participation. Demonstrating fiscal responsibility and religious participation also necessitated connections to the *right* type of fiscal responsibility by patronizing banks rather than playing the numbers and attending the *proper* churches which catered to old Pittsburgh families rather than storefront houses of worship. Social networks were critical in appearing as a fit opportunity for uplift rather than a migrant charity case. Much of the internal conflict within the ULP developed out of a problem assessing which interventions were providing opportunity and which were providing charity to possibly unworthy recipients.

The rapid influx of migrants combined with rigid housing discrimination pushed new migrants into neighborhoods with old Pittsburghers. Gottlieb quoted the *Negro Survey of Pennsylvania*, saying, "We find that the newcomer lives in neighborhoods with the old residents of the city, but there has been very little neighborliness shown the newcomer. . . . He is grouped by himself."[20] Gottlieb continued to quote the survey regarding the attitudes of old Pittsburghers toward new migrants, saying, "This group have [sic] always considered themselves somewhat superior to the 'outlander.'"[21] The tension between old Pittsburghers and the newcomers extended into many areas of life including courtship and marriage, employment, religious expression, family organization, and education.

In emphasizing the social gatekeeping role played by old Pittsburghers through the organization of the ULP, Gottlieb argued, "the goal of acculturating rural blacks to the League's notion of 'efficient' urban life led to attacks on the migrant's own culture. The black professionals insisted that manners and habits of living learned in the South must be dropped before the migrants could become permanent urban dwellers. The League's campaign to reform southern blacks served to protect and maintain the status of Pittsburgh's leading blacks."[22] In this way, old Pittsburghers formed the bedrock of the elite and professional class in Pittsburgh through their access to social networks that they excluded incoming migrants from. Southern Black migrants came for work and opportunity, but they had to build new social networks from within the groups of other southern migrants who predominantly joined the working class through industrial and service work.

As Black Pittsburghers returned from World War II and the Modern Black Freedom Movement began, access to new skilled labor through the Fair Employment Practices Commission (FEPC) along with training through military service grew the professional middle class. Efforts by formal organizations like the ULP and the NAACP made some inroads into areas of fair housing, public accommodations, and upgrading primarily middle-class Black workers into skilled labor positions. As the growth of the Black population of Pittsburgh steadied, the pressures of new migrants being integrated into the social fabric of the neighborhood lessened while the pressure of discrimination against Black residents grew. With the growth of the working-class population, and the middle-class population to a lesser degree, a cross-class alliance developed that mobilized Pittsburgh's Black community into a more coordinated effort to attack racism and Jim Crowism. The Hill District became their city within a city that provided a Black-controlled public space to coordinate efforts against racism and a space where formal and informal social networks could connect Black Pittsburghers across class lines.

In the early decades of the twentieth century, African Americans across classes formed bonds within their neighborhoods. Business, political, and cultural institutions united African Americans within segregated urban spaces, but intraracial tensions persisted. Internal migration of African Americans from the South exacerbated preexisting class tensions within the African American community in Pittsburgh and stretched the racial and spatial bonds within the African American community. Over time, the bond deteriorated as middle-class African Americans made small gains in social and economic mobility. Pittsburgh's African American working class and working poor fought through the changing geography of their streets to forge new uses of street spaces and new social connections that middle-class reformers frowned upon. These uses did not adhere to notions of social propriety but instead allowed for militant and even violent expressions of discontent. This transformation reveals an important schism within the African American community but more importantly sheds light on how African Americans used public spaces to push for class-specific notions of equality.

Sociologists conducted the earliest studies of African Americans in the city. They studied the way African Americans adapted to the urban environment from their rural origins. These studies emphasized differences between rural and urban environments and illuminated the stresses that African Americans experienced in transitioning to an urban geography, but it was not until the mid- to late twentieth century that historians critically investigated space as a factor in African American urban history. In early historical studies of African Americans in the city, geography of the city often appeared as a boundary rather than as a dynamic space, the uses of which changed over time.

Other historians may question the typicality of a city like Pittsburgh, Pennsylvania. Laurence Glasco suggested that African American Pittsburgh suffered from a "double burden" of segregation and geography that differed from other northern Rust Belt cities.[23] These related issues of segregation and geography do not make Pittsburgh's African American community that different from African American communities in other northern cities. While Pittsburgh has many features of natural geography that make travel within the city difficult, African Americans united within their neighborhoods and within the Hill District, which formed a central hub that disparate African Americans returned to for cultural cohesion. Other cites did not have the same features of natural geography but their built environment often presented challenges to African American cohesion.

Pittsburgh had many similarities with other northern industrial cities. Chicago, Cleveland, Detroit, and Philadelphia all had sizable African American populations prior to the Great Migrations from 1918–45. These migrations brought an influx of African Americans from the South into northern industrial cities like Pittsburgh. Chicago, Philadelphia, Detroit, and Cleveland all experienced similar issues with northern-born African Americans struggling with incoming migrants in segregated African American neighborhoods.

Many historians of African American urban history have acknowledged their debt to St. Clair Drake's and Horace Cayton's work *Black Metropolis*. Critics of the ghetto formation model focused on class relationships within the African American community; they did not fully illuminate class tensions within the working class.[24] Intraracial class tensions within the African American community played out in the homes, jobs, churches, and streets of the neighborhood. *Struggle for the Street* illuminates the ways that the middle class, working class, and working poor interacted in the public arena and shows how those relations changed over time. In the arena of the street, African Americans negotiated with one another and with an ethnically and class-diverse wider world. All of these people used, defined, shared, and competed for street space.

An important case study on Chicago, St. Clair Drake's and Horace Cayton's *Black Metropolis*, posited the existence of class divisions within the African American community.[25] In this work, written in the World War II period, class divisions existed in the Black Belt but they attributed these differences to the color line, economic interest, and social status.[26] Drake and Cayton revealed these divisions present in World War II-era Chicago. While Drake and Cayton saw these differences on the streets of African American neighborhoods in Chicago, few scholars addressed questions of class differences within the African American community of Chicago. In recent scholarship on the cities of Chicago and New York, Thomas J. Sugrue discusses the rise of militancy within the African American community and recognized the differing aims of militant African Americans and their various uses of the street. In his book, *Sweet Land of Liberty*, Sugrue reveals the shifting alliances within the northern civil rights movement, but he does not emphasize the internal class divisions within the African American community present on the streets that informed these shifting alliances.[27] Chicago's African American community faced many of the same challenges as African Americans in Pittsburgh and had similar responses to those challenges. Sugrue linked rising militancy concerned primarily with gaining economic justice to grassroots activism. This grassroots activism developed on the streets and within the working class. Addressing shifting class divisions within the African American community helps explain the different trajectories of the northern civil rights movement.

Davarian L. Baldwin addresses the creation of the "New Negro" in Chicago which sprung from a movement born of migration and "mass cultural forces" within the African American community.[28] Baldwin focused his study on what Drake and Cayton termed "The Black Metropolis" or the African American city within the city of Chicago. He suggested that the Black Metropolis represented a "tactical position from which to galvanize strength toward eventual integration" with the larger white city.[29] Interactions between African Americans on the street called "The Stroll" created a dynamic space for social equality and promoted "promising contact within the work-ing class across the color line without the intrusions of the wealthy who en-couraged antagonisms."[30] Baldwin described the "political potential" of The Stroll and as an "important site where many working-class migrants ac-quired alternative sources of labor and created new kinds of leisure and hence their own routes and rites of respectability."[31] Baldwin also noted, "Within this mass consumer space, Chicago's 'New Negroes' self-consciously negotiated, struggled over, and upheld the categories of race, class, gender, nation, and intellect literally, as academics like to say, 'on the ground' in ways that offer lessons for the present."[32] This process occurred on streets like The Stroll and within the bounded spaces of African American neighborhoods. Baldwin's study reveals many similarities between the Black Metropolis in Chicago and African American street life in Pittsburgh, Pennsylvania. The space of The Stroll allowed migrants and established residents to create their own identity. This process occurred in Pittsburgh as well, as African Americans—both migrants and established residents—created their own visions of proper street use and respectability.

Class conflicts developed at the street level within the African American community in many northern industrial cities, including Pittsburgh. Historical studies on racial uplift by Evelyn Brooks Higginbotham, Stephanie Shaw, and others argued ultimately that racial concerns united African Americans and muted class conflict. This focus on semiprofessional and professional women within the African American community illuminated a neglected section of the population and their specific struggles to develop what Shaw called "socially responsible individualism."[33] These scholars suggested that African American women reformers in the long Progressive Era muted class tensions within the African American community through their struggles to forge their own identity. Kevin Gaines also investigated the role behav-ioral theories played on racial uplift ideology. His focus on elite individuals does not allow him to fully investigate the class tensions that he identified in his work. Touré Reed's book, *Not Alms but Opportunity: The Urban League and The Politics of Racial Uplift*, examines the methods of the ULP to "elevate the material conditions" of African Americans of the better class.[34] This book illuminates the class tensions present between African American reformers and their working-class counterparts. *Struggle for the Street* examines the con-flicts present between middle-class and elite African Americans and those of the working classes who supposedly benefited from their solicitude.

Reform-minded organizations like the ULP espoused a mission for racial uplift and worked to provide aid for working-class migrants and to uplift the poor. Like Reed, Joe William Trotter Jr. examines the surprisingly activist history of the ULP in his book *Pittsburgh and the Urban League Movement: A Century of Social Service and Activism*. His study focuses on the Pittsburgh, Pennsylvania branch of the Urban League and its "impact on the lives of poor and working-class blacks as they made their transition from farm to city."[35] Trotter delves deeply into the crux of the historiographical debate surrounding organizational uplift in the urban North by centering his argument on the nature of the Urban League. Was it primarily a conservative organization that rarely improved the lives of the southern migrants it professed to serve? Or was it instead, a predominantly progressive movement that was successful in its aims to address the hardships of migration, labor exploitation, and poor housing conditions in the urban North? In the end, Trotter concludes that the ULP both shaped and was shaped by the forces for Black liberation in the Steel City and that the ULP "increasingly merged social research and professional social work with social justice, civil rights, worker's rights, and black power struggles."[36] Through analyzing the shifting forces surrounding the ULP, Trotter attends to the prevalence of gender and class bias within the organization in ways that add nuance and depth to our historiographical understanding of the role of women within formal institutional uplift and how working-class African Americans both used and remade programmatic uplift to suit their needs.

Chapter one of this study argues that as African Americans came together around a common experience of racial discrimination within their own city space, differences in patterns of street use developed out of the social networks that developed within the Hill District. During World War I and the 1920s, Wylie Avenue, the main thoroughfare, formed the entrepreneurial and cultural heart of the Hill District, and Black Pittsburgh as a whole. After World War I, demographic shifts increased early class tensions on the streets, including Wylie Avenue. African Americans who professed middle-class values aimed to use street spaces in the Hill District to educate those in the working classes on proper behavior and middle-class social norms. Those in the emerging working class, instead, focused on entertainment and employment within street spaces and accommodated some of the values of the emerging middle class. Differing uses of street spaces allowed middle-class and elite African Americans to create education programs aimed at improving those in the working classes and to limit spaces for their own entertainment. These changing dynamics shaped conflicts between the social networks on the streets of the Hill District.

Chapter two reveals the important function social networks played in the lives of women and children and the role that streets spaces played as play spaces and childcare venues for children of the African American working class. Social reformers worked to close off streets as a viable place for children to utilize in the Hill District. Working-class mothers used neighborhood cooperation to provide safe and affordable childcare for their children, which allowed them to work and provide income for their household economy. These conflicting uses reinforced middle-class ideals of stay-at-home mothering while working-class women promoted a vision of cooperative parenting that utilized neighborhood space in new ways. This conflict shows how the interests of women on the streets of the Hill District as both workers and mothers transformed the streets of the Hill District.

Chapter three claims that working-class African Americans developed their own conceptualization of belonging to the neighborhood that conflicted with middle-class understandings of social respectability. Affiliation as a regular on Wylie Avenue created an environment of camaraderie and a community where neighbors took care of one another. Systems of reciprocity and regular affiliation knit working class and the working poor together within the boundaries of the Lower Hill District. The emerging middle class used respectability politics to reinforce their interpretation of community values that often conflicted with the systems of reciprocity and exchange used by the working class within their streets.

Chapter four argues that through the process of urban renewal, Black workers resisted civic and class-based definitions of their street spaces as vice-ridden and dilapidated and instead, redefined the Lower Hill District in their own terms. Urban renewal revealed the fault lines within the African American community and exposed the class tensions surrounding use of street space, displacement and dispossession of street space, and concerns over housing. Residents of the Lower Hill District used their social networks to lay claim to street spaces that reflected their vision of a neighborhood. As urban renewal dispersed the residents from the Lower Hill into other neighborhoods of the city, their social networks stretched into new areas, always linking them back to the Hill District as the central hub of Black Pittsburgh.

Chapter five contends that street capitalists used systems of reciprocity to move between the social networks of the working class and the elite as well as the boundaries of illegal and legal labor. For many within the Hill District, vice and blight were a problem because the presence of vice on the streets of the neighborhood invited the surveillance of the police and the violence that they brought with them. Many Hill residents named police brutality as a problem in their neighborhood but working-class and middle-class Blacks differed on the solution. For middle-class African Americans, Black policemen were a solution to the twin problems of increasing vice and police brutality. Working-class African Americans were more concerned about intermittent police suppression and violence against them on the streets. In this way, the conflict between street capitalists and divisions over the policing of the streets revealed both increasing class tensions within the Hill District and a rift within the social networks of the Hill District.

Chapter six addresses how African Americans formed alliances across class lines through protest and activism to address the systemic social, political, and economic inequality they faced outside their city within the city. This alliance was a conscious effort to incorporate middle-class concerns over the availability of housing and jobs commensurate with their training and income along with working-class concerns over issues of police brutality and economic opportunity. Formal organizations developed to protest inequality in the city of Pittsburgh and in the nation as a whole. These formal organizations developed out of the informal social networks that had been present in the neighborhood and used the connections across class lines to push for full equality with a unified goal. This alliance across class lines and through social networks emphasized the need for fair housing, good-paying jobs, and political rights. As the alliance fractured, elite and middle-class African Americans relied on more formal mechanisms of power through legal victories and political civil rights, while the working class emphasized informal networks of solidarity with other oppressed people worldwide and antipoverty programs through collective action.

Chapter seven illustrates how this alliance stretched to the breaking point in the mid-1960s as the working classes expressed a different vision of their future that included the possibility of street-based violence. In this way, African Americans used street spaces to foster a public space, or "Street Democracy," where they could express different visions for the future of African Americans in Pittsburgh and in the United States as a whole. As the alliance fractured, middle-class African Americans increasingly retreated from the streets of the neighborhood and their central efforts within the alliance by redefining street spaces as inherently violent. Working-class African Americans redoubled their efforts to address issues of economic injustice and social equality through both violent and nonviolent means, and through those efforts found themselves the target of increasing state-sponsored

violence and surveillance on the streets of Pittsburgh. As the city exploded in outrage following the assassination of Dr. Martin Luther King Jr., the efforts of the formal and informal social networks of the Hill District differed on their response to the murder. Violence became a tool for many of those in the working class, while the formal organizations relied on their traditional mechanisms of nonviolent direct action. The police targeted those who used the theater of the street to express their grief and thereby solidified the view of many within the African American elite that the streets were a violent place rather than a political space.

Overall, the shifting currents of middle-class and working-class African American street use changed over time from a large and vibrant mixed-class use of street space within an African American city within the city, to a place where class lines increasingly divided street use into highly stratified uses constrained by social network affiliation and marred by violence. This change over time reveals the struggle for Black-controlled public space within the African American community in one Rust Belt city while also revealing the vital interplay between social networks and the neighborhood streets in the process of community formation. Pittsburgh and the Hill District form a valuable location to investigate these shifts over time and space, but it is not unique in the process of intraracial community formation. Many works in African American urban history discuss race relations between the African American community and the larger white community living outside the boundaries of the African American segregated city. Still, few look at divisions and convergences within the African American community. This focus on intraracial relations and the shifting class divisions and uses of the streets raises an essential question for scholars on African Americans within the city.

CHAPTER ONE

Wylie Avenue

Crossroads of the World, Hill District, 1918–1930

In the *Pittsburgh Courier*, John L. Clark, or "the Fox" as he was known, wrote a regular column called "Wylie Ave." that allowed readers from all over Pittsburgh to write in and add their observations of life on "the Ave" to his. This column ran in the weekly paper regularly from 1923 to his death in 1961. Rev. B. H. Logan commented on Clark's legacy at the time of his passing, saying, "'The Fox' liked people. He knew people. People in every walk of life sought his advice. He was a real 'Plato of the Pavement.' He numbered ministers, politicians, sports figures, theatrical celebrities, and 'the man and woman of the streets' among his friends. He was equally at ease whether talking with a millionaire businessman, presidential candidate, or personal shepherd [pimp] to the nocturnal sisterhood."[1] Clark's view of the Ave included women, men, numbers runners, pimps, laundresses, children, and the politically connected old Pittsburghers. Clark's "Wylie Ave." allowed his readers to see the creation of a neighborhood and the development of social networks on the streets of the Hill District. This space within the Hill District held the street, stoops, front parlors, barbershops, dance halls, and other spaces of social life that became the urban center of Black life in Pittsburgh. These spaces created room for community development. In African American Pittsburgh, and the Hill District specifically, while the neighborhood was multiethnic, the networks of social behavior and systems of exchange therein united a community and created the "Crossroads of the World." The neighborhood that developed around Wylie Avenue that the Fox chronicled became the center of a social network of Black-controlled public space in the city.

Pittsburgh, Pennsylvania, had a small African American population before the Great Migration spurred the movement of many African Americans in search of jobs in the steel mills and other heavy industries and to escape the constant pressures of racial terror in the South. While northern publications like the *Chicago Defender* cautioned migrants against moving to the North, the *Pittsburgh Courier* formulated a calculated gamble to pull migrants to Pittsburgh and the Hill District. Robert Vann published weekly op-eds in the *Courier* naming "friends and enemies" of the migrants to Pittsburgh.[2]

Although African Americans migrated to cities in the North, like Pittsburgh, for jobs, they entered the workforce at the bottom and faced the problem of "last hired, first fired." Most African Americans occupied positions classified as *unskilled* and faced little prospect of advancement into skilled labor. The jobs open to African Americans were the most dangerous and dirtiest jobs available, but they still offered better pay than most African Americans earned in domestic employment. African American women gained little access to manufacturing training and education in professional positions that would later form the base of women active in the African American middle class.

While early African American residents of Pittsburgh held some skilled labor positions, African American migrants to Pittsburgh primarily remained in common labor positions. These positions were insecure, and African Americans faced high turnover rates in the comparatively few industries that employed them. Women had very few labor options outside of domestic employment. By 1915, the employment of African American men in the steel industry rapidly increased. Still, this expansion led to a cycle of expansion and contraction of jobs that left African American men at the mercy of volatile industry shifts.[3] These shifts caused cycles of unemployment within Pittsburgh's African American community. Still, African Americans were not alone in facing these unemployment cycles. White Pittsburgh residents faced similar problems with the volatile employment climate.

During the first wave of migrations to the urban North, African Americans from many parts of the South migrated to Pittsburgh in search of jobs from the industrial boom of the interwar years. Labor recruiters enticed southern African Americans with the prospect of employment in the urban North. These jobs in the heavy-manufacturing sector allowed many African American men to obtain work to support their families. African American migrants to Pittsburgh, like many other northern industrial cities, used strategies of chain migration to follow family members into opening industries. African American migrants to Pittsburgh were also familiar with urban landscapes. Most of the African American migrants to Pittsburgh migrated from other metropolitan areas.[4] In 1918, Pittsburgh's African American community was a mix of native Pittsburgh African Americans and southern-born African American migrants. Peter Gottlieb argued, "The reciprocal influences of the southern migrants and the established black community strengthened the emerging class divisions among Pittsburgh's blacks."[5] Tensions between new African American migrants and native residents of African American Pittsburgh played out in the developing social networks of Pittsburgh's

African American neighborhoods. Pittsburgh's African American population increased from under 27,000 at the beginning of World War I to over 82,000 by 1945.[6] Likewise, Lance Freeman argued that although Pittsburgh had a large African American population, they were not isolated in all-Black enclaves. Still, the process of ghettoization was accelerating by 1920.[7] This rise of the Black enclave or ghetto could serve as a haven for Black residents to find reprieve from the virulent racism of the North and where they could control the public space of their neighborhood. With this increase of the African American population, new migrants clustered in the city's already populated African American neighborhoods. The white population of the Hill District decreased while the African American population increased rapidly. As African American migrants moved into the Hill District, realtors rented substandard housing to migrants and their families.[8] The living conditions of the Hill District were below standard, and many city agencies decried the poor conditions of the streets of the Hill District.

The Hill District became the central focus of these migrations where the idea of a Black neighborhood was not so much a ghetto, but a possible Black metropolis, a location where you could "uplift the race" in a particular place.[9] Wylie Avenue demonstrated this new consciousness forming in the Hill District. The development of Black-controlled public space was a third way between the accommodationists of Tuskegee and the demands for full equality from the National Association for the Advancement of Colored People (NAACP) and the Niagara Movement. This development of the New Negro on the streets of the neighborhood grew out of the race pride formed through social networks within the Hill District. While outside forces imposed segregation, separation could create room for African Americans to control their own public space.[10] Despite the poor living conditions for most African Americans in the Hill District, residents formed a vibrant community within the confines of separated residential space in Pittsburgh, where the corner of Wylie and Fullerton became the crossroads of the Black world.[11]

The Hill District formed the heart of African American culture in Pittsburgh. Leaders in the business community and fraternal societies encouraged African Americans to develop separate institutions, businesses, medical services, and separate public spaces to serve their community. The Hill District formed the center of this separate city, where the people developed their own institutions and social networks. Although African Americans often faced exclusion from the institutions of white Pittsburgh, their cultural life flowed through the streets of the Hill District. Nightlife in the Hill District was as fine as any city in America. Musicians like Duke Ellington, Lena Horne,

Cab Calloway, and other greats performed in Pittsburgh at the Crawford Grill, on the corner of Centre and Wylie Avenues. While most African Americans in Pittsburgh lived in the Hill District, those living outside of the Hill District traveled to the Hill to experience baseball games, culturally distinctive worship, and to connect with their social networks that were centered there. While African Americans created social networks within their neighborhood, divisions also developed within the Hill District-old Pittsburghers (OPs), and southern born, emerging middle class, and working class.

In the early interwar years, tensions mounted between incoming migrants who brought their cultural patterns of worship and entertainment and the older stock residents of the Hill District. These tensions manifested on neighborhood streets as African Americans presented a united front to those outside their sphere while exhibiting divisions within their neighborhood based on cultural differences. Houses of worship demonstrated early divisions as those African Americans with greater access to wealth and many of those with lighter skin disproportionately belonged to Episcopal, Presbyterian, and Congregational churches. Likewise, those in the working classes tended to belong to Baptist and Methodist congregations.[12] These divisions also manifested in the organizational affiliation and educational attainment of African Americans. While most Blacks in Pittsburgh still occupied the lower levels of employment, the University of Pittsburgh trained an increasing number in industries that allowed them access to a new world of professional work.

For Black Pittsburghers between the two wars, Wylie Avenue was the "Crossroads of the World."[13] It educated, entertained, and employed African Americans in the city of Pittsburgh. The street catered to African Americans of all sorts in the city. Wylie Avenue held many types of businesses, legal and illegal, as well as residential housing and entertainment venues. John L. Clark, a veteran reporter for the *Pittsburgh Courier* who wrote extensively about street life, described it as "a street crossed with juke box and boiler factory . . . it had its churches . . . its legitimate businesses . . . its 'dieties' or 'sassiety folk' . . . its 'honor students' ('yes, Your Honor' . . . 'No, Your Honor' . . . 'please, Your Honor') . . . its night clubs, including black and tan . . . its 'upholstered sewers,' called 'after-hours spots' . . . its gay laughter and its abject sorrow."[14] Consequently, Wylie Avenue also had its supporters and detractors. As the hub of the social network for Black Pittsburghers, many social reformers used the space of "the Ave" to implement their ideas for improvements to the race. Wylie Avenue was a home,

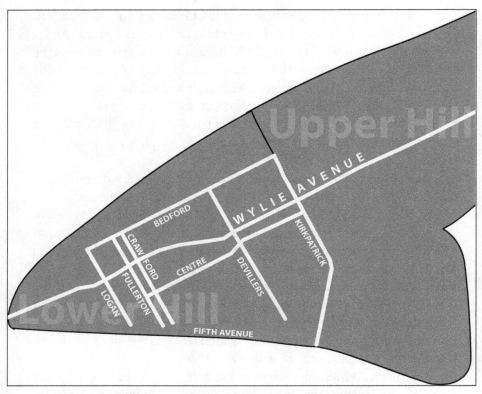

MAP 1.1 Upper and Lower Hill District in Pittsburgh, Pennsylvania.
Jason Klanderud, Altair Media Design, Designer.

a theater, a workplace, and the heart of the Hill District for those in Pittsburgh's African American community. This street offered a location for Pittsburgh's Black community to unify around their common racial experiences while they also struggled on the streets to form their own social networks and cultivate a Black-controlled public space.

By the end of World War I, the Hill District represented the heart of Pittsburgh's African American "city within the city" and Wylie Avenue was the central artery of the Hill District. Wylie Avenue ran through the center of the Hill District, or just the Hill. It was the street that "cocks its head at the welcoming doorway of a church and rests its feet at the gaping iron gateway of the Courthouse and the adjoining jail!"[15] "Arthur," who was born and raised in the Hill District, recalled Wylie Avenue as a community bridge-building street: "Wylie Avenue was more residential, it had little restaurants, bars, clubs, and hotels but since it was in the middle of the hill, closer to Centre

Avenue, it was a good place to be because you had barbershops, the Elks, churches, it was a street that covered everybody; it was a nice street to be on."[16] Longtime Hill District residents recalled the homelike feel of Wylie Avenue. It was the social and cultural heart of the Hill District, and as such, the hub of the developing social network on the streets of the neighborhood.

The heart of the Hill District would not have been possible without the informal work of Black women. Their homes became the central meeting place where social networks formed before spilling out onto the streets of the neighborhood including Wylie Avenue. Their stoops, parlors, and kitchens were the site of neighborhood formation and the place where systems of reciprocity solidified. Wylie Avenue became the parlor of the Black community, the space where you met, talked, ate, and developed relationships. These spaces were the origin of a neighborhood formed through personal connections. Neighbors looked out for one another and participated in systems of exchange. Barbara Gaston, who was born and raised in the Hill District, recalled that "everybody knew everybody" in the neighborhood when she was growing up and "everybody raised your child."[17] These extended kin networks reinforced systems of exchange that both crossed and reified emerging boundaries of social class. The social networks that African American women controlled in the Hill District moved beyond the idea of fictive kin to incorporate actual systems of reciprocity and exchange.[18] The members of these social networks may have been actual kinfolk but more commonly, they were united in a common struggle against the structural forces that formed the metaphysical walls of the urban ghetto. These social networks were the most visible through the hosting of houseguests from around the country. The *Pittsburgh Courier* regularly published the varied ways that African American women used their social connections as hostesses for numerous social events, especially during "FROG Week." In a weekly column, "Talk O' Town," Julia Bumry Jones wrote of the comings and goings of Pittsburgh's Black elite and middle class under her byline, Jules. This column was both a social column and a political call to action for the women of the Hill District. Jules did not shy away from topics that some viewed outside the purview of women. Her column focused on the social world of the Hill District's African American women. While Jules wrote about the comings and goings of the Hill District's women, one major focus of her column was on the illustrious event of the social season, FROG Week.

One of the major African American social clubs in the city was the FROGS. The FROGS took their name from their motto, "Friendly Rivalry

Often Generates Success."[19] This exclusive club for elite African American men met at the Loendi Club and sponsored many events throughout the city during their annual week of events. "Festive Frog Week is here! Society maid, matron club have joined with the organization in planning for plenty of friends and guests. Every evening during the week there will be some place to go; something fun and interesting to attend."[20] The allure of FROG Week charmed middle-class African Americans from Pittsburgh and lured visitors from other cities around the region and country. African American women in the Hill District played hostess to the significant number of guests that came to the city for FROG Week annually. Nearly every article in the *Pittsburgh Courier* that references FROG Week concludes with a listing of the out-of-town houseguests and who they are staying with. The hostesses were often the wives of the Loendi Club members that made up the African American elite in Pittsburgh, but they were also women from all over the Hill District who were forging connections between their African American world and other African American neighborhoods in Chicago, New York, Cleveland, Baltimore, Philadelphia, and many others. The *Courier* regularly published lists of FROG Week visitors as well as regular houseguests throughout the year. These listings of houseguests also reveal intergenerational cooperation as many unmarried women traveled to Pittsburgh for FROG Week to meet or at least mingle with other eligible single people. A 1932 article in the *Courier* names the maids who will be attending the Matron and Maid's Annual Ball as an added attraction for the FROG Week festivities. Hostesses also connected the social world of the Hill District to the larger African American world through their parlors and private spaces.[21] The *Courier* noted the contributions of women to FROG Week when they reported, "While the Frogs are men . . . and professionally and socially prominent . . . it falls to the lovely women to provide much of the enchanting background for much of the glory of the week."[22] This enchanting background took the form of significant social engineering in forging connections between socially prominent families in African American communities around the nation. These social networks were visible through the elite events of FROG Week as well as the ways those connections spilled into the middle-class and working-class events of FROG Week.

Descriptions of FROG Week activities highlighted the glamour and drama of the events while simultaneously emphasizing the elite and, above all, respectable nature of the events, which occurred both inside the Loendi Club and other venues and outdoors in public parks and street spaces. In August 1924, the *Courier* exclaimed, "The Frogs again triumphed! The weather, the spirit, the pleasure were delightful. From early morning until the closing hour of eleven at night, Olympia Park was the scene of a beautiful array of fashionably gowned women and nattily attired men taking in the pastimes, greeting old friends."[23] These outdoor events displayed and connected social networks from the Hill District to the nation.

While some of the events took place in private, the FROGS used outdoor parks where working-class African Americans could observe their events in public venues. Sala Udin recalled watching the men and women enter the Loendi Club from the window of his family apartment when he was a child. This was a special treat for the children because they got to stay up late and see the African American elite men and women dressed up for a night out.[24] The *Pittsburgh Courier* often reported the lavish fashions of the wives of FROGS as well as general descriptions of the affairs themselves. The descriptions included the fabrics and cut of the women's dresses and included references of the relative social standing of the women listed. Out-of-town visitors also earned mention of their clothing as well as the distance they traveled to attend the event.[25] The descriptions of clothing and visitors created an atmosphere of glamour around the FROG event. Other social clubs and fraternal organizations held events limited to current or prospective members and their guests. Although, in warm weather, African American Pittsburgh used public spaces like parks and pools to host their events. Teenie Harris photographed the FROGS as they celebrated FROG Week at Lovuola's Farm (see figure 1.1). These outdoor venues became Black-controlled public spaces where Hill District residents formed social networks that both solidified a neighborhood and worked to develop distinct classes within the Hill District.[26]

The events of FROG Week were both social and educational. The *Pittsburgh Courier* outlined the events of the week, saying, "On Sunday, August 2nd the Symposium at Loendi will feature Professor Anderson of Tuskegee University."[27] The speakers for the FROGS' symposium usually hailed from African American universities and spoke on socially conscious topics. The FROGS advertised these symposia as educational for the race. These talks were explicitly for "race men," and to raise up leaders that would be active toward social and political equality. FROG Week intentionally included educational events alongside social events to allow members and their guests access to the most recent ideas on topics of interest to African Americans. Segregation and efforts to achieve social equality with whites were popular topics for speakers. Speakers educated the FROGS on current efforts to combat social concerns like Jim Crow in the South and de facto segregation in the North, especially

FIGURE 1.1 Men and women gathered at picnic table with soft drink, liquor, and beer bottles, with cooler in grass in foreground, at Lovuola's Farm for Junior Mothers night picnic during FROGS week, July 1959. Charles "Teenie" Harris (American, 1908–98), black-and-white, Kodak safety film, H: 4 in. × W: 5 in. (10.20 × 12.70 cm), Carnegie Museum of Art, Pittsburgh: Heinz Family Fund, 2001.35.13832, © Carnegie Museum of Art, Charles "Teenie" Harris Archive.

in professional employment and housing. The FROGS emphasized the importance of these events to the whole race, but they limited them to elite men.

The FROGS also used their influence to help organizations by fundraising and drawing attention to specific events or causes. In 1926, the FROGS launched a popularity contest for young women tied to subscriptions to the *Courier*. The contest stressed the beauty and composure of the young women who entered. The *Courier* described most of the young women as debutants and members of "the young set." These young women personified the virtues of beauty, charm, kindness, and timidity.[28] To receive votes these women solicited subscriptions to the *Pittsburgh Courier* from their friends and neighbors. Young women used their connections through social networks of clubs, recreational associations, and relationships within the neighborhood to solicit subscriptions on the streets to gain points for the contest. While this type of activity from young middle-class women would apparently violate the standards of behavior for middle-class women on the street, middle-class and elite African Americans linked this particular activity with civic virtue as it occurred during daylight hours and under the, presumed, supervision of adults. The winner of the contest in Pittsburgh received over one million votes. The national winner traveled to Pittsburgh from Evanston, Illinois, to attend FROG Week in Pittsburgh. The number of entrants and the success of the contest led the FROGS to award an additional winner. The winners all attended a ball in their honor at Duquesne Gardens in addition to their prizes. The *Courier* presented these contestants as the daughters of the privileged classes of African Americans, but they also were willing to work for votes out in the streets.

FROG Week brought Pittsburgh's African American community into the public spotlight. The *Courier* published the details of FROG events for weeks before and after, idealizing the elite world the FROGS and their guests occupied. FROG Week drew visitors from other African American communities across the country to Pittsburgh. Many of these visitors and others aspiring to "hop with the FROGS" wanted to know the proper standards of dress and behavior required to attend FROG events and coveted the invitation from a member that gained them entry into the event. The coverage of FROG events focused on their pageantry. FROG events occurred in a combination of private clubs, street spaces, public parks, and private homes. Events like the annual baseball outing encouraged participants to display their less formal attire while they attended events in the public, while the Matron's Formal required evening wear. Reporters described the clothing of participants, the food and beverage served, the entertainment provided, and even the smallest detail of the setting surrounding those attending. Columns describing the activities of those within this sphere commonly appeared within the *Pittsburgh Courier*. Apparently, readers enjoyed vicariously participating in these *society* events although they could not attend them in person. These descriptions transported the reader into the rarified spaces occupied by Pittsburgh's Black elite.

While not all members of the FROGS or their guests were elite, they were socially connected within Pittsburgh's African American community. The location of these events removed attendees from the streets. The public spaces appropriate for FROGS and other society events were exclusive. FROGS limited their events to members and their guests, thereby limiting the spaces used for these events to places where they could regulate attendance such as public halls, membership clubs, and public parks. In that way, these venues were closed public spaces. Pittsburgh's African American society used closed public spaces to socialize and educate members of their class, while at the same time using open public spaces to attempt to educate the working classes. This behavior separated the classes into those fit to socialize with and those requiring education. The work of the FROGS built a separate class from the social networking of African American women. The networks formed by Hill District women crossed class boundaries and showed how the FROGS were not able to isolate working-class residents from the events, even though the tone of the FROGS events displayed more than a little paternalism.

The official events of FROG Week were for members only. The FROGS and their guests limited their events to those of the elite and middle classes, who were "race men," but the festive atmosphere of the events included the areas of the street commonly occupied by those of the working classes for their entertainment. The formal events in the Loendi Club often spilled onto Wylie Avenue after the end of the official festivities. Nightclubs and after-hours joints welcomed both the working classes and the society folks straight from FROG Week festivities.[29] The working classes reaped a portion of the benefit of FROG Week, from the visitors from out of town to the increased entertainment and socializing occurring in the city by all the social networks in the Hill District.

Working African Americans spent their leisure time on the streets as well. Street spaces offered a variety of entertainment, both legal and illegal, for people in the Hill District after working hours. African American members of labor unions often spent their leisure time socializing with other African American union members through social clubs. The society pages of the *Pittsburgh Courier* listed the leisure activities of the elite and middle class, but also listed the activities of fraternal and union orders. In September 1930, the *Courier* announced an upcoming dance and card party at the Fifth Ward Progressive Club. Sponsored by the Pittsburgh Chapter No. 62 of the National Association of Colored Waiters and Hotel Employees, this event represented the first of "a series of brilliant social affairs" planned by the organization. The planning committee "spared no expense" in making the event a success, including offering prizes to the best card players.[30] Working African Americans often held different societal positions based on their associations. Union membership, whether officially recognized or as an informal association awaiting recognition, offered African American men some level of social standing. Union membership apparently raised the social standing of an African American man somewhat within the community, but it did not affect a man's social standing as much as membership in a club or fraternal order.

FROG Week provided some social activities for African Americans in the emerging working class during their off-work hours. The neighborhood benefited from sponsored events and special rates during FROG Week. The *Pittsburgh Courier* reported sale prices in all kinds of establishments from the beauty parlor to the grocery store. These prices were available to members of the community. The *Courier* advertised special "FROG Week" admission prices at the Triangle Theater, accenting the names of the stars and enticing patrons with the names of popular movies.[31] African Americans in the working classes benefited from the price reduction of some forms of middle-class or elite entertainment, but they also created their own festivities during FROG Week.

The emerging African American elite were not as insulated from the working class as they may have liked to believe. Informal social networks connected individuals across class lines through relationships, and importantly through systems of exchange and reciprocity. Elite African Americans could not enclose all street spaces in the Hill District during FROG Week. In Chester L. Washington's column, "Deep Wylie," he commented on the interaction between elites and the working classes, saying: "Society folk, rubbed elbows with the denizens of the underworld. And all joined in making heap big whoopee. The best of order prevailed, however, in all of the night rendezvous, and entertainers, musicians, waiters and café owners reaped a joyous jingling return from the nightly celebrations."[32] Places of business all along Wylie Avenue prepared for the arrival of FROG Week. A *Courier* reporter described the effect of FROG Week on the cultural and commercial life of the community: "Everything perts up Frog Week. The butcher, the baker, the candlestick maker are polishing up their shingles and adding a touch or two to their windows in anticipation of some real business. They are acting wisely, for Frog patrons are high class and the up-to-date business establishment attracts their attention and trade."[33] These connections, both legal and illegal, gave the events of FROG Week a celebratory flair that affected the whole community.

Many of the social events sponsored on the streets of the Hill District often catered to the same clientele of African Americans. Organizations often paired indoor events like benefit concerts and public talks with outdoor events like picnics and fairs to maximize exposure to neighborhood social networks. Organizations carefully planned their events to avoid overlap so that a majority of the middle-class African American community could attend. The dates of events were particularly important. Many street festivals and community events occurred in the late spring. The Urban League of Pittsburgh's (ULP) committee worried about the timing of the event "because one or two of the large affairs is to be held among Colored people have been planned for the last part of April which we wish to avoid."[34] The ULP anticipated a large turnout for their street fairs. The events raised money for the ULP's social programs and operating budget with the benefit of providing a way for middle-class African Americans to display idealized African American women and entertainment for those members of the community that could afford the ticket price. Street events utilized neighborhood social networks to gain access to their desired clientele. Pageants were an important mechanism of formal organizations to leverage social networks and systems of exchange to connect to goals of racial uplift in the working class.

The May Day pageant functioned as a fundraiser and community social event in conjunction with the ULP's May health and recreation fair. Annual health fairs, sponsored by the ULP, focused on improving the race by educating African Americans about health and "modern scientific advances." A 1924 *Pittsburgh Courier* report illustrated the need for these fairs: "In Pittsburgh last year 90 out of every 1000 white babies born, died before they were one year old, while 146 out of every 1000 Negro babies born, died before they were one year old. This fact alone gives added importance to the contests each year."[35] The health fair and Better Baby contest included lectures for mothers on health, disease prevention, and the *proper* way to care for their babies, a program targeted toward African American women in the Hill District.

These events linked social networks within the Hill District through combined street displays such as parades and picnics with health clinics for African Americans, while focusing on poor sanitary and public health conditions on the streets and attempts to remedy those conditions in a type of social respectability. Better Baby contests divided children into age groups and then assessed them based on scientific characteristics. Better Baby contests also included baby clinics to address the health needs of children. The health campaigns of the Urban League focused on areas of the city with high infant mortality rates. The clinic included, "a complete physical examination which will be given to each child brought to the clinic, advice to mothers for the proper care, diet, and remedial treatment for defective conditions." The clinic also provided "moving pictures and other entertainment for the adults and children, and milk for the babies."[36] These fairs also addressed public health concerns like the spread of tuberculosis and pneumonia. The African American middle class linked their values with public health and racial uplift. Urban modernity through clean streets and neighborhoods demonstrated the race's fitness for equality and human rights.

African American organizations used street spaces to extend medical services for poor and working-class Black families to their existing social networks.[37] Few African Americans allowed home visits from social service institutions, but many reformers believed entertainment was an effective way of reaching the working classes with vital information on public health.[38] Street spaces allowed reformers to present information in an entertaining way without the pressures and stigma of home-based interventions. Public health matters were best addressed in the public sphere.

Health fairs took place on the streets of African American neighborhoods, including the Hill District. Street cleanup campaigns used health fairs as a tool to gather groups from local schools and churches to clean alleyways and sidewalks, while public health committees presented information on prevention through leaflets on street corners. Public performances and parades also displayed a more entertaining vision of public health for African Americans in the Hill District.[39] Cleanliness and hygiene were major components of the campaign as well as a focus on neighborhood improvement. While the generally better-off African American residents of the Middle and Upper Hill District escaped notice, public health advocates expressed the greatest concern over the streets of the Lower Hill District. The Tuberculosis League of Pittsburgh reported on tuberculosis rates among African Americans in Pittsburgh. In their report they called special attention to the Lower Hill, saying, "The Lower Hill District, which is predominantly a rooming house neighborhood, and which is the most congested section of the city, showed more infection arising from sources without the home than did any other district."[40] The Lower Hill District had a reputation as unclean. This reputation developed from perceptions that cleanliness of street spaces equated with cleanliness of character. Progressive reformers urged public health as an avenue for social mobility and racial uplift. Cleanliness of public spaces indicated modernization and a society committed to civic morality. In this case, public cleanliness equaled civic godliness.

The ULP sponsored a visible display of public health in the form of a health parade through the Hill District with schoolchildren leading the way. African Americans with middle-class values approved of this visible presence of children on the streets of the Hill District. Children emphasized the hope

African American reformers had that the next generation of African American Pittsburghers would learn the lessons of public health and civic virtue. The children prepared banners for the parade emphasizing health-related virtues. The children's banners would "display all manners of advice concerning personal hygiene, home cleanliness, and neighborhood improvement, and will be quite worth the effort in the districts in which they will be used."[41] This campaign also included street cleaning and sanitation assistance to give "the districts in which colored people live largely in the city of Pittsburgh . . . an opportunity to get such a cleaning up as never been given before with the cooperation of the children and residents of these districts."[42] Parades displayed public values on the streets of the Hill District. Children exemplified the concept of racial uplift. Reformers believed that education of children provided a way to improve the behavior and habits of the young to transform future generations of African Americans.

African American adults in the Hill District used their social networks to access entertainment as well as to navigate racial discrimination in Pittsburgh. Working-class adults frequented the bars and after-hours clubs of Fullerton Street, while middle-class African Americans had access to fraternal orders, upscale bars, and private clubs. Marcia Donnell, whose father worked in the steel mills and whose mother was a church musician, recalled how middle-class African Americans pooled their money to get into more exclusive clubs, saying, "Then later when I became a young adult then we had a club. When we wanted to go out, we would go to a nightclub. They were like bars that were on a higher standard. We would put our money together and go as a group. And that's how I got to go to the bigger entertainment. We had plenty of entertainment here in the Hill District. So, if we weren't welcome somewhere else, we didn't miss it."[43] Robert Vickers, whose father also worked in the steel industry while his mother stayed at home, recalled going to nightclubs with his wife and other friends, saying, "By the time you worked and came home, maybe on the weekends you would go out now and then. We went to the Crawford Grill, the Hurricane and some of the neighborhood bars; we would get together with some of our friends. We would go out with the wives; we went out as couples. Maybe now and then I would go out with the fellows but mostly we went out as couples."[44] Sarah Tomlin, a daughter of a domestic worker, recalled that nightclubs limited the people who attended to those in certain social networks through passwords, special hours, and having to be recommended by a member to attend. She stated, "Some clubs you couldn't walk right in. There was someone there to greet you. With a bar you could just walk in."[45] Tomlin recalled attending local bars and some clubs, but she did not have the connections necessary to attend the clubs of the middle class or elite. Bars and nightclubs offered adult African Americans a place to gather for superior music and entertainment in their neighborhood.

Fraternal orders and clubs formalized social networks within the neighborhood. The society page in the *Pittsburgh Courier* often listed many social activities outside of the church realm. St. Clair Drake and Horace Cayton noted a social separation between middle-class African Americans who affiliated with the church and those who did not.[46] This separation also appeared in Pittsburgh's Hill District and larger African American community. Sarah Tomlin recalled that, "A lot went to church and a lot didn't."[47] Tomlin recalled going out to nightclubs and bars on Saturday night, but she cautioned that "religious people were different," from those who routinely went out on the weekends.[48] The ULP dedicated a committee to social and recreational activities for African Americans in Pittsburgh. For adults, the ULP sponsored formal lectures, dinners, the Urban League Follies, and other dramatic and artistic presentations open for African American attendance.[49] The NAACP also pushed for greater access to venues through legal action in their Public Accommodations Committee.[50] Venues established African American nights when Pittsburgh's African American community could use the space. This racially segregated use of space limited the times African Americans could use large venues.[51] As the concentration of African Americans who espoused middle-class values grew within Pittsburgh's African American community, they used their economic and social advantages to limit events to those of their own social networks. In this way, elite and middle-class African Americans closed off public spaces to reserve them for class-specific uses. These closed public spaces allowed the elite classes of African Americans to create spaces tailored to their own social networks.

Middle-class and elite African Americans who did not affiliate with the church pursued other options for recreation and social activities both on the streets and through social clubs. Social clubs offered middle-class African Americans an opportunity to form social relationships with members of their own developing social class as well as members of the African American elite. While some clubs limited their membership to elite African Americans only, most clubs allowed middle-class African Americans to join with the recommendation of a present member. Members of the same social club often held similar values. Lee K. Frank described the characteristics of the social network he observed in a predominantly African American social club, saying, "Such areas as family background and connections, friendships, moral attitudes, amount and kind of education, success in occupation, wealth or lack of it, and prestige of religious, economic, and racial affiliation, all contribute to social class distinction."[52] Frank also claimed all respondent members of the club held conscious class attitudes toward members of other classes.

This class consciousness led members of the social club to form social networks with other members of the same social class outside of the club buildings. Middle-class and elite African Americans socialized with other members of their class or better. Social clubs allowed them to display their class affiliation in public ways that enforced separation between classes. Elite and middle-class African Americans used public displays of class affiliation through social clubs to separate themselves visually from other African Americans. Street spaces and other public venues allowed members of African American social clubs to display their emerging class affiliation.[53] Street corners allowed members of the African American elite classes to display wealth through their dress, their possessions, even the types of transportation they used, while also displaying their status through their social relationships on the streets of the Hill District and other African American neighborhoods in Pittsburgh.

African Americans in the Hill District developed early class divisions out of their competing visions of appropriate street use. African American reformers linked public health with civic virtue and middle-class status through appropriate use of street spaces in the Hill District. These reformers, often women, developed social networks that defined respectable and appropriate uses of street spaces for women and children. African American organizations created formal social networks that exemplified middle-class values and used their influence on existing social networks to educate poorer African Americans on social respectability.

Working-class African Americans' participation in street-based fairs and other programming developed by the ULP and NAACP did not imply a tacit acceptance of middle-class values. Instead, they used the carnival atmosphere of the events to take part in after-work activities on their own terms that developed informal social networks through entertainment.[54] Press releases in the *Pittsburgh Courier* emphasized the high attendance rates for street fairs among African Americans in the Hill District.[55] Marcia Donnell recalled street fairs in the Hill District as a child. She emphasized how well attended the events were and how the whole neighborhood came out for the events.[56] Middle-class African Americans like Ms. Donnell's family or Mr. Vickers recalled their attendance at street fairs in the Hill District while working-class African American families like Odessa Wilson and Helen

Mendoza also recalled attending street fairs in the Hill District. In the public portions of street fairs, working-class African Americans mingled with elite and middle-class African Americans while enjoying the carnival atmosphere of celebrations surrounding the Fourth of July and other important dates in the Hill District. These fairs provided a venue for African Americans across class lines to come together and enjoy entertainment and culturally relevant expressions of racial solidarity in their own separate city.

Working-class African Americans used street spaces as places to work, play, and generally escape the confines of, often substandard, housing in the Hill District. Recreation programs aimed to provide working-class children with an alternative to street spaces for play, and church programs sought to provide alternatives to bars and nightclubs for adults in the working class. These street uses by the working class did not conform to the ideals set by African American elites or by social service professionals within the African American middle class. Reformers expected men's presence on the streets of African American neighborhoods, but they expressed concern over the visible presence of women and children on the streets.

During the period from World War I through the 1920s, African Americans in the Hill District developed social networks focused on their common experience of racial discrimination and the attendant social and political injustice they collectively faced. The interests of the race dominated the thoughts of African Americans in the Hill District. This led African Americans to come together within their neighborhoods to create and promote the idea of a city of their own within the larger city. While they did not always agree on the best ways to use street spaces, middle-class, elite, and working-class African Americans often experienced street spaces together through events like street fairs, parades, picnics, and daily interaction through formal and informal social networks. These interactions formed the foundation of the larger African American community in Pittsburgh and made the Hill District the heart of African American Pittsburgh. African Americans in Pittsburgh used the streets to cultivate their own social networks through formal clubs and organizations and through informal interactions in the neighborhood. Social networks continued to play a critical role in the development of the Hill District but the divergence between formal and informal social networks reinforced emerging class differences in the Hill. These differences solidified into more distinctly stratified classes with different goals and visions for appropriate street use in the Hill District, and these divisions continued on the streets through conflicts over housing, urban redevelopment, and illegal labor in African American neighborhoods within Pittsburgh.

CHAPTER TWO

Bedford Avenue
Street Reformers and Social Mothering, 1917–1940

In the spring of 1937, Odessa Wilson walked home from the Rose Street School in the Hill District. On her way home she walked past other streets where children played stick ball, pitched pennies, and played dolls on the front stoops or on the streets of the neighborhood. Odessa did not go into her small apartment that day. Like other weekdays, Odessa's mother would not be home that night. Odessa's mother worked as a domestic servant to a family in Squirrel Hill, a wealthy neighborhood to the east of the Hill District. Her mother "stayed on the job" which meant that she lived at her employer's home during the week and was only able to come home on the weekends. Odessa's father worked during the day, so a neighbor took care of her after school along with other children from her block. Odessa's mother used a system of reciprocity to arrange childcare for her daughter when other outlets were not available. These social mothers met a need for parents in the neighborhood and often cared for many children of the working class in the Hill District. Working-class mothers used the streets as play spaces and a refuge from the often-cramped quarters of overcrowded housing in the Lower Hill District. The social networks that they formed functioned through a system of reciprocity based on the exchange of favors, gifts, and care work for those in their community and on their neighborhood streets.

Streets offered the space for children to play games with one another and to develop community bonds with the other adults in their neighborhood. Odessa was one of many children who remember a block mother taking care of all the neighborhood children on a particular street. These mothers worked together to meet the childcare needs of their neighborhood without reliance on state mechanisms of support or the heavily supervised play recommended by social scientists in an effort to combat their fears of social degeneration from incoming migration and a developing concept of blight. Black professional social workers pushed highly structured and surveilled play on the residents of the Hill District. The systems of reciprocity that allowed the block mother to function as the love and law on the streets of the Hill did not meet the strident demand to structure children's play and ensure that they were developing into properly respectable members of society. Social workers argued that this performance of respectability would ensure the white community's acceptance of African Americans and give rise to equality for the Black community as a whole. Many of these social workers were not mothers themselves so their understanding of children and childcare was developed from books rather than from experience with children, especially children from the working class or the working poor. The neighborhood systems of reciprocity allowed working Black women to care for their children in a way that fostered communal bonds rather than individual relationships, but the community-oriented systems did not welcome outside oversight and surveillance. Social workers worried that by allowing this social mothering to take place, such actions would not secure broad respectability for African American women and therefore the race as a whole. Motherhood needed to be reformed to move away from community constructions and toward a scientifically managed version that would align with professional, respectable womanhood.

In the summer of 1929, Mr. Ira De A. Reid, an African American sociologist, along with his team of social scientists, collected data on the streets of the Hill District, Pittsburgh's largest African American neighborhood. Through Reid's investigation of the living conditions in the Hill District, his team of middle-class African Americans surveyed issues of cleanliness of street spaces and recreation, which they viewed as linked to crime and delinquency. His study addressed many of the believed indicators leading to juvenile delinquency. As a result, Reid and others saw increased presence of children on the streets of the Hill District as a marker of social maladjustment. Professionals feared the Hill District's changing demographics brought on by the migration of southern-born African Americans to northern industrial cities, and used social science methodology to both confirm their fears and to fight against the stigma associated with the perception of increasing social disorganization on the streets of the Hill District. This report highlighted the difficult negotiations between socially conscious middle-class and elite African Americans and their working-class clients.

Middle-class reformers emphasized values like thrift, public health, and education in their uses of the streets. Through events like Better Baby contests, street fairs, public health displays, and cleanup campaigns, middle-class African Americans defined street spaces as places for education and entertainment where women and children could be present in defined ways that did not violate respectable norms. Reformers used social science methodology and social surveys like the large-scale survey conducted by Reid and his team to make recommendations for policy changes that would implement middle-class values within the African American community. Reid's committee noted the changing composition of the Hill District during the 1920s. During World War I, European immigration slowed while demand for manufactured goods and wartime necessity created good jobs in the manufacturing sector. Pittsburgh, which had particularly relied on European immigration to fill its industrial jobs, turned instead to African Americans from the South. With the opening of higher-paying jobs, the older-stock immigrants were able to move from the Hill District to other parts of the city that were developing outside of the industrial corridor.[1] The recommendations from Reid's survey stated, "Though the Italian and Jewish populations are leaving the Hill District, the Negro population in this area is increasing as are the populations of other immigrant peoples."[2] African Americans claimed the Hill and its street spaces as the cultural center of African American Pittsburgh. While African Americans concentrated in the Hill District, it became more of a haven for them as they created their own social networks and a space of their own.

The Hill was one of the few neighborhoods where African American migrants could obtain housing in the city. Reid addressed the need to study the conditions of African Americans in the Hill District in his opening letter to Mr. Ihlder, saying, "let us consider discriminations or segregation, for example. That whites suffer similar discriminations does not void the discriminations against Negroes. It is true, however, that there are any number of discriminatory practices exercised against Negroes in Pittsburgh that are in no way applicable to any other whole racial group."[3] The social conditions of other ethnic groups in the Hill District concerned reformers, but African Americans faced special circumstances based on racial discrimination that other ethnic groups did not face. Reid contended that race played a pivotal role in the lives of Pittsburgh's African American community. The societal deterioration that other ethnic groups experienced was not equal to the struggles present in the African American community in Pittsburgh. This concept differed from the dominant ideology of the day in the field of sociology, which presented the hopeful idea that African Americans were similar to other ethnic groups experiencing social disorganization as a part of urban migration.[4] For many professionals, the transition of African Americans from rural southerners to urban northerners was a far more dramatic transition than the effects of racial discrimination on their lives.

The Urban League of Pittsburgh (ULP), the National Association for the Advancement of Colored People (NAACP), the Young Men's Christian Association (YMCA), and the Young Women's Christian Association (YWCA) all expressed interest in the outcome of Reid's study. Reid argued that these organizations would be best suited to implement these recommendations within the African American community because of their "fundamental principles" including "necessary social programs . . . when these are not undertaken by other agencies, or when no other agency exists to foster them."[5] The organizations Reid recommended stressed middle-class standards of propriety while Reid's committee suggested many practical reforms more compatible with working-class values and norms. The Hill District was transformed block by block during the Great Migration as European immigrants who were gaining access to whiteness moved to the emerging neighborhoods that opened for their use. It was common to find areas that were densely African American alongside streets that were primarily Armenian or Syrian. The immigrants that remained in the Hill District were from nations that were darker, more foreign, and therefore had a harder time integrating into the larger white city. The ULP focused its reform work on incoming migrants. Their emphasis on resettlement in housing and employment for African Americans relocating from the South revealed a significant need for migrants. While it was common for families to migrate in a chain, with one member resettling first to be followed by other family members, unscrupulous work recruiters and other dangers lurked for migrants moving North. One significant challenge came from the old-stock African American residents of northern cities. The old Pittsburghers held on to their hard-won status with a tenacious grip. Reid's report highlighted the difficult negotiations between socially conscious middle-class and elite African Americans and their working-class clients as well as tensions between northern-born and southern-born Pittsburghers.

White social scientists working within the social service system also investigated racial tensions between white social workers and their African American clients. In Olga Verin Kreisberg's dissertation for Smith College's social work program, she illustrated tensions between white reformers and their middle-class African American clients for child guidance.[6] Kreisberg noted a large degree of "colorism" in the African American clients in the clinic with African Americans of lighter skin color having greater financial means and those of darker skin color tending toward poorer means.[7] Kreisberg used the work of E. Franklin Frasier to outline the hypothesis of her study. She wanted to understand the degree of "racial feeling" among African American children and the effect of those feelings on the counselor-client relationship. She also noted the varying degrees of hostility African American clients brought with them into a social service agency.[8]

The conflicts between social workers and their clients were not limited to external relationships but also occurred on the neighborhood streets. Occasionally the conflict was internal as well. Marcia Donnell, a long-time resident of the Hill District and a former social worker, recalled how social workers often checked with neighbors to see if a man was living in a residence before providing relief to the women and children. Much of the available relief predicated on the family having no available male breadwinner.[9] Donnell was concerned with this method since it "broke up families because a man couldn't get a job that paid enough to support his family but if he stayed around, they couldn't get relief."[10] She also questioned the ethics of neighbors reporting on other neighbors. In her opinion, working-class parents often faced tough decisions regarding the support of their families and the raising of their children and those in a position to help did not usually help in the best possible way.

The ULP created programming to educate women on proper, hygienic, and scientific methods of child-rearing. If working-class women failed to incorporate these lessons through the carrot of street entertainment, the court remained a viable stick for enforcing proper child-rearing.[11] The social science methodology of the Chicago School emphasized the power of structural and environmental forces in the lives of children. This model encouraged institutional and organizational responses to the threat of juvenile delinquency. Trained social workers envisioned street spaces as a place to cultivate both neighborhood cohesion and social propriety but with specific aims in mind. These actions within the African American community would be a tool to gain racial acceptance from the larger white culture in the city. Interracial coalitions of reformers used the tools of the professional social workers to reinforce their vision of neighborhood spaces. In this vision, working-class African Americans would learn the proper way of conducting themselves, gaining skilled employment, raising "better babies," and uplifting the race. Middle-class African Americans had to compete with entertainment directed to the working class and working poor. Reformers in the Urban League believed juvenile delinquency and social disorder were increasing in African American neighborhoods and pervasive public health problems, like infant mortality and tuberculosis, were indicators that African American reformers needed to do more to combat these public problems.[12]

For reformers, the presence of children on the streets indicated that they were at risk for delinquent behavior. Children played on the streets, and they also used street spaces as workplaces for informal and formal work. Middle-class Black women worked to create structured play spaces for children and often disapproved of children on the streets as workers. Official outlets like the *Pittsburgh Courier* occasionally differed from reform organizations in that they emphasized values like thrift, hard work, and hustle for children employed on the streets, while organizations like the ULP emphasized the need for structured play spaces that would steer children away from entertainment and work. African American reformers also viewed children as a vehicle to reform the community. Children's participation in health fairs, Better Baby contests, and other public health campaigns supposedly educated future generations of African Americans on proper health and social behavior. Therefore, professional African Americans often focused much of their reform efforts on defining proper social behavior and parenting for primarily working-class children in the Hill District to reinforce middle-class values within the African American community.

The junior section of the *Pittsburgh Courier* emphasized the desired physical characteristics promoted by these reformers by including photographs of two young boys described as "fine robust sons."[13] These photos visually demonstrated the characteristics of a healthy child. One of the toddler boys, dressed only in a diaper, displayed a stout form with thick arms and legs with rolls of baby fat. The other toddler also displayed characteristics of a healthy weight and diet. The *Courier* stated, "These dandy boys are great boosters of the *Courier's* Junior Section and plan to join the Kiddies' Klub real soon. Although they are a bit mischievous at times as boys usually are their mother said: 'Well, I suppose they are regular fellows.'"[14] The junior section also included health-related information for mothers of young children and for the children themselves. Health rhymes were a regular component of the section as well as "Letters to Glad-Girl," a write in column where readers could get advice, usually consisting of cultivating the middle-class virtues of thrift, cleanliness, and hard work.

Children's visible presence on street spaces in the Hill District defied many middle-class reform notions of respectability and fed fears of increasing social disorganization and juvenile delinquency. African American reformers struggled to uphold a respectable view of African American social life and culture in the context of many so-called progressive white reformers arguing that African Americans were ill suited for urban life and resorting to legal codes to enforce discriminatory policies on the streets of the Hill District. African American reformers both tolerated and accepted men's presence on the streets as a natural part of street life, but women's and children's presence on the streets, especially as workers, was highly suspect. Concerns over juvenile delinquency and vagrancy led to an emphasis on recreation programs to instill middle-class values in children and access to playgrounds to limit unstructured play on the streets of the Hill District and other African American neighborhoods.[15] The streets of the Hill District often served as a place where children spent their time when they were not in school, a place where they developed their own social networks. Children were active members of social networks on their own terms.

Discussions of juvenile delinquency within the African American community focused on the presence of children on the streets and stoops for entertainment and the need for increased structured playground spaces and recreational activities to prevent unstructured play in order to halt the spread of delinquent behavior on the streets.[16] Organizations working within the African American community stressed internal recreation programs as an alternative to the streets. Organizations like the ULP and the NAACP used the streets of African American neighborhoods to educate their neighbors regarding new medical treatments for tuberculosis and prenatal care as well as civil rights and employment issues. Reformers from these institutions focused their efforts on education and uplift of the working class and working poor. Public health officials protested the unsanitary conditions of the streets of the Hill District and used a combination of education and entertainment to combat the problems of overcrowding and poor sanitation as a mechanism to show racial fitness for equality.

Reformers in the ULP believed juvenile delinquency and social disorder were increasing in African American neighborhoods and the pervasive public health problems, like infant mortality and tuberculosis, were indicators that African American reformers needed to do more on the streets in African American neighborhoods to combat these public problems.[17] ULP records focused on the philosophical need for change while the *Pittsburgh Courier* documented the actions taking place on the streets. It was primarily women in the ULP who tackled issues of juvenile delinquency and public health as they took on the task of reforming the streets and the race.

Organizations like the ULP and the NAACP, both nationally and locally in Pittsburgh, contained many academically trained, African American social workers and sociologists from the University of Pittsburgh and other schools built on the Chicago School of Sociology's model. This training manifested itself in the policies and procedures of these organizations toward the working class and poor on the streets of Pittsburgh.[18] African American sociologists trained at the University of Pittsburgh used "social disorganization theory" to underscore the importance of structured play for children as a method to uplift the race and combat crime and delinquency.[19] Reform efforts developed in the middle class aimed at modernizing the streets of Pittsburgh, and focused on defining street use while limiting unstructured entertainment and vice on the streets.[20]

Social approval of children on the streets was heavily gendered. Fewer people frowned on the presence of young men or boys on the streets, either for play or for work, but young women or girls did not enjoy the same freedoms. The *Courier* Newsies Club presented the characteristics of thrift and hustling as a natural part of young men that needed cultivation to be useful later in their life. Salesmanship depended on the ability to be thrifty, and young men could gain the knowledge of how to sell through their association with the *Courier* Newsies Club. Young boys participating in street work in a capacity associated with the *Pittsburgh Courier* relied on the *Courier's* reputation as a respectable institution within the African American community to promote a type of respectable street participation for young boys rather than the unapproved activities of errand running and other questionable activities.[21] Barbara Gaston recalled her older brother's activities on the streets to earn money, saying, "My brothers shined shoes, they delivered papers, they swept out driveways, they swept out sidewalks, they'd go to the store for people, that's how they made their money."[22] Many young men participated in this type of enterprise as a way to make some money, but many African American reformers distrusted this type of behavior on the streets as potentially dangerous and possibly leading to increasing vice. Members of the ULP expressed great concern over perceived increasing juvenile delinquency in African American neighborhoods all over the United States and Pittsburgh, with its large population of southern migrants exhibiting greater potential for social disorganization in the eyes of African American reformers than other comparable northern cities of similar size.[23]

The *Pittsburgh Courier* used African American newspaper boys to distribute the paper within the Hill District. One anonymously authored column criticized the life of a newspaper boy and the hours that they kept as a part of their job. The author discussed his conversation with "Jim," a nine-year-old paperboy, who returned to his home around two in the morning. Jim's story was a common one. His mother married young and moved from Georgia to Pittsburgh in search of work, when her husband left her with the children and did not return. Jim and his brother both worked to help support their family. Jim faced truancy charges and the author suggested Jim was risking a future of juvenile delinquency.[24] Barbara Gaston recalled many children working jobs for their family and these jobs were essential for the economic viability of the family.[25] African American professionals fought over children working in street spaces. On one hand, children played a vital role in family economic stability for the working class; on the other hand, these same children posed a cultural risk if they were delinquent. African Americans often faced stereotypical views from other ethnic white residents of the Hill District for large numbers of lazy or disrespectful children. African American reformers suggested stronger enforcement of mandatory education and truancy laws as well as programs of structured recreation as remedies to the problem of children on the streets of the Hill District.

Many working residents of the Hill District lived in small apartments that city officials considered some of the least maintained in the city. These apartments often had little room for the family other than sleeping spaces. Children routinely used outdoor spaces for playing and took advantage of the services at local centers, like the YMCA, the Irene Kauffman Settlement House, and in the early 1930s, the Kay Boys' Club, as well as recreational programming at the local churches for entertainment. Children played games on the streets, worked as newspaper boys, and ran errands for adults. Many long-time residents of the Hill District recall playing on the streets as children. They played games like kick the can, tag, and street ball with neighboring children and played with dolls together. They also frequented the few playgrounds available in their neighborhood.[26] Children created and reinforced their own social networks on the streets of their neighborhood. While the goals of street-based entertainment often differed between the working class and the middle class, African Americans often crossed class lines during street-based entertainment.

Street-based entertainment included its own rules that united the children of the neighborhood in common play. Robert Vickers recalled, "Oh yes, we played games outside. One thing I remember very much was that when the streetlights came on you must be sitting on the porch. If you weren't sitting on the porch, you were in trouble."[27] Vickers' family lived a predominantly middle-class lifestyle. His father worked for U.S. Steel and his mother was a homemaker. They also owned their home in the Hill District, which was a distinct difference from the high rate of leasing for African Americans in the Hill District. Team play was common for the children of the Hill. Vickers recalled playing primarily with his siblings, saying, "We played games amongst ourselves. I played softball, baseball, basketball. We played neighborhood sports, we had little neighborhood teams. Those are the things we did. It seemed like back then there were a lot of kids in the neighborhood so there were a lot of things to do and kids to play with."[28] Children in the neighborhood created their own structures for play. These structures were occasionally in line with middle-class ethics of social responsibility, but often they were seen as disorganized and rife with risk.

Children's presence on the street without proper supervision indicated potential social disorganization in the community. Discussions of juvenile delinquency within the African American community focused on the presence of children on the streets and stoops for entertainment and the need for increased structured playground spaces and recreational activities.[29] Limiting children's social free time or steering them into structured play was one way of controlling working-class children on the streets.[30] Ira Reid had noted a need for a "preventive and social rehabilitation program similar to that of the Big Brother and Big Sister Movements."[31] The "Wylie Ave." column in the *Pittsburgh Courier* advertised a desire to start a Big Brother organization in 1923 stating, "We are thinking seriously of starting a Big Brother Club to bring some Christmas cheer to some destitute colored families."[32] Organizations working within the Hill District stressed internal recreation programs as an alternative to the streets. African Americans had limited access to recreational outlets.

The YMCA and YWCA were available for limited use by African American youth but only the YMCA had recreational facilities. In 1931 a group of concerned citizens including Mrs. Charles Longnecker and Mr. George L. Hailman of the board of managers of the Pittsburgh Newsboys' Home and Homer S. Brown and Harry K. Craft of the YMCA worked to establish the Kay Boys' Club at 2380 Bedford Avenue in the Hill District.[33] Many residents recalled using the services of the Kay Boys' Club and other recreation centers as an alternative to playing in the streets. The YWCA formed segregated Girl Scout troops to give young African American women a chance to participate in recreational clubs. The YMCA allowed African American groups to use their gymnasium but the demand for the facility was far greater than what the YMCA allowed. In reality, working-class children used street spaces for entertainment and used available recreation centers when they could, especially to play group games like basketball that required special equipment.

The Pittsburgh branch of the Urban League invested a lot of attention and funding into plans to construct or refurbish playground areas within the Hill District and other African American neighborhoods in Pittsburgh. The ULP praised affiliated homemakers' auxiliary clubs as they established playgrounds in African American neighborhoods.[34] Editorials in the *Pittsburgh Courier* stressed not only the physical danger to children playing unsupervised on the streets, but also the moral danger this placed on them. For the author of the editorial, play in the streets left urban African American children vulnerable to "EVIL COMPANIONSHIP" and served as their "apprenticeship" to a life of crime and vice. These evils could be combatted by proper access to recreational facilities provided by the city or the church. These two institutions had a "civic responsibility" to invest in the future of the neighborhood children in this manner.[35]

Most social workers expressed a belief that children played in the streets because they had no other options within a reasonable distance to their homes. The streets and alleyways were close and readily available and if an alternative were as convenient, children would naturally move toward more structured play. Reformers pushed the city government to improve recreation facilities in the Hill District and used the rationale of massive internal migration to the Hill District to underscore the problems of overcrowding and potential social disorganization.[36] In a 1939 editorial in the *Pittsburgh Courier*, the author addressed the perceived need for a playground, especially for African American children after the accidental death of Angelo Leonard while playing on the streets, saying:

> There was no place in all that section of the Hill District beckoning little Angelo away from the dangers of traffic or other street or play hazards. He simply had no place to play.
>
> May it not be appropriately asserted that Angelo Leonard is dead because he had no place to play? May it not be said of hundreds of other children, particularly black children, in that benighted district, that they run the risks of disease, delinquency and picket fences on the streets because they have no place to play?
>
> The Lower Centre avenue district needs a playground for all children, Mayor Scully. A playground will remove the risk to life of other Angelos, black and white. It will give them some escape from so much that is dark and dirty and narrow and indifferent to child welfare in this, one of the most congested districts of the city.[37]

Urban League homemakers' clubs looked for space to convert into playground areas for children to get them out of street spaces. Professional discussions of delinquency prevention focused on children's presence on the streets as a marker of both social disorganization and juvenile delinquency.[38] Reformers focused on creating playground spaces for children in the Hill District. There was a paucity of venues for children to play away from street spaces; the YMCA, YWCA, and Irene Kauffman Settlement House offered limited and controlled play spaces for African American children. Those locations offered segregated venues for play, but the majority of working-class African American children in the Hill District did not have consistent access to play away from street spaces.[39]

For African American social workers, structured play was as important as the location of the play. Streets themselves were unstructured and thus physically and morally dangerous while playgrounds offered a combination of enclosed, structured play and the supervision of professional "recreation experts" who were best equipped to instill societal values in the vulnerable youth of the African American working class and to steer children away from the dangers of the streets.[40]

Additionally, Reid's survey also stressed the "organized" nature of the play offered to African American children in perceived opposition to the unstructured play children engaged in on the streets of the Hill District. African American women who worked as social workers emphasized their training in child development to stress the importance of structured play for the social and moral development of children. Play also had to incorporate "fresh air" to counteract the detrimental influence of overcrowded housing and limited diets. M. E. Hubbard suggested that working-class mothers took in too many boarders in order to meet family financial obligations, which contributed to the general overcrowding of neighborhoods like the Hill District.[41] Overcrowding, crime, and generally dirty streets were not only a "public health" issue, but a moral one as well. Social workers not only associated the physical cleanliness of the neighborhood with its moral health, but they also believed the physical look of the streets indicated to the larger white society that African Americans were not fit for equal citizenship. This was an issue for the whole race.

Play on the streets of the Hill District was not the only area of conflict between African American social workers and working-class mothers. Concerns over available or adequate childcare fueled debates over the role of women in the workforce and as examples of African American female respectability especially during the interwar period. Even when working-class African American mothers could get work, childcare posed a problem. Middle-class reformers praised the ideal of a homemaker providing childcare, but the reality for working-class African Americans, and some in the middle class, included two working parents, and sometimes working children. Employment on the streets varied in its legality, but it remained a common activity for working-class African American men, women, and primarily children. Working-class African American women who worked outside of the home used street spaces as their workplaces and occasionally used them for child-care as well. These uses of the street often violated middle-class values and led reformers to view working-class street use as an indication of the neighborhood's decline. Working parents did not often have the option of having a parent stay at home. Instead, the neighborhood used social cooperation to meet their childcare needs. In much of the Hill District, working-class neighbors cared for the social needs of the community through their relationships to one another.

Odessa Wilson recalled a popular solution for the children of working parents; neighbors often took turns caring for local children until their parents returned from work. Wilson recalled: "My mother worked in housekeeping. . . . A neighbor lady took care of me until my mother came home on the weekend."[42] Wilson and many of the other working-class African American children in the Hill District had a neighbor caring for them during the week while their parents worked. Wilson also recalled, "The neighbor lady took care of some other kids too and we'd go together [to church] on Sunday."[43] Children played on the streets while they waited for their parents to get home from work. These cooperative relationships between working-class African American women allowed for neighborhood cohesion within the streets of the Hill District. Children played with other children in the same city block. Neighborhood women were often called the honorific "aunt" or "miss" to designate the respect shown to women who were commonly available to watch out for the children of other working parents.

Barbara Gaston, who was born in the Hill District, also recalled unconventional arrangements for childcare when she was a child, saying, "you could go from door to door everybody watched out for your child if you were working, my mom worked, my dad worked, I knew I could go to somebody else's house and get something to eat."[44] Gaston also recalled having Kool-Aid on Miss Sarah's porch with the other neighborhood kids and equally knowing that if Miss Sarah told you to do something that it was important that you listened or your parents would be aware of your disobedience as soon as they returned home. She also stressed the links within the working class in the larger neighborhood. She recalled that as a child she knew people within a five-block radius and that all the children in the neighborhood walked to school. This action allowed for other adults to participate in the upbringing of the neighborhood children and for the children to form relationships with one another on the streets. Charlotte Boxley recalled walking home past a neighbor's house and having him inquire about her grades in school and offer her rewards of penny candy from the corner store for making the high honor roll.[45] These interactions between children and adults on the streets of the neighborhood reinforced connections within the African American community and confounded middle-class assumptions of increasing delinquency on the streets of the Hill District.

Reformers expressed concern over the numbers of children on the streets of the Hill District. The Urban League and the NAACP both had committees dedicated to creating organized recreational activities for African American children. J. Warren Madden wrote a letter to Miss Stella E. Hartman, the field secretary of the Hill District community council, addressing perceived crime and delinquency in the Hill District. Madden related his ideas for members of the Law Observance and Enforcement Committee, saying: "My ideas are very simple. The members of the Committee should keep their eyes open, and their ears open for reports from other people as to conditions in the district concerning crime and the attitude and effectiveness of public authority toward it. If numbers are being sold indiscriminately even to school children, if prostitution is common, if saloons are selling liquor to minors, if health and sanitation laws are being violated, if policing is inadequate or indifferent, those are matters of great importance to the community."[46] Madden advocated vigilance from the members of the community, those with respectable values and proper ties to influential members of city government. The concern over the whereabouts of African American children on the streets of the Hill District also appeared in reform literature as a method of delinquency prevention. In the *Pittsburgh Courier*, John L. Clark wrote, "One of our readers offers a solution to juvenile delinquency. She proposes: 'keep all women out of the taverns, night clubs, and speakeasies, and give them more time to be mothers to their children, wives to their husbands, and friends with their neighbors.'"[47] This concern about the behavior of women and children defined middle-class African American respectability.

The Urban League of Pittsburgh often sponsored Better Baby contests as a part of its health week programming. This contest, like other baby contests, evaluated children on standards of public health and used the contest as a forum to educate mothers on proper health, sanitation, and child-rearing.[48] The goal of educating the working classes extended beyond the boundaries of public space into the private space of the home and the family as well. The Urban League created programming to educate African American women on proper, hygienic, and scientific methods of child-rearing. If working-class women failed to incorporate these lessons, the court remained a viable option for ensuring proper child-rearing.[49] The social science methodology of the

Chicago School emphasized structural and environmental forces' power in the lives of children. This model encouraged institutional and organizational responses to the threat of juvenile delinquency.

For working-class African American mothers, the standards of social scientists were difficult to meet. For many in the working class, the church filled the dual roles of character education and recreation for children and often served as an alternative to street spaces for children. Churches offered afterschool programs, vacation Bible schools, gym programs, and spaces for Girl and Boy Scout troops to meet, all while providing centers for community development.[50] Elbert Grey Sr. recalled the role of the church in preventing street violence among children and fostering community cohesion. He stated, "The churches were very important at that particular point in time. The churches were always open. They always had activities, family activities and activities for the youth in the community. The recreation centers were open. There was a lot of competition, friendly competition, throughout the community and we in turn went to other communities and competed. There was always something for us to do that kept us out of harm's way."[51] African American churches like Bidwell Presbyterian and "Brother Dan" and "Sister Ann" churches all held programs designed for both the social and spiritual health of the community as a whole, across class lines. Marcia Donnell also recalled the role of the church in the lives of the neighborhood children, saying, "In those days, you had Sunday School and Vacation Bible School so you would bring your neighbor's children and your neighbors— neighbors' children, everybody's children. So, children had the opportunity to learn even if their parents were the ones in the bars until closing every night."[52] Children had opportunities to play and access to education through the churches. Middle-class reformers approved of this type of activity for children while they questioned the presence of children on the streets of the Hill District.

Working-class African Americans often took advantage of the labor of all family members, including children, especially during hard economic times like the Depression. The *Courier* published a junior edition catering to children and youth in the city. The junior pages included games and puzzles for children as well as health-related information. Health rhymes and household tips for mothers raising children filled the page along with information on the *Courier* Newsies Club. The Newsies Club offered an opportunity for young boys to deliver papers for extra cash. In a later advertisement, the *Courier* asked parents, "What does your boy do after school?" This advertisement encouraged parents to have their sons join the *Pittsburgh Courier* Newsies Club to deliver papers after school hours as a way to "start Him on the Road to Thrift and Business Activities—Encourage Him on to Success by Starting Him RIGHT."[53] The *Courier* marketed the Newsies Club as business training for young boys. In a related article in the junior section headlined "Scores of Hustling Lads Get Splendid Training in Thrift and Salesmanship" the *Courier* argued: "Business training of a nature which will prove invaluable in later life is being gathered by dozens of local boys who are active young salesmen—members of *The Pittsburgh Courier* Newsies' Club. This group has proven to be one of the most rapidly growing associations of youths who have united to co-operate along business lines in the city."[54]

African American children from the working classes also formed their own social networks on the streets. While gang activity in the strict sense would not develop until later in the period, African American children did form social groups on the streets of the Hill District. Cum Posey reminisced about the relationships he had with other working-class children on Wylie Avenue, saying:

> John "Kid" Bates was the boss. Not only of "Dickie" and "Jimmy" his brothers, but of Wylie Avenue from Washington street to Arthur street, and all the side streets. . . . When he loaned a dollar out, you paid it back on the day and hour promised or you were "called in." We don't know when or how "Kid" came to power or how he kept his power, as he ruled through putting fear into all. . . . We don't think the Third Ward will ever be ruled by a colored or white man as it was ruled by "Kid" Bates.[55]

Street gangs of youth in the Hill District and other African American neighborhoods claimed territories of street space and fiercely defended that street space from intruders, whether adults or other gangs.

Elbert R. Grey Sr. recalled his childhood in the Northside neighborhood of Pittsburgh as one of street violence. He stated, "Being a new kid on the block always entails the kids that reside in the community testing you. There were many instances where I had to fight to survive. It was situations where focus wasn't on education, focus was on staying alive, it's kind of difficult to focus on education when you're being chased home from school or attempts are being made to bully you. You have to fight. You have to stand up."[56] Gray also recalled gangs on the streets of his childhood. African American street gangs existed alongside white street gangs and both shared similar behavioral patterns including traveling in groups, territorial claim on street spaces, and little oversight from adults. Levels of violence from street gangs varied by their strength and few gangs had any interaction with drugs in this period. Gray remembered territorial squabbles among the small African American street gangs on the Northside where they pushed back against other African American gangs for the limited space on streets dominated by African American residents. White residents lived in parallel street spaces where white street gangs dominated. Gray recalled taking a circuitous route home from school to avoid territories controlled by white gangs.[57] While the Northside had significant youth gang activity, the *Pittsburgh Courier* suggested that the Hill District had the highest concentration of youth gangs.[58] Children faced violence in the streets from other children and from adults in street spaces. Gang violence on the streets through the World War II period focused on fist fighting and other hand combat with few incidences of knife fighting. Reformers emphasized the prevalence of knife fighting and shoplifting among children in gangs and decried what they viewed as rising levels of delinquency in the African American community.[59]

Working-class African American children often worked to help supplement the family's income while middle-class children often had more free time to participate in recreational activities put on by social organizations. The boys participating in recreation programs at the YMCA were often children of the middle class. African American women did not have the same quantity or quality of recreational opportunity. Ira De Reid recommended the construction of a year-round recreation center with a pool open to African American use. He focused on recreational opportunities for African American children as a way to limit delinquency and control their presence on the streets of the Hill and other neighborhoods. Reid stated, "The recreation situation, as are other social situations, is fraught with difficulties. None of the three streets closed for general play purposes in Pittsburgh are located in the Hill District."[60] Apparently, the city routinely closed some streets for children to use as play spaces in the summer months, but the Hill District did not have any of these reserved street spaces. Many long-time residents of the Hill District recalled using street spaces to play. Marcia Donnell recalled, "Children played games on the street. We did a lot at the Y and at the other centers. But we did a lot of hide and seek, the giant, Simon Says, those kind of games, were prevalent, there were different games on different streets. If you're going to play ball and you don't have everybody, it doesn't really matter, you played with who you have."[61] Odessa Wilson also remembered playing on the streets, saying, "We played outside. We played with Doll babies and stuff like that. We went to the playground."[62] Helen Mendoza also played on the streets of the Hill District. She recalled how children played on the streets, saying: "The Hill district was somewhere to play. I ran up and down the street to play. We roller-skated. We skated in the streets. We used to take ladybugs and put them on our ears. We played hopscotch on the streets."[63]

Through the interwar period, ideas changed about the primary causes of social disorganization and perceived delinquency. In 1947 an editorial in the *Courier* chided residents of the Hill District for their reliance on "city officials" to accomplish the changes middle-class reformers wished to see on the streets. This editorial reinforced the common correlation between cleanliness of street spaces and virtue while simultaneously shifting the responsibility onto the poor and working-class residents of a "horrible block" within the Hill District. To this author, "good schools, transportation, libraries and playgrounds were available to EVERYBODY in the neighborhood," therefore the residents must be without "community responsibility and pride."[64] This editorial advocated for a group of citizens "determined to cultivate and maintain high standards."[65] These statements signaled a greater willingness to use the power of the legal system to enforce standards born out of structural understandings of racial uplift to enforce cooperation from the working class. While African American women faced common dilemmas balancing motherhood with their work they responded in differing ways. Social workers professionalized motherhood and held themselves up as experts to be emulated, while working-class mothers used their social connections to cultivate a collective understanding of motherhood that prioritized cooperation over competition. For the children who played on the streets of the Hill District, the interwar period brought many changes to their neighborhood. The development of more jobs for their mothers and fathers opened new opportunities for family support. The triumph of social scientists and scientific management allowed for new intervention from state and city authorities in their attempt to manage the streets of the Hill. While children continued to use street spaces for play and work, they were more often pushed into formalized play spaces and moved out of the streets as middle-class reformers defined streets as a place of vice and blight. These definitions would build during the interwar period and pave the way for massive renewal projects in the early postwar period. The social mothers would continue their conflict with the Black social workers in the neighborhood, but the focus of these fights changed as social workers and other Black professionals worked to demonstrate the fitness of African Americans for full equality while the working class continued their reliance on systems of reciprocity to demonstrate that they had their own values that could lead to racial uplift rather than reliance on purely middle-class values alone. These challenges continued to play out on the streets of the Hill District as the neighborhood transformed with increasing migration in the postwar period and through the crucible of urban renewal. The systems of reciprocity that built neighborhood cohesion in the working class continued to function through these challenges as more members were incorporated into the system, but the struggle between African American women over children and their use of the street only foreshadowed the conflicts between different understandings of the importance of both formal and informal systems of power on the streets and the role both types of power would play in the formation of a cohesive vision for full African American equality.

CHAPTER THREE

Deep Wylie
The Struggle for Working-Class Social World, 1930–1950

In the early interwar period, William A. Harris, known around Wylie Avenue as "Woogie," ventured up to New York City with Gus Greenlee and brought the numbers back to Pittsburgh. Woogie Harris was a well-known figure on the streets of the Hill District in Pittsburgh. Harris was the older brother of Teenie Harris and the owner of the Crystal Barbershop and Billiards Hall on Wylie Avenue. His shop was the place to get the up-to-the-minute haircut or shave along with the hottest stories coming off the Avenue. Woogie's shop also served as a hub of information on the people, politics, and informal economy in the Lower Hill District. This site was one of many spaces where legal and illegal overlapped and where the boundaries between respectability and doing work for the race blurred. Residents of the Hill District used social networks to frame their street spaces and to create systems of reciprocity to define who was in their class and who was outside of it, but these systems often could not entirely exclude members of the working class.

Street capitalists like Harris, Greenlee, and others, often operated out of a sense of reciprocity. Much like the fabled Robin Hood, their work was technically illegal, potentially immoral, and certainly questionable. They used the profits of their business to invest in the community and uplift the race in their own way. Those in the emerging middle class struggled to balance an explicit use of respectability politics to ingratiate themselves into the wider culture of Pittsburgh with the culture of the streets that honored street capitalists for their prowess in gambling and their generosity toward the African American community as a whole. This distinction between those who contributed to the community and those who took from the community through their work formed the basis for who was a part of the social world of Wylie Avenue, a regular, and who was a source of blight on the streets. The perception of vice also posed a problem for Pittsburgh's Black community as it opened up street spaces to increasingly violent police action and state suppression. The African American community built their own systems of reciprocity and power within the larger city through the social networks in their neighborhood. Street spaces nurtured the early development of race consciousness as African American Pittsburghers struggled across class lines to define their community.

In urban neighborhoods where African Americans lived and worked, the streets formed the arteries that moved goods and people in and out. The streets of urban neighborhoods were not static lines on a map or boundaries demarcating one region of urban space from another. Instead, streets functioned as spaces: spaces of labor, commerce, ideas, politics, and power. African Americans faced particular problems accessing the usual avenues of formal power within American cities, but they formed their own networks of information and ideas in segregated neighborhoods. These networks of informal power challenged formal notions of social hierarchy within the community and created conflicts along and within the color line. These streets were sites of struggle and cultural development. During the Modern Black Freedom Movement, African American Pittsburghers formed alliance-based systems of reciprocity with the working class and based on the streets of the neighborhood to combat social and economic injustice. The streets became a theater of battle as African Americans used the visibility of streets to display the outcomes of systemic inequality in the urban North, including frequent charges of police brutality and violence.

During the early years of the northern civil rights movement, street capitalists used their networks of informal power to amass large and questionable fortunes, but these networks all functioned through communal systems of reciprocity. The combination of legal and illegal enterprise often garnered a side-eye from African Americans invested in cultural respectability. But for those enmeshed in systems of reciprocity, the promise that social debts would be paid kept few from openly disputing their labor. As the movement for equality and human rights progressed, African Americans used their informal networks to advance their cause, until some gained access to more formal networks of power and the alliance between classes collapsed amid urban redevelopment and increasing street violence.

Woogie Harris, one of preeminent street capitalists of the Hill District, used loans from his variety of legal and illegal enterprises to finance many of the businesses that lined the shopping area up and down Wylie Avenue. These businesses formed the central nexus of streets along the Wylie Avenue corridor which situated legal and illegal enterprise below and alongside residential streets. Many longtime residents of the Hill District remember the variety of goods available within the boundaries of their neighborhoods. Black-owned businesses and those owned by other ethnic minorities within the Hill District that catered to African American Pittsburgh coveted the spaces along the central business district up and down Wylie Avenue. De-wayne Ketchum recalled his father Theodore's tailor shop along Wylie Ave. in the Lower Hill District and the important role it played in the neighbor-hood. Like much of the shopping area, the storefront faced the Ave. while the second and third floors provided space for storage and living quarters.[1] This shop was not unusual in its vertical organization. Ketchum's tailor shop also was not unusual in its combination of legal and extralegal labor. Ket-chum used his storefront as a neighborhood pawn shop and also held money for the numbers men along Wylie Avenue. Wylie Avenue was a business space as well as a living space for many within the neighborhood. This central ar-tery was a meeting place for many working-class African Americans after the workday was done. It was viewed as a street that did not sleep since patrons were often on the Avenue during business hours and late into the morning.

Young men and women maneuvered through the shops up and down the Avenue, especially during the late hours of the night. For many working-class African American migrants, affiliation as a regular on Wylie Avenue created an environment of camaraderie and a social network where regulars took care of one another. Regulars were a part of the system of reciprocity in the neigh-borhood. In one instance, the *Pittsburgh Courier* reported that an entertainer's mother died, and a group of his associates collected money to get him home for her funeral. John L. Clark commented, "Because he was a 'regular' fellow it was not held against him as is the case in the higher strata. Nobody asked why he hadn't saved for such an occasion."[2] This association of those who were "regulars" suggests that the neighborhood held distinctions between those who were a part of their system and those who were outside. The arti-cle implies class distinctions, but those distinctions seem based on attitudes and social connections rather than economics. The designation of "regular" applied to those who viewed the street as their community and who partici-pated in its system of informal power. Wylie Ave. regulars carried specific val-ues that did not necessarily reach the standard set by middle-class African Americans. Regulars valued their own community and participation in the life of the street. Regulars could be men or women, rich or poor, but they all spent a great deal of time on the streets of the Hill District.

Street capitalists, like regulars, were kin to many within the working class and often invested their profits toward the advancement of the community. As the last hired, first fired, many working-class Blacks embraced illegal or quasilegal labor as an alternative to labor insecurity. The streets of urban neighborhoods became spaces where men and women worked in both for-mal and informal ways. Prostitutes and jitney drivers faced labor issues in their street work like competition, labor discipline, and encroachment. Residents of the Hill District also faced violence in the form of police brutality and increasing censure from middle-class reformers for increasing disreputable behavior on the streets. Street capitalists, by their position across the legal boundaries of labor, navigated class divisions within the African American community in unique ways. Middle-class African Americans expressed ambivalence, followed by growing hostility between legal and extralegal work. They struggled to deal with the most successful street capitalists, especially those who ascended into the ranks of the African American elite through combinations of illegal and legal labor. Clark's column also showed how interconnected the so-called respectable world of the African American middle class were with the "underworld" in the Hill District. Clark writes,

> By this time it should be generally known that the Avenue is a clearing house for inside knowledge or "the low down" on the "respectables" who reside in our city. Men and women slide by on false reputations in other sections but down here they must "be themselves."
>
> A common practice of toying with the underworld is charged up against professionals and business men of the slicker type. In their own homes they are accepted as puritans or stoics. It is not unusual for one of these men to mount platforms and spout off at the mount against conditions which they, in practical life, help to develop.[3]

Over time, the developing middle class disavowed those who "toyed with the underworld" as they were able to access more formal networks of power. Aspiring middle-class residents of the Hill cut working-class residents out of their social networks as a way of defining their separate class status. The relationships between these members of the neighborhood often shifted over time and through the street spaces of the Lower Hill.

Working-class street capitalists participated in street life in both legal and illegal ways throughout the period leading up to World War II. Charles Harris Jr. recalled his father Teenie Harris's life in Pittsburgh and his work in the Hill District. In an oral history interview, Harris described the interplay between legal and illegal labor in the Hill District among friends and associates of Teenie Harris. Harris recalled George Harris, of no relation to the photographer, who owned a confectionary on the corner of Wylie Avenue. The confectionary sold soft drinks and ice cream to the local population as well as small groceries. Harris's confectionary was a gathering place for African Americans in the Hill District and did a brisk business in the late evening, often staying open twenty-four hours a day.

Teenie Harris photographed two girls standing in front of Harris's confectionary (see figure 3.1). In the storefront window you see a sampling of the wares including detective novellas, smoking paraphernalia, and advertisements for soft drinks. Street corner shops like Harris's were meeting places for African Americans across classes but in the evenings working-class African Americans and those participating in illegal business thrived in the same gathering places.[4] Charles Harris Jr. also noted that George Harris ran numbers games out of his confectionary in the evening hours. This illegal lottery was the "economic engine of the Hill District."[5] Numbers runners operated in the space between legal and illegal labor.

Numbers businesses often operated out of legal street corner businesses. Restaurants, barbershops, nightclubs, convenience stores, and other venues with large numbers of customers going in and out often served as fronts for illegal labor in the Hill District. Street transactions moved into affiliated businesses and back out into street spaces as these legal fronts sheltered street-based transactions from the eyes and intervention of authorities. Marcia Donnell recalled the prevalence of the numbers in the Hill District, saying:

> The numbers were very, very, very popular. So you could yell out
> the house "what were the numbers" we didn't know nothing about the
> word "lottery" "what were the numbers" and because of me growing
> up here and in my teens I really knew what was going on but as a
> young girl you could play something called "the last figure" can you
> imagine, you have three digits and then you had what was called "I'm
> going to play the last figure" you could get like two dollars if you
> played the last figure for a quarter. When you think that gasoline,
> I mean when I was in my twenties gasoline was like twenty-nine cents
> a gallon, so you can imagine what it was when I was a young girl so if
> you could hit for a quarter and get two dollars you could get a lot.[6]

For many in the neighborhood, the prize from hitting the numbers was an incentive to play and fueled the practice in the Hill District.[7]

The bookies running the numbers held a place of prestige in the community even though their enterprise was strictly illegal. Winnings from hitting the numbers was the economic engine of the Hill District. Harris recalled his Uncle William "Woogie" Harris's interaction with both legal and illegal enterprise. Woogie operated a barbershop and pool hall in the Hill District. While these businesses were legal, Woogie also ran numbers out of the pool hall.[8] Woogie Harris also had an informal business partnership with another Hill resident who excelled in both legal and illegal enterprise, Gus Greenlee.

FIGURE 3.1 Dolores Stanton and Eleanor Hughes Griffin standing in front of
George Harris's confectionery store, 2121 Wylie Avenue, Hill District, July 1937.
Charles "Teenie" Harris (American, 1908–98), gelatin silver print, H: 10 in. ×
W: 7¹⁵⁄₁₆ in. (25.40 × 20.16 cm), Carnegie Museum of Art, Pittsburgh: Purchase:
Second Century Acquisition Fund and Gift of Milton and Nancy Washington,
1996.55.17, © Carnegie Museum of Art, Charles "Teenie" Harris Archive.

"Leroy Jones," who was born in the Hill District, recalled, "Numbers men like Woogie Harris and the Greenlees gave food out, started a football league, they helped the community out. Numbers men were a blessing to us. That's when the white men wanted to take it over."[9] As long as the numbers men contributed to the community most residents ignored their illegal activities. As a part of a thriving underground economy, Harris and Greenlee offered loans for business start-ups or for African American children to attend school. African Americans across class lines respected Harris and Greenlee for their philanthropy, even if they did not approve of their illegal activities. Harris and Greenlee also bought a section of row houses in Homewood along Frankstown Avenue. They then rented the row houses to African American families for what they could afford.[10] This allowed African Americans to move into quality rental housing that was affordable in an emerging Black neighborhood.

Street capitalists used loans and favors to connect to a broad coalition of social networks across class lines. Harris stated that during the Depression, Gus Greenlee "went to New York to find out about Numbers and brought them back to Pittsburgh."[11] Greenlee loaned money to Teenie Harris to open his photography studio on Centre Avenue in the Hill District. While African Americans like Woogie Harris, Gus Greenlee, and George Harris occupied the boundaries between formal and informal labor, they also crossed the boundaries between African American elites and the working class. Working-class African Americans relied on bookies for community support. On Wylie Avenue, a write-in letter advised African Americans facing jail time in Allegheny County jail to not waste time calling the bail bondsman until they spoke to their bookie.[12] The bookie would have the money to post cash bail and would often loan it on better terms than the bail bondsman. Bookies also held positions of varying esteem within the African American community. Working-class African Americans often used connections with both legal and illegal labor to increase their financial ability, and the streets of the Hill District offered a venue to explore both types of labor options.

As elsewhere in industrial America, the onset of the Great Depression weakened the economic and institutional underpinnings of Pittsburgh's African American community, but class divisions persisted on the streets of the Hill District as middle- and working-class African Americans dealt with the effects of the economic downturn. Middle-class African Americans expressed ambivalence, and occasionally hostility, about the blurring of the lines between legal and extralegal work during this period, while working-class Blacks more readily embraced these systems of reciprocity within the informal economy (including numbers games, prostitution, and jitney driving) to help make ends meet. The emerging middle class used the spaces of the streets of the Hill District to construct their own social networks that increasingly excluded members of the working class as they defined their space for "race men" and their women.

Pittsburgh was home to a number of African Americans who had ascended to high social status within the community. Many African Americans of means gravitated to fraternal orders and clubs as a way of reforming social networks with other members of their social class rather than from within the systems of reciprocity present in the neighborhood streets. The FROGs were one such group within the Hill District. Their name stands for Friendly Rivalry Often Generates Success, and they operated out of the Loendi Club. The *Pittsburgh Courier* reported plans for FROG Week in 1930, saying: "Frog Week, two magic words indicative of gaiety and joy and cordial hospitality, will hold the spotlight of Pittsburgh's social world this year beginning with August 3rd and extending through to the 9th. This welcome announcement, heralding a local season of festivities which fashionable folk everywhere look forward to, was released by the officers of the popular Frogs Club Tuesday. According to the present plans of the club members, Frog Week this year will be bigger and better than ever."[13] While this report claims that FROG Week would proceed in much the same fashion as previous years, the article also implied a degree of concern regarding whether FROG Week would take place. In 1932, Jule, a society reporter for the *Courier* declared, "Old Man Depression was completely side-tracked," during FROG Week.[14] Earlier in the year, another African American club, "The Ducks," also planned a ham and egg fry in Highland Park along with a "Depression Dance."[15] Groups like the Ducks shifted the traditional emphasis on fashion in elite African American entertainment by hosting a Depression Dance featuring "old clothes."[16] The Ducks commented, "Can you imagine attending a dance and not having to think of what to wear? The Ducks have made that decision. There will be no new dresses. Wear just what you have been wearing and come along."[17] The Ducks also promised that the event offered "a full measure of real entertainment at a depression price."[18] Other members of African American high society commended the Ducks for their novel idea of a Depression dance and hailed their event as a highlight of FROG Week.[19]

African Americans occupying the social level of the FROGs seemingly held different opinions on the state of the Depression from their working-class and working-poor neighbors. In November of 1930, the *Courier* sponsored a charity drive for the working class and working poor stating, "this drive is not intended to help people who never work, who are habitually idle and who refuse to work, but it is devoted to the people who are industrious in normal times, but who are now; because of the lack of employment, destitute and without funds, but not without honor and character."[20] This drive focused on providing necessities like food, shoes, coal, and underwear for those unemployed in the working classes. The *Courier* editor stated: "It will be a sad day for our community when our little ones who have been accustomed to some expression of Christmas at Christmas time learn this year that this community is so poor and so impoverished, so Santa Claus is so niggardly and so selfish that he cannot visit the little folks as he has in years gone by. They must not know and feel the actual sting of deprivation and poverty."[21] Elite African Americans expressed varying degrees of social obligation toward the poor, emphasizing their position as self-described leaders of the race.

In a response to a published debate between African American elites on the subject of how best to deal with African American poor, John L. Clark castigated the self-titled African American leadership for their "antics" and for doing "nothing" to help those "faced with actual starvation."[22] Clark goes on to say, "If our poor and hungry had to depend on Negro organizations for aid they would be even worse off than they are now."[23] African American elites who were somewhat insulated from the full effect of the Depression responded in different ways than the African American middle class and especially Blacks in the working class.

Middle-class and professional African Americans faced significant insecurity over employment and access to a living wage. This economic insecurity translated into concerns over the possibility of increasing juvenile delinquency and crime during a period of economic hardship. Many in the middle class attempted to ameliorate the effects of the Depression on children on the streets. J. H. N. Waring Jr., a well-known educator, weighed the implications of an extended Depression on African American children in Pennsylvania including "the disappearance of the home" which would lead to "a large number [developing] in social and criminal delinquents" or joining the estimated 200,000 strong "army of vagrants" across the country.[24] To Waring, the economic troubles magnified social disorder within the African American community and children, especially the adolescent children of the working class and the working poor, who faced the most potential harm from a continued economic depression.

As the Depression moved on, New Deal programs reached into the African American community and the continuing presence of African American laborers in less desirable positions allowed some African Americans to maintain their economic status. Street spaces became increasingly politicized as African Americans expressed their discontent over the racially uneven effects of the Depression. A local resident worried that the economic hardships would produce radical feelings in the children of the Hill District, saying: "Of such things are criminals made; of such things are Communists and Bolsheviks born, and our little folks must not grow up believing that this great country, and especially this great community, cannot have Santa Claus visit them this year."[25] The fear of many middle-class and elite African Americans that economic hardship would bolster the small African American communist numbers or radicalize the working classes drove many middle-class African Americans to embrace liberalism through Franklin D. Roosevelt's New Deal.

African Americans in Pittsburgh felt the Depression in their neighborhoods and on the streets of the Hill District. African Americans in the Hill did not feel these effects evenly across class lines. Class divisions continued on the streets through differing responses to the economic conditions of the Depression and the demographic changes of the Great Migration. These early divisions between the middle class and working class developed over fear of delinquency and crime from those in the middle class and toleration of illegal labor by those in the working class. Under the influence of the Great Depression, middle-class Blacks expressed some ambivalence over precisely how they should react.

Rayford W. Logan, assistant director of the Association for the Study of Negro Life and History, also addressed concerns about the potential effects of a long Depression in his address to the Twenty-fourth Annual Conference of the NAACP in Pittsburgh in 1933. Logan argued that "liberal thought" and "radicalism" were growing among African Americans since the Great War. Logan declared, "A new radicalism among American Negroes stimulated by the migration northward from the south, the World War, and the Depression is spreading steadily."[26] These concerns by middle-class and professional observers of the working classes revealed increasing tensions between those in the professional classes who downplayed the severity of the Depression and those in the working classes who felt the Depression keenly. African Americans in Pittsburgh displayed these disagreements on the streets through divergent uses of street spaces in their neighborhoods.

African American workers complained that they were the "first fired and last hired," and as such they felt "the depression first and [were] the last to feel relief when the depression [wa]s over."[27] Unprecedented unemployment within the African American community combined with racial discrimination in relief programs placed heavy burdens on working-class African Americans. African Americans typically held "drudgery" jobs; one writer for the *Courier* claimed that the Depression for African Americans was "largely an impression" because African Americans already did the jobs that white Pittsburghers did not want to do.[28] Although African Americans held the lowest caliber jobs in the city, working-class African Americans still faced unemployment, which exacerbated class differences among African Americans. One writer in the *Courier* compared economic conditions among working-class African Americans to the period before emancipation and declared "conditions are now worse than during the period before 1865."[29]

Poor African Americans faced problems as they skimped on food and fuel during the Depression. Algernon B. Jackson, MD revealed a disturbing trend of young children reporting symptoms of lead poising from families using old battery casings as fuel.[30] For many working-class and working poor African Americans, the Depression changed their neighborhood in dramatic ways. The lack of coal for heating and shabby clothing were only a few of the changes. Local businesses failed, while others, perhaps less viable, emerged, and still others survived the hardships of the Depression. John L. Clark outlined the changes to the Ave in his column, "Wylie Ave.," stating:

> From Fullerton to Logan, one gets the impression at night that conditions have not changed. Bright street lights and the hustling auto traffic tend to make one overlook the fact that many changes have taken place. Sammy Rosenfield operates only one store now. Jeff, the tailor, has been replaced by a beanery two doors above Townsend Street. The Avenue restaurant, taken over by Kid Welch, is just a memory. This is also true of Norvell's Hotel. Max Goodman (Mack's) at Logan Street holds the spotlight at this intersection — although admitting that the going is rough. Dining car employees are no longer quartered in this block, having been transferred to the "Y" at Centre Avenue and Francis Street. In the "dark stretch" — Logan to Congress — Jackson's Undertaking Establishment remains active. And George Nelson continues to make, alter, and press clothes at the same old spot.[31]

Illegal laborers also felt the sting of the Depression on their work. The *Courier* reported, "Members of the 'fifth-estate,' the rum runners, are feeling the effects of the depression along with legitimate business."[32] Illegal business often benefitted and suffered from the same cycles as legal enterprise, but it is difficult to discern the true cost to illegal business because of the lack of reporting. As for prostitution, it is possible that the Depression increased the number of women practicing prostitution in the Hill District.[33]

The *Courier* reported the tale of a cabbie who helped an African American woman escape conviction for prostitution by setting up an informant to rescind his testimony. In the article, the author tells the story of Eleanor, described as "only about 24, reddish brown-skinned, five feet four and in perfect proportion,"[34] and outlines her fall from respectability into the world of implied prostitution. Eleanor worked in an office as a secretary where she became involved with a married man she worked for. When she lost that job, her reputation was so damaged within the community that she had trouble getting a job. Eventually, Eleanor was arrested "along with several other ladies who shared the big house on the side street."[35] The cabbie conspired with Sally Weldon, "a colored girl who is about as white as a woman can be. In addition, she has blonde hair," and Jeff Fischer, a federal narcotics agent. Sally flirted with the informant and eventually planted a packet of cocaine on him that Fischer then "discovered" in exchange for him "leaving town for six weeks." Fischer claimed he would "not report" the cocaine on the informant. The court dismissed Eleanor's case for lack of evidence.[36] This episode shows how members of the working class did not necessarily frown on prostitution and other illegal labor. The cabbie in this article showed compassion for how Eleanor got into prostitution and helped her avoid conviction for her actions. He did express relief that Eleanor would not return to prostitution after her near escape, but his use of narcotics agents and another African American woman shows how working-class African Americans, illegal laborers, and law enforcement could work together.

In the *Pittsburgh Courier*, John L. Clark revealed the conflict between those espousing middle-class values and those that operated within the systems of reciprocity by saying:

One "Well Wisher" wrote in to chastise a businessman on the Avenue:

Dear Sir:
I happened to be in your place of business the other evening. There were two fellows started to argue with one another and finally one threatened to throw the other out. I also noticed fellows and girls pulling and running each other down the aisle, which looked very bad. I also noticed different fellows standing around playing what they call the dozens with each other. I had a party of friends with me and when they saw what was going on they would not stay. I will say you have a

wonderful place of business; your service is excellent. You have done more for the people on the Hill than any other man has done. We appreciate it. But if you want the patronage of the better class of people in Pittsburgh and elsewhere you certainly will have to have better order, particularly in the restaurant. I wish you would give this immediate attention. It may mean better business for you.[37]

Clark asked his readers in response, "Now, who ever heard of a restaurant on the Avenue thriving on patronage of the 'better class?'"[38] This example illustrates the conflict between African Americans within the Hill District. Although the event the writer referenced occurred primarily inside the doors of a business on the Ave, the conflict between African Americans who viewed themselves as part of "the better class" wished to change the behavior of others and limit certain areas of the Hill District to those of the same class.

Women also participated in life on the streets of the Hill District. African American women worked in businesses and restaurants along the Avenue as well as in prostitution and other forms of illegal labor. The lines between these groups often blurred and were a point of contention between African Americans in the Hill District. In "Wylie Ave.," Clark defended the virtue of waitresses at the establishments on the Ave from charges of prostitution and other illegal labor. He stated:

There is an impression about Avenue waitresses, or girls who work at anything on the Avenue, which needs correction. At afternoon teas, private dinners or scatter-brained sorority affairs many of the titled proselytes create or repeat lies, which have no foundation.

They do with their own girls what they condemn the white man for doing with the entire race. All girls of the Avenue are thrown into one immoral classification and discussed as such. To these simple women there is no distinction between a girl who earns her living as a waitress and one who advertises herself as a common prostitute.

As a matter of fact the majority of waitresses have better minds and stronger character than those girls who sometimes are forced to take the name of a doctor or lawyer. The waitress not only works with her feet, hands, and mind every day, but subjects her character to a daily test. And it is surprising to know that only a small percentage of those tests leave bad results.[39]

Clark condemned other African American women for their uncharitable attitude toward Black waitresses who were working class. These waitresses spent a great deal of time in the company of men on the Ave, but the streets were their workplace. Working-class African Americans did not assign the same standards of respectability to women working on the street. Waitresses often worked in a vulnerable position between legitimate labor and illegitimate labor. Many of the restaurants and lunch counters were legitimate businesses and operated as such. On the other hand, many women worked at unlicensed beer gardens and other bars as servers and proprietors. These women faced more perceived censure and a stronger association with prostitution.

According to the *Pittsburgh Post*, many African Americans of all classes expressed outrage at unchecked vice in the Hill District, yet few African Americans participated in meetings designed to address the issue.[40] This view, from a white newspaper, typified the view of the majority of Pittsburghers outside the Hill District. For many, the Hill District was a center of vice and crime in the Steel City. The white press suggested that vice was out of control in the Hill District. As one *Courier* reporter responded,

> A prejudiced reporter, a "cracker" city editor and an exaggerated misstatement of many of the facts, has led to the revoking of the dance license of the now famous Paramount Inn, 1213 Wylie Avenue, has caused a storm of vigorous protest against an article appearing in Tuesday morning's Pittsburgh Post. . . . The paragraphs which have aroused the ire of the Hill and caused a feeling of racial animosity throughout the entire city, allege that white girls of tender ages, of the so called "flapper" type, are running wild in the numerous "black and tan" cabarets, in the plague spot of a city infested with vice.[41]

Church attendance or affiliation played a major role in African American tolerance of vice. The quotation from the *Pittsburgh Post* suggested that churches had launched their own investigation and "revealed unspeakable conditions."[42] The reporter from the *Courier* refuted these specific charges, but the campaign linking the Hill District to increasing vice continued in the white press. Churches focused on more than cleaning up vice in the Hill but also on a "language 'clean-up'" as well. The *Courier* reported on a campaign to address the "vulgar and unprintable language, which one hears at almost every step throughout a stroll through the Hill District." In this article, the author stated, "On the street corners, in public places and floating through the windows of private homes, the filthy talk comes in a seemingly endless stream, and many a woman has been seen to hang her head in shame as she passes hurriedly by. . . . The language is vulgar and depicts the users as having little or no respect for our Negro womanhood."[43] The author defined African American womanhood as genteel, refined, and church affiliated. These definitions corresponded with African American middle-class notions of respectability. The concern over vice and language continued well into the interwar period. Chester L. Washington said, "Raids Razed Deep Wylie from stem to stern over the past weekend. The cops couldn't have swept the district any more effectively with a broom. They broke down doors with crowbars. And they took away scores of men and women on every conceivable charge. The Bluecoats, however, missed the lower end of the Avenue, just below the seething Black Belt."[44]

Washington also elaborated on relationships between idealized African American men and women on the Avenue. For women in the professionalizing middle class, it was critical to distance themselves from the systems of reciprocity at play in the working class. Individualism and the ability to separate yourself from the systems of reciprocity at work in the neighborhood were the markers of middle-class social status and a convenient fiction that allowed professional African American women a way to claim the virtues associated with idealized African American womanhood.

For women who depended on systems of reciprocity to meet their basic needs, life was often more complicated in the Hill District. Threats of arrest for prostitution or illegal liquor sales were common for African American women in the Hill District. Ira De A. Reid documented that 71 percent of the arrests among African Americans resulted from visiting or keeping disorderly or bawdy houses. This ranked second out of the most common causes for African American arrests in 1928.[45] Both African American and white residents of the Hill District faced arrest for keeping or visiting houses of prostitution. Raids had little effect in shutting down prostitution on the Hill. The top three vices listed in Reid's report were: "(1) Gambling and policy playing, (2) Illegal manufacture and sale of liquor, and (3) Prostitution and its related vices."[46] Reid described a status divide between prostitutes, namely those who worked out of a disorderly house and those who worked on the street. Over the period, home-based prostitution declined as automobile and street-based prostitution increased.

For African American men, gambling and being good with cards signified the masculine ideal, while African American women were supposed to be faithful, church attending, and beautiful. These feminine characteristics also imparted luck to men on the Avenue.[47] The ideal woman presented by men on the Avenue was not always consistent with women's behavior on the Avenue. Female gamblers were not unusual on Wylie Avenue John L. Clark suggested "the best poker game in town is staged right here on the Avenue. Men and women play every night with a fifty-cent limit. Squabblers and cheaters are barred and the game is 'cut' only when staged in three other homes in the circuit. Waitresses, barmaids, and housewives have been known to drop $150 in a night. Several 'numbers' men drop in just as regularly 'drop' their bundle."[48] Working-class African Americans differed on their perspective on gambling and on illegal activity on the Avenue, but their opinion often coincided with their church attendance or affiliation.[49]

Sex work flourished along Wylie Ave. throughout the period. Many African Americans along the Ave suggested prostitution did not always violate the morals of the working class, but there were those in the middle class who disapproved. Map 3.1 details the side streets Reid lists in his report and shows their proximity to Wylie Avenue. Cribs along the alleys off Wylie Avenue operated as locations for sex work in the Hill District.[50] Vice cleanup campaigns focused on the allies and side streets off Wylie Avenue. Reformers and patrons alike knew the alleys and side streets along Wylie and Fullerton offered ample opportunity for illegal entertainment in the Hill District. Teenie Harris documented the conditions along Wylie Avenue in the Hill District.[51] In this period, prostitution also occurred in houses or salons along Epiphany Street and other streets in the Lower Hill District. Other women practiced prostitution out of their own homes.

While most African American prostitutes served members of their own race, some race mixing did occur, primarily with the Italian and Slav laborers who also resided in the Hill District. Reid quoted James Forbes from the Pittsburgh Survey stating that among African Americans, "the largest number [of colored girls] living as prostitutes in Pittsburgh found places in the alley houses of the Hill District."[52] While Forbes conducted this survey in an earlier period, Reid acknowledged that much of Forbes's findings remained accurate in the late 1920s. Prostitution thrived in the Hill District because of a large population of African American and other working-class laborers and a seeming lack of concern over the actions of women on the streets from the majority of the working classes. Members of the African American middle class expressed great concern over the presence of prostitution on the streets of their neighborhood and chided police and city officials over ineffectual raids they saw as a political tool to gain favor rather than an effective method for rooting out prostitution and vice from their neighborhood.[53] The raids were often ineffective because the plans for them were leaked to the targets before the raid could be started. Many of the people involved in informal labor were in close relation and in social networks with those outside of the

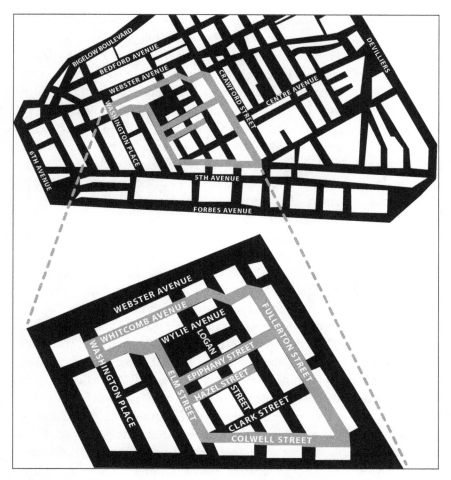

MAP 3.1 Prostitution locations in the Lower Hill District before urban renewal. Jason Klanderud, Altair Media Design, Designer.

informal economy. Bawdy houses used the laundry down the street, women who worked at an illegal beer garden had family that worked at the grocery. The economic and social lives of the Hill District were intertwined.

Participation in extralegal labor like numbers running, prostitution, or jitney driving did not automatically disqualify a person from respectability within the systems of reciprocity at work within the Hill District. John L. Clark defined multiple types of respectability, saying: "Negroes have numerous ways of determining the respectability of people. The ditch digger or unskilled laborer are automatically disqualified because of the way in which they earn a livelihood. The prerequisite to respectability, in the opinion of most Negroes, is a white collar and a college degree. It matters very little whether the wearer of the white collar or the holder of the degree engages in legal or illegal practices. As long as he is so equipped he is respectable."[54] Clark's column showed the relationships between those of perceived respectability and those who operated as "regulars" on Wylie Avenue. He did not suggest that the Avenue did not have any concept of respectability; it just differed from how others in the African American community, particularly those in the middle class, perceived respectability.[55] John L. Clark's column also showed how interconnected the so-called respectable world of the African American middle class was with the "underworld" in the Hill District. Clark discussed the "inside knowledge" of certain "respectables" who often toyed with the "underworld" of the Avenue while maintaining a public facade of middle-class virtue. The interactions between those African Americans traditionally described as the middle class and those described as the "underworld" also make such distinctions based on economics alone difficult. Values and behaviors make for a clearer distinction in some cases. The reform workers who declare progressive values claimed a middle-class identity while the "regulars" on the Avenue claim an identity associated with their neighborhood and working-class affiliation. Instead, those who participated within the system of reciprocity at work within the Hill District could claim status in the neighborhood, while some who had more access to formal power in the form of education or wealth were able to separate themselves from the informal systems at work within the neighborhood. The professionalizing middle class could access some forms of formal power due to their education and employment. Many of the African American women trained at the University of Pittsburgh in the emerging social work program worked to implement the social science training they received to uplift their neighborhood by instituting formal programs to reform the informal networks of the neighborhood into modern, scientific, and structured social systems that would demonstrate the fitness of African Americans for full citizenship.

For African Americans who lived and worked in the Hill District, their relationship with street capitalists and social networks changed during the interwar period. The financial hardships of the Great Depression caused more of the residents of the Hill District to rely on their neighborhood-based systems of reciprocity to meet their needs. These systems used the spaces of the neighborhood streets to build and sustain connections between African Americans across class lines. These systems incorporated those working in both legal and illegal labor as well as those doing primarily reproductive labor. The capitalists of the street were individuals that crossed the boundaries between the legal and illegal worlds of the Hill District, and they created a system of informal power that allowed affiliation as a regular along the Avenue to carry a degree of power within the neighborhood. By the beginning of World War II, however, Pittsburgh's Black community forged cross-class alliances and pushed for victory against fascism abroad and racism at home. Whereas earlier cross-class uses of the streets revolved around such events as baby contests, street fairs, and parades, by the war's end, the streets of African American Pittsburgh had taken on new and more highly politicized multiclass uses. As African American veterans returned from World War II focused on gaining access to formal power networks of voting, equal employment, and fair housing, they planned to use formal respectability to access those power networks within the city as a whole. The world of the street capitalists and their networks of informal power posed a liability to those who were trying to leverage economic mobility into formal political power.

CHAPTER FOUR

Webster Avenue

Blight, Renewal, or Negro Removal, 1945–1960

In the mid-1950s, Theodore Ketchum received a notification from the Urban Redevelopment Authority (URA) informing him that he would have to relocate his tailor shop from 1414 Wylie Avenue in the Lower Hill District to make way for the construction of the Civic Arena. Ketchum's Tailor Shop was one of many African American businesses affected by redevelopment of the Lower Hill District. It was a part of a vibrant shopping district along the Wylie Avenue and Fullerton Street corridor. The Crawford Grille and the Crystal Palace Barbershop were along Wylie Ave., as was Goodes Pharmacy and Harris's Confectionary. These shops all faced relocation as a part of the redevelopment of the Lower Hill District along with about 8,000 residents. After much discussion and debate, Ketchum moved his shop further uptown into the Middle Hill to 5 Erin Street between Wylie and Centre Avenues, where many Lower Hill residents who were able to afford the rents secured space. Like most affected by the efforts to redefine the streets of the Lower Hill, Ketchum's Tailor Shop moved into the Middle Hill after considering moving out to the developing African American neighborhood of Homewood. Businesses and residents tried to outmaneuver the URA as the city of Pittsburgh used eminent domain legislation to redefine the streets of the Lower Hill District as blighted and in need of renewal. The URA gained broad authority to define areas of the neighborhood, but the residents of the Hill District did not accept these definitions without contesting them and using their social networks to push back against them. The influence of *urban renewal* demolished much of the Lower Hill District while also transforming and dispersing the residents and their social networks throughout the Hill District and into emerging African American neighborhoods like Homewood and East Liberty.[1]

Urban renewal, which developed as a response from the city to the "Double V" campaign and efforts by the African American community to address social and economic inequality, changed the physical and social street spaces of the Hill District as middle-class and working-class African Americans struggled to define the streets of their neighborhood to their best advantage. Through parades and other street-based actions, African American

Pittsburghers pushed for better access to jobs and fair housing. The efforts of middle-class reformers to address issues of economic inequality within the Hill District transformed the streets of the neighborhood. This transformation changed many of the streets of the Lower Hill District into *blighted* areas requiring change to make them habitable for *respectable* people. While some residents of the Hill District welcomed these definitions, others resisted defining their neighborhood and their social world as something degenerate. African Americans struggled across class lines over acceptable uses of street spaces, prevailing definitions of street spaces, and perceptions of varied respectability for people on the streets of Pittsburgh. Street-based expressions of neighborhood reciprocity, like parades and street fairs, continued as a way of fostering a sense of community and solidifying social networks within the Hill District. But the intrusion of the larger city, with its definitions of blighted street space, into the Hill District increased class tensions among African Americans in Pittsburgh. Beginning after World War II, urban renewal initiatives that pushed through Pittsburgh focused on the "golden triangle" of downtown Pittsburgh. Wylie Avenue or simply "the Ave," was the dominant artery of the Hill District and in many ways the social world of African American Pittsburgh. Many elite and middle-class African Americans welcomed renewal of the lower section of Wylie Avenue as a method of curtailing abuses by absentee landlords and possibly opening up more access to Black homeownership, while many working-class African Americans resented intrusions into street spaces defined as their neighborhood.

African American migrants faced poor housing conditions in the Lower Hill District. Overcrowding, poor housing stock, and absentee landlords led to severe deterioration of the lower section of the Hill District.[2] Many working-class African American families and recent migrants from the South lived in the Lower Hill District. Incoming migrants and other members of the African American working class faced declining prospects for employment as employment in the steel industry declined. Blacks faced numerous instances of discrimination in manufacturing, technology, transportation, building trades, and other industries. A growing African American population collided with a tight job market for African Americans in nonmenial labor and increased the divide between those who obtained skilled and professional positions and those who were unable to breach that barrier. Urban redevelopment separated and redefined the working-class neighborhood of the Lower Hill District from the relatively more prosperous neighborhood of the Upper Hill. Over the period of urban renewal, the divide between working-class African Americans and those within the middle class widened both socially and spatially.

The "Double V" campaign encouraged African Americans to pursue a double victory for democracy, both home and abroad. Victory at home would give African Americans the civil liberty they desired and believed they were fighting for abroad. African American's push for democracy at home was contested from many directions. This campaign also occurred across class lines as middle-class and working-class African Americans forged a tentative alliance to push for social and economic equality. In 1943, the *Pittsburgh Courier* printed an editorial and cartoon entitled "The Convenient Accused" which showed a disoriented "Uncle Sam" after a beating from a large white man with a club confronting a small African American paperboy. The editorial stated:

> When some heinous CRIME is committed, the canny criminal looks around for some convenient person to accuse in order to thwart JUSTICE. The latest illustration of this natural bent is the increasingly frequent charge hurled at the NEGRO NEWSPAPERS that they are disrupting NATIONAL UNITY and thereby impairing the war effort. This is widely BELIEVED because certain classes of people WANT it to be believed . . . If the Negro is angry about being discriminated against, SEGREGATED and called names in the armed services, the remedy is not to end this treatment, but to SUPPRESS the Negro newspapers which report it.
>
> If the Negro is DISGRUNTLED because he is barred from nine-tenths of the hotels, restaurants, theaters and amusement places in the United States, the way to make him HAPPY is not to abolish racial ostracism, but to censor Negro newspapers for voicing his discontent. If the Negro is mad because he is BARRED from most skilled and professional work in war industries except for a few "token" jobs, the way to appease him is to clamp down on his ONLY means of expression.[3]

African Americans clearly presented their case for social equality and the rhetoric of "fighting for democracy" was not lost on the majority of African Americans who faced discrimination daily. White Americans did not take African American agitation for civil rights lightly. African Americans who pushed for victory at home faced labels of "traitor" at worst and "unpatriotic agitation" at best; these labels aggravated already tense race relations in American cities.[4]

FIGURE 4.1 Soldiers from 372nd Infantry marching in parade, Fifth Avenue, Downtown, July 1942. Charles "Teenie" Harris (American, 1908–98), gelatin silver print mounted on cardboard, H: 7½ in. × W: 9½ in. (19.05 × 23.97 cm), Carnegie Museum of Art, Pittsburgh: Gift of the Estate of Charles "Teenie" Harris, 1996.69.137, © Carnegie Museum of Art, Charles "Teenie" Harris Archive.

As veterans returned from World War II, the desire for increased employment opportunities and for government intervention to assist in preventing crime and blight as well as increasing the availability of good quality housing for all Americans coincided with a reminder of the national service provided by African American veterans. Parades had been a common feature of the Hill District since before World War I, but the influx of migrants during the Great Migration had swelled the numbers of African Americans in the Hill District and increased the political imagery of parades on the streets of the Hill District. These parades were common in the Hill District and Wylie Avenue was a common route.

In figure 4.1, Teenie Harris photographed a military parade down Fifth Avenue. Both African American and white spectators watched the march while a young African American boy imitated the marchers in the background of the photo.[5] The community supported their soldiers and expressed their pride in the African American soldiers and their service to the country. Parades were a feature on the streets of the Hill District, both formally organized parades and informal parades. Many organizations sponsored formal parades including the Knights of Pythias, the Urban League, and The Elks who all used streets spaces as a venue to show off the strength of their organization or to promote specific events.[6] Members displayed their regalia and encouraged all visitors from other urban areas to exemplify African American pride and unity. These formal parades often used the main thoroughfares of the Hill District, primarily Wylie Avenue. In an article on a Better Baby contest sponsored by the Urban League, the reporter mentions a "little girl's doll carriage parade" under the direction of Miss R. J. Taylor from the Young Women's Christian Association (YWCA).[7] This doll parade reinforced the role of young African American girls as future mothers and gave young girls a chance to display their personal possessions. Professional organizations like the Business and Professional Association also used parades to promote their vision for African American life in Pittsburgh.

The Business and Professional Association (BPA) planned a parade as part of Negro Trade Week, a celebration of African American–owned businesses. This "mammoth parade through the Hill District will be the feature of Monday Evening, September 18, presenting all fraternal, civic, and social organizations of this city."[8] The BPA's trade week presented a large formal parade through the streets of the Hill District, featuring bands, pageant winners, military displays, and drum corps.[9] These parades sponsored by approved organizations happened frequently on the streets of the Hill District. Many had common features of marching units, bands, pageant winners, decorated cars, and representatives of various fraternal and social organizations, but city officials did not grant all requests for parade permits. In 1934, two members of the Communist Party in Pittsburgh formally requested a permit to stage a parade through the Hill District and police declined their request. Police then jailed the two members for refusing to leave the station without a permit.[10] Formal parades united the community and made social networks visible on the streets. Displays of public values such as service to the community, beauty, and order linked African Americans in the Hill District.

Many residents of the Hill District recalled the parades as a highlight of the neighborhood experience. Marcia Donnell recalled following the parades as a young child, saying: "We would have parades from one end of the Hill District down to the other, and I would follow it but we wouldn't go downtown. Kids would follow it. You would follow the parade and our majorettes were beautiful. Young teenage girls and they would march and strut and we'd have the bands, yes a parade in the hill district was a big thing."[11] African Americans in the Hill District benefitted from the parades. LeRoy recalled, "Parades happened all the time, it seemed like every other weekend. We also had big picnics at Kenmore field. We had 15–18 parades a year. Sometimes you didn't know what the parade was about."[12] The formal parades united the community and were a venue for public display of racial pride. Barbara Gaston recalled her time as a featured majorette and beauty queen in the Hill District, saying:

> The Black Hill district always ran a big parade every year it was called the Hill District Parade, they picked the best of the best. It wasn't about your looks it was about your talent. And I had learned it [baton]. I learned it from watching other people. I pick up things very easily. I made myself practice and my dad made me practice. I slept with my baton, I ate with my baton, and then I started having parades in the Hill District myself to get the kids to learn. You know, to learn that it's fun to march it's fun to do something that people look at you in a different light. Back in the day that I marched, we had the big white boots, the short skirts, you know knee length and we were dressed now days you see majorettes they ain't got on too much of anything, they have something on they would catch a cold in. We were dressed, we were proud. We didn't walk, we strutted. And in the process of strutting we knew how to do it and we did it with pride and the band behind us played with pride.[13]

Everyone came out for the parades. They were a source of community pride and a way for African Americans across classes to come together around a common racial identity.

African Americans across classes came together around the community displays of solidarity. Odessa Wilson recalled, "Oh, yeah. The whole neighborhood went."[14] Parades were an important way African Americans used street spaces within their neighborhood for entertainment, racial pride, and solidarity. Parades flowed through the central arteries of the neighborhood and allowed African Americans across class lines to gather and support one another and to see positive racial images displayed in a public setting. "Arthur," a lifelong resident of the Hill District, also remembered the parades and the route they took through the Hill District, saying, "At certain times of the year there were parades—real nice parades. One thing you could always count on was that the parades would come down Wylie Ave. It basically followed the route of the 85 Bedford Streetcar."[15] In this way, Wylie Avenue functioned as a showcase for social values and racial pride as the central thoroughfare through the Hill District. Formal parades were common, but informal parades also functioned as a mechanism for fostering social network development and cross-class interaction within the Hill District.

Informal parades could happen for almost any occasion. Sundays offered an opportunity for African Americans to display their Sunday best clothing as they walked to services at one of the African American churches located in the Hill District. Rev. John Welch recalled street parades in the Hill District on Sunday afternoons as a child. He recalled traveling from Homewood to the Hill District on Sundays to attend church services and following church, African American families would walk through the Hill District in their Sunday best. These informal parades allowed African American adults and children to participate in a cultural display of values. Welch recalled his pride in the community on those Sunday parades. The trip to the Hill District also presented an opportunity to get a treat from George Harris's confectionary on Wylie Ave. He remembers Sundays in the Hill District fondly as a time of fostering connection among African Americans in Pittsburgh.[16] African Americans from all classes and neighborhoods around Pittsburgh journeyed to the Hill on Sundays to attend services. The most lavish informal parades happened on Easter Sunday, as many churches and clubs held special programs and brunches for members. Dewayne Ketchum suggested that the informal parades were a display of race and neighborhood pride. These parades were a way of gathering the community together on the streets of the neighborhood.[17] Informal parades celebrated the culture of the streets of the neighborhood and provided a way for African American Pittsburghers to unite around common experiences and demonstrate their pride in their people.

Parades inspired pride in Pittsburgh's African American community, but they could also create fear in Pittsburgh's white communities. A report entitled "The Police and Minority Groups" designed to "present constructive, practical suggestions on police techniques for preventing riots and improving relations between different groups" stated: "A series of demonstrations (parade, mass meetings, etc.) were scheduled to protest the lack of jobs for Negroes in public utilities. . . . Rumor and fear reached such proportions that responsible citizens urged the superintendent of police to withdraw permits of meeting and parades already issued to the demonstrators. The superintendent refused to withdraw the permits but instructed his policemen that they were to maintain complete neutrality in their efforts to preserve or restore order."[18] Police relied on the visible presence of African American police officers on the streets and in the streetcars in African American neighborhoods to quell any potential unrest while recognizing the potential power of street gatherings like parades. When African American veterans returned to the Hill District, parades served as a way to mobilize social networks toward the ending of racism and economic injustice.

Over time, the Double V campaign coalesced around a strong commitment to beating fascism abroad and discrimination at home. With the increasing pressure on the federal government from this organized national campaign, President Franklin D. Roosevelt signed Executive Order 8802 in 1941 that created the Fair Employment Practices Committee (FEPC) that desegregated wartime industries. Through efforts pertaining to wartime hiring, African Americans in the Hill District and throughout Pittsburgh fought for legal jobs that would pay fair wages like the jobs within the Pittsburgh public transit system. The FEPC received numerous complaints from African American residents of Pittsburgh against the Pittsburgh Railway Corporation. Complainants argued that the Pittsburgh Railway Corporation discriminated against them because of their race. African American applicants faced spurious reasons for their refusal. These complaints all listed impressive qualifications, but none of the applicants received a call back for an interview. The FEPC investigated these complaints and worked to integrate African American "operators in the Pittsburgh system."[19] The FEPC examiners reported limited success in integrating African American hires into the Pittsburg Railway Corporation. In November of 1944, Milo Manly reported to James Fleming, the regional director, saying, "The company, through C. D. Palmer, commercial manager, on October 4, 1944 advised examiner that the board of Trustees has decided that the employment of Negroes in operating jobs was not 'practical' and, therefore, the management would not consider the applications received from Negroes."[20] African Americans in Pittsburgh pushed for access to transit jobs as operators as a way of gaining access to a skilled position in a necessary industry for the Hill District and the war effort. Residents of the Hill District used their social networks to learn about open positions and to flood employment offices with applications from African American residents.

Transit operators held a visible job on the streets of Pittsburgh and therefore were a visible representation of discrimination to many African Americans in Pittsburgh. The Greater Pittsburgh Citizens' Coordinating Committee (GPCCC) organized an emergency conference to address the "local transportation problem" in Pittsburgh.[21] This report described Pittsburgh as a major industrial center, a part of the "arsenal of Democracy." Because of this Pittsburgh production occupied a strategic position in the war effort. The report stated:

> We who live here know that not all workers can travel to and from these vital jobs in their own cars or even in car-pools. The buses, trains, and streetcars, have a role to play in keeping up production. To fulfill this role, it seems to us, who (we grant) are not experts on this matter of the operation of a transit system, that a well defined and WORKING system of transportation is necessary. We who have waited interminably for cars, who have been late on the job because of such waiting, who have been crushed, irritated, and fatigued upon riding to and from the job wonder if our transportation system does meet the above-mentioned qualifications for fulfilling this role. Properly serviced busses and cars, sufficient number of operators, operators who are not fatigued by doubling back on their shifts, are a factor in the maintenance of this type of service.[22]

The report went on to list other northern cities that utilized African American labor to meet transit needs during wartime. African Americans, both women and returning servicemen, applied for positions as transit operators. The GPCCC defined the attitude of the Pittsburgh Railways Company, saying, "Obviously, both management and the unions are of one mind that Negroes must not, and will not, be employed as operators with the Pittsburgh Railways Company."[23] The company responded, suggesting that current operators "would have a violent reaction against such workers. This violent reaction might well culminate in a curtailment of service. Since the railways have a serious responsibility to discharge in the matter of transporting war worker to and from their jobs the management could not undertake any move which might cause such a curtailment of service."[24] The GPCCC argued African Americans pushed for employment as transit operators because of their civic ethics and used their social networks to advance candidates for transit jobs.

Labor shortages during the war and the importance of transit services to necessary war industries compelled African Americans to pursue jobs within the transit system. The GPCCC concluded, "For these ethical reasons and the contribution which would be made to unity on the home front we felt that Negroes should be employed as operators. For the practical reasons that there is an untapped source of both man and womanpower in Pittsburgh which could alleviate a manpower shortage, cut down accidents, provide better overall service, etc. we felt that Negroes should be employed as operators."[25] African Americans in Pittsburgh expressed their civic concern in the arena of transit jobs as well as on the streets themselves. Public transit connected the neighborhoods where African Americans lived to the areas where they worked. In a period where African Americans gained increased access to jobs otherwise barred to them via wartime shortages, public transit played a critical role in getting African Americans to their places of employment, but the visible lack of African American operators on streetcars and buses pushed African Americans to work toward employment as transit operators. African Americans faced significant difficulty gaining access to legal employment that paid a living wage. The streetcars and busses, like the streets themselves under urban renewal, became a site of resistance as African Americans in the Hill District pushed for equal access to fair employment and economic equality.[26]

During the Second Great Migration, Pittsburgh began heavy investment in an urban development program entitled Renaissance I. Renaissance I linked public interest through eminent domain legislation from the local and state governments and private industry, primarily Mellon Bank, in a bold plan for urban renewal. The proposed redevelopment focused primarily on the central business district. State and city government granted the Allegheny Conference on Community Development broad authority to demolish and reconstruct large portions of the area surrounding the "golden triangle." This transformation put the Lower Hill District right in the path of the URA as the African American neighborhood of the Hill District sat atop increasingly coveted land for the development of the area connecting the central business district with the affluent and University of Pittsburgh–dominated Oakland neighborhood. Urban renewal was a response from the city of Pittsburgh to increasing demands from African Americans for fair employment and equal access to housing under the guise of improvement for all residents of the city.

Members of the city government viewed urban renewal as a chance to improve the city and reduce poverty, but many working-class African Americans viewed urban renewal as Negro removal.[27] Within Pittsburgh's African American community, urban renewal intensified class divisions and divided social networks on the streets. Substandard plumbing, paving issues, prevalence of vice and juvenile delinquency, and deteriorating housing stock all led to the city labeling the Lower Hill District as a blighted area. Reformers and city officials targeted lower Wylie Avenue below Crawford Avenue as a place where renewal could transform the face of African American Pittsburgh.

Middle-class African Americans tried to establish the Upper Hill as a cultural bastion of middle-class values and African American high culture, while reaffirming the working-class areas of the Hill District as blighted. This split amplified the tensions between working-class and middle-class African Americans as they contested the meanings and uses of street spaces within Pittsburgh's most prominent African American neighborhood.

Beginning in the 1950s, urban renewal initiatives pushed through Pittsburgh focused on the "golden triangle" of downtown Pittsburgh. The city focused on questions of blight in African American neighborhoods with a special focus on the street spaces of the Hill District. Social scientists had questioned the living conditions in the Hill District since Reid's social survey in the late 1920s. In the 1950s, conditions had not changed significantly. Middle-class African Americans worried that their neighborhood would be associated with degeneracy and blight. They sought to separate themselves from the perceived taint of blight, which reinforced and even intensified the stratification of social networks on the streets, but the emergence of the Modern Black Freedom Movement tempered their diversions before they exploded with the advent of Black Power. By the mid-1960s, middle-class African Americans coopted the term blight and used it to describe working-class social activities on the streets in opposition to their respectable uses of street spaces. This split showed the tensions between working-class and middle-class African Americans as well as those who culturally associated with the social networks of the street.

The streets of the Lower Hill formed the boundaries of a diverse neighborhood. African Americans shared the Lower Hill with white immigrants. Map 4.1 outlines the boundaries of the Lower Hill District. City reformers defined this area as blighted and in desperate need of urban renewal.[28] Renaissance I made room for construction of the "Civic Arena, the Crosstown Parkway, and some housing."[29] In 1950 the city of Pittsburgh declared, "The Lower Hill is 'blighted.' That is the official verdict of the City Planning Commission. In its meeting Tuesday, the Commission gave the first legal impetus to the ultimate redevelopment of the area."[30] African Americans across classes questioned the motives of redevelopment officials. Paul Jones expressed his concerns in a *Courier* article, saying, "When Jack Robin [first Chairman of the Urban Redevelopment Authority] says that present living patterns in the Hill are 'undesirable, unacceptable, and unendurable.' Just what does he mean? Is he simply slurring life there? Is he seeking to justify redevelopment with a slogan? Or does his statement give a measured evaluation of the way Negroes actually live in the Hill?"[31] Civic leaders and social

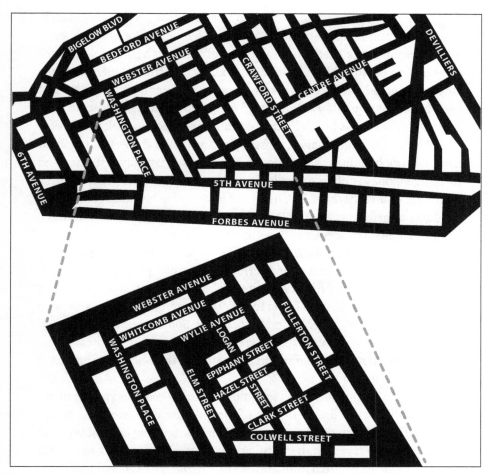

MAP 4.1 Streets of the Lower Hill District, before the Civic Arena.
Jason Klanderud, Altair Media Design, Designer.

services workers also considered conditions in the Hill District detrimental to the public health of African Americans. The unsanitary and dangerous street spaces of the Lower Hill District required a swift remedy but displaced residents, especially of the white working class and African American middle class, needed access to housing in emerging suburbs and *better* neighborhoods within the city. African American organizations shifted their focus from integrating new migrants into the city to the theme of housing access while simultaneously emphasizing the need for renewal to ensure safe and clean street spaces in the Lower Hill District to promote respectable social networks.

Working-class African Americans also faced a shortage of housing outside of the renewal area. Longstanding issues of absentee landlords and deteriorating housing stock led the Urban League of Pittsburgh (ULP) to argue for increased access to public housing assignments for African Americans. In a study conducted for the ULP, researchers stated, "Rental housing has not been built in any quantity in Pittsburgh for Negro occupancy except in public housing. There has been a limited amount of new homes built which were available for the Negro market (possibly 300 to 400) in the Pittsburgh area. Land for new buildings that is open to Negroes is drastically restricted and mortgage money is often unavailable or is available at less favorable terms than is the case with whites."[32] The lack of low-income housing for displaced residents transformed the Hill District as working-class African Americans struggled to find replacement homes in other neighborhoods. African American residents of the Lower Hill District faced particular hardships finding replacement housing because of discriminatory rental practices and neighborhood resistance to African American suburbanization. In map 4.2, you can see the Hill District in relation to the other emerging African American neighborhoods of Homewood and East Liberty. Some of the displaced residents from the Lower Hill District were able to find housing in these areas, but many residents faced significant disruption to their housing and had to leave the Hill District.

The right of eminent domain gave the URA unprecedented power to define the Hill District, but residents of the Hill also contested this power through their social networks. The available public housing in Pittsburgh did not have enough room for the working-class displaced residents of the Hill District. A *Courier* editorial from the fall of 1950 concerned about insufficient low-income housing stated, "Atty. Richard L. Jones of the Pittsburgh Housing Authority says that there are 30,000 families not now served who qualify for admission to the public housing projects. In the present projects there are only some 5,600 families. . . . Whether one likes it or not, from a political point of view, the Government has provided subsidies for housing for people in this economic group whom the private housers have not reached."[33] Others complained that the process of urban renewal allowed the wealthy to acquire land at below market rates and through back-room deals that occurred at the expense of poor urban residents. The same editorial continued by questioning the role of federal and city governments, saying, "There is frequent grumbling, as in The Press, against this [so-called] subsidy for the poor. But what about another subsidy? The monies given to Redevelopment

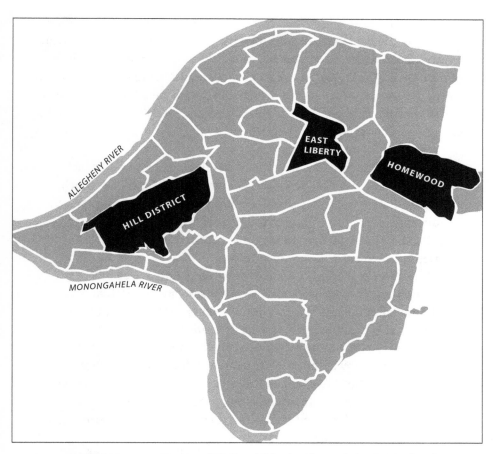

MAP 4.2 Highest concentration of Black neighborhood population in Pittsburgh. Jason Klanderud, Altair Media Design, Designer.

authorities by the Federal and State governments are subsidies for private builders. When private builders think of redeveloping an area like the lower Hill District they say they cannot afford to buy the properties already on the land so they ask the Government to do that for them. The Government does so. That's a subsidy for the rich. You don't read The Press complaining about that."[34] The residents of the Lower Hill who did not qualify for public housing faced stiff racial quotas and therefore did not have plentiful options for replacement housing. Redevelopment of the Lower Hill benefited city officials and private corporations much more than the residents displaced by urban renewal.

African American leaders also feared secret agreements between private industry and city governments through the process of urban renewal, fears which appeared correct. R. Maurice Moss, the associate executive director of the national Urban League, wrote a confidential letter to Mr. Alexander J. Allen, the executive secretary of the Pittsburgh branch, addressing the proposed urban renewal of the Lower Hill District and the collusion between the city government and private corporations, saying:

I have a theory which has slowly been developing in my mind which I would like to outline for you in the deepest of confidence, but which I would like for you to check and see how near I come to being correct. You might check this with [Percival] Prattis because he, of all the folks in Pittsburgh, would have an awareness about this sort of thing. As briefly as I can put it, here is my theorem:

The Allegheny County Committee on Community Development is financed largely by Mellon and department store money. It desires to take over all of the planning for the future Pittsburgh. The one planning body which it did not control was the Federation of Social Agencies. Certain of the Committee's leaders, a couple of years ago, announced a plan for clearing away the property between Fifth Avenue and Bigelow Boulevard and Sixth Avenue and Fullerton Street and rehabilitating it by the erection of a civic auditorium, parking facilities, perks, etc. This would have been developed with private capital, with some governmental assistance through redevelopment program.

The Mellon interests now own most of the land up to the Sixth Avenue boundaries. Above that line, the district is inhabited by Negroes, Italians, Jews, Greeks, and Syrians. If they were to be displaced, other living quarters would have to be provided, and there just aren't any available spaces that convenient to the Golden Triangle.

Now who might be expected to protest such a displacement? The Urban League, because of the Negroes involved; the American Service Institute, because of the other racial groups; the Community Councils and the Pittsburgh Housing Authority, for obvious reasons; and the Public Charities Association, because it has favored and promoted legislation in this area of human relations.

If my theory is correct then you have not heard the last of this with the compromise reached on last Wednesday, for these interests will now bide their time until a more auspicious period. I would really be interested in your reactions to the preceding.[35]

Moss's assessment of the urban renewal and those who would oppose it was eerily prophetic. Public and private money and interests shaped the streets of the Lower Hill District while displacing the ethnic white and African American residents in the neighborhood. The Urban League protested the plans for renewal of the Lower Hill because housing discrimination still prevented African Americans from accessing housing based on their ability to afford quality homes.

The Pittsburgh branch of the National Association for the Advancement of Colored People (NAACP) protested the lack of available housing for African Americans with the financial means to afford to move out of the redevelopment area. The general secretary of the Pittsburgh branch of the NAACP, Mrs. Marion Jordon, wrote to the *Pittsburgh Post-Gazette*, a mainstream newspaper, accenting the role of the federal government in creating segregated housing funds through the Federal Housing Authority and the Veterans Administration, saying, "many Americans have not realized that there is no constitutional right which would insure them the 'right' to exclude others on the basis of color, religion, or origin. A neighborhood is not the exclusive domain of any group of citizens. Rather those who meet the financial requirements are entitled to live there."[36] Jordon, along with many others within the African American elite of the Hill District pushed for the right to buy any home that their means would allow. African Americans with the means to purchase housing in other areas of the city that did not have street spaces labeled as blighted faced many obstacles to their goal.

Middle-class African Americans faced difficulty in finding housing in the private market. An Urban League study concluded "that private housing [was] not available in sufficient quantity to meet the Negro demand and that the attitude of the white community [created] the problem."[37] Middle-class African American organizations stressed the respectability of their membership and advocated that ignorance alone prompted white neighborhoods to resist middle-class African American migration into their neighborhood. An Urban League statement described the plight of African Americans moving into new neighborhoods, saying, "The Negro family seeking to buy a home or rent a dwelling in neighborhoods other than the traditionally 'Negro' areas is almost always met with resistance. Often this comes from white neighbors. More often it is evident in the fact that real estate brokers will not rent or sell a building to Negroes other than in the known 'Negro' or transitional areas."[38] The conditions of the streets in the Hill District and other African American neighborhoods led many middle-class African Americans to believe that renewal offered a method of improving the race by improving their living conditions on the streets of the Lower Hill. Elite members of the Loendi Club took advantage of assistance from many notable people in finding a "suitable location" to relocate their clubhouse. A *Courier* article inducing members to attend a special meeting reinforced the club's connections to members of the URA and city government.[39] The amount of governmental and institutional help this club received to relocate out of the redevelopment area emphasized how little other businesses and organizations received and even more, how little assistance residents of the Lower Hill received in gaining access to housing outside of the redevelopment area.

The Irene Kauffman Settlement House (IKS) also held a number of forums addressing the question, "Will redevelopment mean better housing for Negroes?"[40] At one of these forums, James T. Goode, a Beltzhoover real estate agent, spoke on the "problems involved in obtaining better homes and property for Negro buyers."[41] Marcia Donnell recalled the problem of purchasing quality housing in the Hill District. When she married, Donnell and her husband looked for property in the Hill because she wanted to stay in the neighborhood, but they were unable to find a home that fit their standards. She recalled, "Those who could afford them were buying homes in Wilkinsburg, Homewood, and Beechview."[42] The housing stock in the Hill District was often in disrepair and generally overcrowded. Donnell and her husband both worked and generally had a good income, so they were able to afford property near the Southside where she worked for the welfare department. Donnell's experience in moving to find suitable housing echoes that of many two-income families or others with middle-class aspirations in the Hill District.

Urban renewal transformed street spaces in the Lower Hill. One of the major projects of the redevelopment of the Lower Hill was the construction of the Crosstown Boulevard. This highway bypasses the Hill District and moves traffic from downtown into the Oakland section of the city. In 1953, Jack P. Robin of the Pittsburgh Redevelopment Authority acknowledged that the building of the Crosstown Parkway would affect residents in the Lower Hill, saying, "some attempts may be made in 1953 to get started on rights of way for new streets which will bring about a juncture of Wylie Avenue, below Crawford, and Centre Avenue: and Bedford Avenue, below Crawford, and Webster Avenue."[43] These changes in the street patterns of the Lower Hill paved the way for redevelopment by moving people away from their travel patterns within their neighborhood. The changes also limited the number of people traveling through the Hill District with the construction of the Crosstown Boulevard.

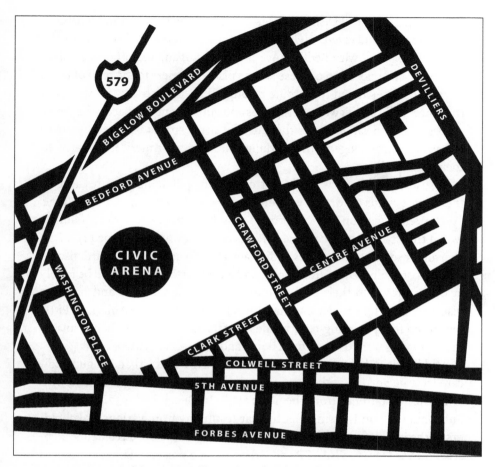

MAP 4.3 Streets of the Lower Hill District, after the Civic Arena.
Jason Klanderud, Altair Media Design, Designer.

The construction of the Civic Arena dramatically transformed the Lower
Hill District. Map 4.3 details the destruction of the former street plan of the
Lower Hill District and the subsequent rerouting of many of the major
streets, including Wylie Avenue.[44] The area of the Lower Hill called "Deep
Wylie" faced almost total destruction to make way for the new arena. The
Courier reported when the Public Auditorium Authority of Pittsburgh and
Allegheny County authorized The Pennsylvania Drilling Company to drill
some test bores to gather samples of the earth under the proposed arena
site. These tests took place along Wylie Avenue and Logan Street and many
of the cross streets. The *Courier* stated, "In order to complete the arena, the

majority of Lower Hill District streets will have to be rerouted and tenement houses vacated and razed. Wylie Avenue, the main street in this area, is to be relocated together with Bedford Avenue, Elm, Logan, and other secondary streets."[45] The relocation of these streets placed barriers to the path of these streets and interrupted their route through the Hill District. The streets of the Lower Hill District were workplaces and entertainment spaces; they were spaces where social networks thrived. The street spaces rerouted by urban redevelopment changed how working-class African Americans related to their neighborhood.

Displaced residents who did not qualify for public housing because of their single status or for many other reasons concerned John L. Clark. In his "Wylie Ave." column, he questioned whether African American families would truly be able to access the benefits of the newly redeveloped Hill District and revealed the anxieties of displaced families that faced "burdensome trolley costs going to and from work" and fears that "the people will be rudely evicted, thrown to their own resources to find new homes and business places."[46] The Hill District was the cultural center of African American Pittsburgh and many working-class residents of the Lower Hill felt their displacement as exiles from their cultural home and their social networks.

Middle-class African Americans in the NAACP and Urban League dedicated a large portion of their programming to the problems associated with relocation of families from the Lower Hill. In December 1957, the Senate Subcommittee on Housing met to hear testimony from various stakeholders in the issue of urban renewal and housing for displaced residents. Representatives from the NAACP and Urban League presented major concerns regarding the relocation of families from the development district. Residents relocating out of the Lower Hill demonstrated an alarming trend of increasing residential segregation and patterns of relocation favoring white ethnic residents of the Lower Hill. The Commission on Human Relations also stressed the dangers of increased residential segregation, saying, "The relocation of families from the lower hill redevelopment project dramatically reveals a 25-year trend and at the same time accelerates the process. The trend shows a decrease in integrated neighborhoods and serious overcrowding in areas given over to the Negro."[47] For members of the African American middle class, access to housing based on merit was an important marker of status and an obvious area of discrimination.

The National Housing Act, through its urban redevelopment and urban renewal provisions, has both benefited and harmed members of minority groups. . . . Likewise, the administration has failed to take the necessary steps to prevent the transfer of the conditions which cause slum and blight to other areas of the community. In large measure this it due to failure to provide the same or a greater number of dwelling units as the number demolished in the redeveloped area. It is also due to lack of safeguards which would make possible the securing of housing on a non-discriminatory basis.[48]

For this organization, and many others focused on the problems of relocation, the solution to this problem of housing rested on a simple supply-and-demand issue. If the housing supply was made available to all based on merit, the issues associated with high demand and overcrowding would dissipate. Others within the NAACP and Urban League were not completely convinced that a market solution would resolve the issue in its entirety.

Many middle-class and elite African Americans suggested, "It is the middle-income Negro who is hardest hit by the shortage of housing."[49] The availability of affordable housing occupied a majority of the discussion of urban redevelopment. Organizations like the Urban League and the NAACP focused on opening the private housing market to individuals based on their income. Middle-class reformers viewed overcrowding and slums as moral issues that threatened all of African American Pittsburgh, saying, "We, of the Urban League, know that the artificially stimulated concentration of demand by Negroes; this unbearable shortage, this criminally dangerous overcrowding in the scant housing available have combined to form a vicious and threatening pattern of high rents (taken from low incomes) excessive disease rates, social maladjustments and crime."[50] To middle-class and elite African Americans, urban redevelopment programs classified street spaces as blighted and therefore street spaces represented a liability if they encouraged governmental intervention to eliminate blight without also opening access to housing in other neighborhoods of the city.

For some, the problems of relocation illuminated opportunities to uplift African American residents of the Hill. The American Services Institute described their positive view of the relocation effort. They argued, "in [the Urban Redevelopment Authority's] efforts to encourage rehabilitation and conservation to prevent such blight, it faces an unparalleled opportunity which requires the cities' minorities and majorities to voluntarily share responsibility together, to help themselves and each other."[51] For some within the African American middle class, renewal efforts in the Lower Hill could reform the working classes and transform their neighborhood into something respectable for all African Americans.

The streets of the redevelopment area were not the only casualties of redevelopment. The businesses in the redevelopment area were also transformed. George Barbour reported: "Because of the large investment, Uncle Sam will keep the new owners under close scrutiny for forty years."[52] Government regulations allowed cultural establishments like art galleries, museums, and libraries as well as professional office spaces and shops, but they prohibited "auto service station, blueprinting establishment, boarding house, cleaning and dressing of poultry or animals, feed store, funeral home, hospital for animals, pawn shop, pet shop, rescue mission, second-hand sales shop, and trailer sales and supply."[53] The restrictions placed on businesses demonstrated a strong preference for those businesses requiring a large amount of capital investment to operate rather than those businesses that served more of a working-class clientele. Barbour also outlined the many "landmarks" in the way of redevelopment. Most of the institutions affected by renewal plans were those serving the working poor and other working-class African Americans.

Street spaces perceived as blighted or dangerous received special focus. In 1957, Councilman Paul F. Jones clashed with Homer Green, then the director of the Department of Lands and Buildings, over a vacant lot adjacent to the Miller Street School. Councilman Jones argued he had personally asked Greene to "do something about that lot." Green had "sent men to do all that could be done 'without spending a lot of money.'"[54] The public expressed interest in this issue. When the city council held a meeting on this "eyesore," representatives from local churches and the Hill District Community Council came to make their voices heard. Greene argued that his agency had done what they could but for the protestors it was not enough. Greene wanted the URA to meet him "half-way," but the public concern over a street space defined as hazardous took precedence.[55]

Middle-class and elite members of the Business and Professional Men's Association and other interested parties met with Jack P. Robin, the head of the URA, "to discuss the announced plans as they apply to the Loendi and other institutions in the Lower Hill."[56] Concerns over the nature of renewal had businessmen asking, "Does the blue print call for restaurants, hotels, barber shops, grocery and drug stores, taverns, and other businesses operated by Negroes?"[57] For John L. Clark, the answer to that question was paramount. He stated in his column, "Answers on these last questions are not clear. And, the Column believes it is now time to find out from the Urban Redevelopment Authority if it is true that Negroes will be shunted to another slum district and left there?"[58] These concerns over the fate of African Americans living and doing business in the area targeted by developers appeared regularly in the *Courier* for years leading up to the destruction of the Lower Hill.

The Hill District Community Council held a conference to discuss how the redevelopment plans for the Hill District would affect middle-class African Americans on the Hill. According to the *Courier*, "About 125 teachers, social workers, heads of organizations and interested citizens took part in the conference."[59] The URA opened an office in the Lower Hill to answer questions displaced residents had as a part of the process. The URA urged residents of the Lower Hill to "not become alarmed and not be in a hurry to move."[60] While the URA tried to reassure African Americans that there was no need for sudden flight from the redevelopment area there actually were few places for displaced residents to go.

Middle-class professionals all had different perspectives on what housing reforms working-class African Americans in the Hill needed. Paul L. Jones wrote, "The insurance man will show you where six people live in a filthy, damp, two-room apartment, and have to bathe in a wash tub since there is no bathroom. The nurse will point out where a man stepped out on a back porch he didn't suspect to be rotten, and dropped thirty feet to the ground. The visitor will lead you to a house where sixty-four people share one bathroom."[61] Many middle-class and elite African Americans moved into the Upper Hill. The availability of affordable housing for African Americans with the means to purchase homes on the private market dominated the discussion of urban redevelopment. The *Courier* suggested, "Many families in the affected area probably will be relocated in the city's low-rent housing projects. For those who do not fall within the special 'clearance area' income limits of the authority, real estate listing services will be available."[62] The limited availability of housing for low-income African Americans as well as the fact that their social networks were largely shut out of the conversation around renewal meant that working-class African Americans were largely cleared from the Lower Hill and the URA lost track of where more than 3,000 residents from the removal area ended up.

Homewood was an emerging African American neighborhood where both middle-class and working-class African Americans relocated throughout the period of urban renewal. Movement of African American residents transformed the Hill District and caused ripple effects in other Pittsburgh neighborhoods as African Americans wrestled with the meanings of urban renewal on the streets of their neighborhoods. Transformations of street spaces in the Hill District pushed African Americans into other neighborhoods within Pittsburgh. Homewood had a small African American population prior to urban renewal in the Hill, but the demolition of homes and businesses in the Lower Hill pushed African Americans into emerging neighborhoods as especially middle-class African Americans moved into Homewood. Middle-class residents of Homewood did not want migrants from the Lower Hill to transfer "slum conditions" into Homewood.

Marion Jordan, executive secretary of the NAACP, addressed the concerns of her organization regarding the transference of "some of the same conditions responsible for deterioration of the lower Hill District" to Homewood and other emerging African American neighborhoods in Pittsburgh.[63] She stated, "It is the policy of NAACP that unless Urban Redevelopment and Relocation plans provide adequate and non-segregated housing, we must oppose such plans."[64] African Americans in other African American neighborhoods looked skeptically at the redevelopment of the Lower Hill because of concerns that the "blight" from the Lower Hill would relocate into their neighborhood. The president of the Homewood Community Improvement Association (HCIA), William S. Howell, commented on the number of saloons relocating to Homewood, saying,

> On Frankstown Ave. between Lang and Braddock Aves, a distance of about five blocks, there are now 11 liquor dispensing establishments. He added that he has been advised that two additional ones will be located there in the future as many saloon owners, located in the redevelopment areas of the Hill District, are desirous of locating in these blocks. He explained that "Frankstown Ave in Homewood has every indication of becoming a duplicate of Fullerton St. in the Hill District . . . a haven for intoxicated individuals who have no respect for the good citizens of the community."[65]

This sentiment was common in African American suburbs. African Americans who had escaped the ghetto had no desire to see it relocated to their neighborhoods. African Americans also expressed concern over lack of available housing and a feeling of enclosure into a Negro ghetto within the Hill District. The Homewood-Brushton Chamber of Commerce fought a plan to build a shopping center in their neighborhood mostly populated by businesses relocating from the Lower Hill.[66]

In the opinion of many people in Homewood, Frankstown Avenue was becoming the new Wylie Avenue and that was not a desirable change in their eyes. The Commission on Human Relations reiterated the concerns of many when they described the demographic state of the Lower Hill, saying, "85% of the Negro families from the Lower Hill have moved into areas of already heavy concentration of the Negro population. The remaining 15% move into small pocket areas or blocks which are totally occupied by Negroes. Likewise, you will see that the white families have moved into areas largely occupied by whites."[67] This research showed increasing segregation in the migration of displaced residents from the Lower Hill. Residents of Homewood stressed increasing housing segregation, increased crime, and juvenile delinquency, as well as increased overcrowding. Residents linked these new developments on the streets to the rapid influx of African American refugees from the Lower Hill District renewal project.

Middle-class African Americans stressed increased segregation, especially in neighborhood composition and housing. Though the Hill District remained a racially mixed neighborhood, the portion of African American residents increased as ethnic white residents successfully gained housing in other emerging suburbs or white-dominated areas. The migration of African American residents from the Lower Hill to other African American neighborhoods within the city also transformed neighborhoods like Homewood-Brushton as African American migrants from the Hill settled in Homewood. Mrs. Marion Jordon reiterated the feelings of many middle-class African Americans when she described the changes occurring in Homewood, saying:

> These facts indicate the following: 1- Negro families in the Redevelopment area are being housed in segregated neighborhoods. Urban redevelopment has done little to change the existing pattern of residential segregation. 2- As a result of slum clearance in the lower Hill, other areas, such as the upper Hill and the Homewood-Brushton area are now experiencing over-crowding, exploitation by real estate dealers, and transference of some of the same conditions responsible for deterioration of the lower Hill District. 3- We are convinced that human planning and concern for displaced persons, were not sufficiently emphasized in advance of physical planning. It is the policy of NAACP that unless Urban Redevelopment and Relocation plans provide adequate and non-segregated housing, we must oppose such plans.[68]

The primary goal of the NAACP was helping middle-class African Americans gain access to housing in neighborhoods outside of their traditional neighborhoods. Many middle-class African Americans feared Homewood would develop the same kinds of problems associated with the Lower Hill. Business relocation to Homewood from the Lower Hill also concerned middle-class African American residents of Homewood. Many of the businesses facing relocation served the working classes and those seeking entertainment on the streets rather than more respectable pastimes. Homewood Avenue and Frankstown Avenue served as primary relocation areas for businesses relocating from the Lower Hill.

Middle-class residents of Homewood objected when real estate developers proposed a new shopping center along Homewood Avenue. Some objected to the shopping center because they claimed Homewood needed "more homes and not shopping centers," but the city council had "also promised merchants of the Lower Hill District aid in relocating their businesses."[69] Residents feared both residential overcrowding and an increase in crime and vice in their neighborhood. Homewood Avenue was the main thoroughfare of Homewood-Brushton, and residents did not fully support construction of a shopping center in what they viewed as a primarily residential neighborhood. The residents of Homewood did not uniformly welcome relocated residents from Wylie Avenue or the Lower Hill District. White residents complained they were being pushed out to provide additional housing for African Americans from the redevelopment district.

White renters complained to George Barbour of the *Courier* that they did not have the option to purchase the homes that they rented before realtors offered them to African American buyers. However, Barbour reported, "a Sterrett Street family said they had been given the opportunity to buy, but 'we turned it down because we thought the price was too high.'"[70] Many prospective buyers thought the prices in Homewood were inflated. White residents felt displaced with the influx of African American buyers moving into Homewood. Unfortunately, this internal migration exacerbated tensions between African American and white residents in a neighborhood known for its peaceable integration. Homewood absorbed many of the African American families from the Hill District with the means to purchase their own housing, while those who could not afford to purchase and were ineligible for public housing projects faced a tight rental market and an increasing housing shortage for African Americans.

In 1950, the *Courier* reported new home building had declined for the second month. The reporter stated, "The less new houses built barrier thus becomes another rail in the housing enclosure fencing Negros in the Hill District Ghetto in which most of them live. . . . Meanwhile the Urban

Redevelopment Authority was literally cutting the land from under some 1,600 Third Ward residents by declaring the area in which they live 'blighted' and making plans for commercial buildings and super town apartments."[71] Many African Americans felt the city was taking their homes from them in favor of interests in the private sector and leaving them few options for adequate housing to replace what they had lost.

Those African Americans who secured housing in the Upper Hill wanted to remain in a familiar neighborhood. In 1956, the *Courier* reported 57 percent of displaced residents from the Lower Hill "would move to the Upper Hill District."[72] Many of the residents of the Hill District were familiar with the patterns and culture of the Hill. Other neighborhoods were further away and different culturally. Some African Americans wanted to move to East Liberty, Homewood, or other neighborhoods throughout the city, but the vast majority wanted to stay in the Hill District.

When the URA defined areas of the Upper Hill as blighted and posited urban renewal projects, African Americans of some means protested what they viewed as increasing encroachment on one of the few areas where they could acquire housing. In 1957, Mayor David L. Lawrence requested "at least $5,000,000 from the federal government for each of the next 10 years in order to move ahead with the renewal of deteriorating neighborhoods in a 'realistic and meaningful pattern.'"[73] The city asked for funds from the U.S. Senate Subcommittee on Housing to construct three new public housing projects. One of the areas on the list for redevelopment was now the Upper Hill. The *Courier's* report from the subcommittee's hearing described the proposed projects stating:

> The three projects for which Director Theodore L. Hazlett Jr. said the Urban Redevelopment Authority soon will apply for survey and planning advances are as follows:
> (1) THE UPPER HILL DISTRICT.
> A largely blighted and overcrowded area of 150 acres between Crawford and Devilliers St.; adjacent to the 95 acre Lower Hill District, now in the last stages of clearance preparatory to redevelopment.
> According to Mr. Hazlett, the major portion is beyond rehabilitation and should be cleared and redeveloped, requiring about $20,000,000 in Federal money and necessitating relocation of an estimated 3,640 families (compared to 1,900 in the Lower Hill). It is believed to be suitable mostly for new residential uses, with some parts of it for cultural, recreational, and commercial purposes.[74]

This definition of the Upper Hill as blighted concerned many of the African American residents of Pittsburgh. Additionally, the Upper Hill was not the only African American neighborhood under the shadow of redevelopment plans; Manchester, Wood's Run, and East Liberty all had sizable African American populations and the mayor named them as probable redevelopment sites. In many of the Northside African American neighborhoods, redevelopment would not bring improved housing but instead offered increased space for the transit authority and other industrial uses. The displaced residents from these proposed developments had few places to go. The city and African American organizations differed greatly on the numbers of families displaced by renewal programs.

In the Upper Hill, residents protested the installation of "radio and television towers, Bell Telephone installations, Cab Company sending and receiving stations, and other electronics equipment, which is being placed in the district."[75] Some African Americans expressed concern over real estate speculation in areas defined as blighted. In the Upper Hill the *Courier* suggested, "According to reports reaching the *Courier*, real estate speculators have already moved into the area, seeking to purchase property in the affected district, apparently with the idea of later peddling it to the Redevelopment Authority at an inflated price."[76] The URA cautioned homeowners against this type of scam but the label of blighted neighborhood marked areas as ripe for redevelopment, and the influx of state and federal money drew those who wanted to take advantage of the unprecedented amounts of money available to acquire properties in redevelopment areas. In addition to these concerns, residents acknowledged the difficulties African Americans faced in finding replacement housing. A reporter in the *Courier* quoted Roland Sawyer stating, "Why won't the City Council help us to maintain this section? You gentlemen know the problems confronting Negroes in our city. We can't move anywhere. You know that in the urban redevelopment program now being put into effect in our city . . . one of which all of us are proud . . . that Negroes have very few places to move. But they are moving into the upper Hill District. They're spending hundreds of thousands of dollars in building new homes. And they're doing all this with very little help from the city."[77] The possibility of affordable housing for African Americans with some means drove some to seek better housing opportunities in other Pittsburgh neighborhoods like Homewood.

Middle-class African Americans welcomed redevelopment in some ways. Hazel Garland described renewal in the Lower Hill: "One will hardly be able to recognize Pittsburgh in just a few more years. Certainly, everyone has noticed the new face which the downtown section has put on during the past year. And all of us are looking forward to the redevelopment plan which is slated in the Hill District."[78] The residents of the area slated for redevelopment, however, were not excited over the limited prospects for relocating their residences and businesses.

Proposed redevelopment of the Upper Hill District caused middle-class African Americans to change their tone on the topic of redevelopment. Middle-class and elite African Americans turned their focus to issues of discrimination in housing and public accommodations. To middle-class and elite African Americans, urban redevelopment programs classified street spaces as "blighted" and therefore street spaces represented a liability if they encouraged governmental intervention through eminent domain legislation to eliminate blight. Urban redevelopment focused on the conditions of homes and streets in the Hill District. Middle-class African Americans desired access to improved housing and hoped that renewal efforts would open up space for African Americans to purchase homes in the Hill District and other areas of the city. The URA and other governmental organizations viewed these programs in conjunction with public housing efforts as a solution to the problem of relocating residents of the Lower Hill redevelopment area. Unfortunately, public housing protests in the Northside and Southside succeeded in squashing plans to provide housing for working-class African Americans displaced by redevelopment.

Working-class African Americans identified with the systems of reciprocity in their neighborhood and were reluctant to leave. Those African Americans who had means to afford better housing faced the "reluctance of banks and mortgage companies to grant loans in the face of the rapid depreciation of property values on the so-called 'Hill.'"[79] John L. Clark discussed African American opinions on the redevelopment of the Hill District and the relocation of businesses, churches, and the working-class and working-poor residents of the Lower Hill. He questioned the lack of planning for African American–owned businesses in the redevelopment plans. Furthermore, Clark asked, "Will the 'new hill' be tenanted only by whites of different races and established as a segregated part of the city, where Negroes will not live or operate businesses?"[80] Middle-class and elite African Americans faced problems relocating living spaces and businesses. They viewed the Hill as their neighborhood and worried about the city's plan to assist in relocation.

Working-class and working-poor African Americans also complained about the resettlement plan. Clark wrote, "Pittsburgh's dreamers and idealists, who have participated in the city's urban redevelopment program, will be surprised to hear that many Negroes would be better satisfied with a resettlement plan which would not destroy their identity or drastically change their places of residence."[81] Other residents expressed concern that the redevelopment plans and objections to them were racially motivated. A 1950 editorial demanded, "New housing must be found for those whom the redevelopment district cannot absorb for one reason or another. The Southside and the Northside housing projects will provide some of this housing. When the Northside Protest Committee asks: 'Do you want the Hill District here?' they really mean, 'Are you going to permit Negroes from the Hill District to be moved into our neighborhood.'"[82] In the Northside, protestors erected fences and "in general, asked that slums be cleaned out by keeping slum residents where they are."[83] These protests against public housing projects in the Northside led to a two-year court battle which *killed* this North side public housing project.[84]

African American residents of the Lower Hill faced many problems in relocating to other areas of the city. Working-class and working-poor African Americans had limited opportunities for replacement housing. Public housing projects or affordable rental properties were not available for all of the displaced residents and protests limited new project construction of public housing in both the Northside and Southside neighborhoods. In 1955, the NAACP raised concerns over the relocation of African American families from the Lower Hill. The *Courier* reported, "The Rev. Charles S. Spivey, new chairman of the NAACP housing committee, told the URA meeting, presided over by Mayor David L. Lawrence that the implied understanding seems to be that prospective Negro home buyers will move to areas like the Hill District, the Northside, Beltzhoover, and Homewood-Brushton, where Negroes currently live in large numbers."[85] The NAACP was concerned that the city wanted to transfer one African American blighted slum to other neighborhoods where middle-class African Americans had established a foothold as homeowners.

For African Americans in the Hill District, the period of urban renewal in the Lower Hill District was a period of uncertainty and adaptation. The use of parades as a source of race pride and display foreshadowed the street-based protests that would become iconic during the Modern Black Freedom Movement in the city by displaying the strength and pride of a unified neighborhood. The response of the city to increased pressures following World War II to provide equal access to fair employment and housing led to an emphasis on urban renewal as a mechanism to *improve* the city at the expense of African Americans in the Hill District. The struggles on the streets of the Hill District for access to skilled positions in the transit authority were a part of a developing struggle between African Americans who were committed to improving their race as a whole and those who had formerly relied on neighborhood systems of reciprocity and social networks to meet their needs on the streets of the Hill. As those streets fell to the press of urban renewal, African Americans were dispersed through the city into emerging African American neighborhoods like East Liberty, Homewood, Beltzhoover, and the Northside. These internal migrations changed the neighborhood of the Hill District by stretching the neighborhood systems at work in the Lower Hill District and displacing many of the residents throughout the remaining Hill District and the city as a whole. The ensuing divisions that developed as middle-class African Americans pushed for access to housing based on income increased the divide between working-class and middle-class African Americans in the Hill District. Overall, urban renewal pushed African Americans in Pittsburgh to develop a cohesive response to economic inequality, but that response was heavily influenced by the interests of the middle class, while the working class was increasingly pushed into public housing where they relied on social networks to maintain their connection to the Lower Hill District.

CHAPTER FIVE

Dinwiddie Street
Street Capitalists and Policing of the Hill, 1950–1960

In the spring of 1950, the Hill District lost a great sportsman, a husband, a father, and one of the most notorious numbers men and pimps in the Black community. Leon Clark, better known as Pigmeat, died as he lived, near one in the morning at the home of his friend Squirrel Woods following a weekend-long party.[1] Pigmeat left behind a wife and three small children along with a legacy as one of the prominent characters along the Ave. His connections to other street capitalists like Gus Greenlee and Woogie Harris placed him in the center of complex negotiations between social networks and legitimized use of street spaces and social networks that were increasingly delegitimized by African American reformers in the middle class. The ensuing conflict let to increasing police presence on the streets of the Hill. In figure 5.1, Teenie Harris documented mourners at Pigmeat's funeral. In the image, residents of the Hill District line up to pay their respects. Most of the mourners are women in simple coats, but their flowers are extravagant and in the later part of the line, you can see women with fur stoles included among the mourners. Clearly, Pigmeat was a resident of the Hill District who was integrally connected across lines of class and legality. Pigmeat appeared to operate as a legitimate sports manager and promoter for boxers and other athletes, but his reputation as a numbers man and pimp far outpaced his legitimate work. He operated his illegal business out of the Crawford Grille No. One, a location notorious for hot Jazz, good food, and an impressive variety of available illegal activities. Pigmeat was not the only street capitalist that operated out of the Crawford's premiere location along the heart of the Hill District's Wylie Avenue corridor. This site was one of many spaces where legal and illegal overlapped and where the boundaries between respectability and doing work for the race blurred.

Street capitalists like Pigmeat and others often operated out of a sense of reciprocity. Although their work was technically illegal, immoral, and certainly questionable, they used the profits of their business to invest in the community and uplift the race in their own way. Those in the emerging middle class struggled to balance an explicit use of respectability politics to ingratiate themselves into the wider culture of Pittsburgh alongside the

FIGURE 5.1 Funeral procession for Leon "Pigmeat" Clark, with women holding floral arrangement, including Ruby Wheeler Woods front right, on Webster Avenue, Hill District, April 19, 1950. Charles "Teenie" Harris (American, 1908–98), black-and-white: Kodak safety film, H: 4 in. × W: 5 in. (10.20 × 12.70 cm), Carnegie Museum of Art, Pittsburgh: Heinz Family Fund, 2001.35.3241, © Carnegie Museum of Art, Charles "Teenie" Harris Archive.

social networks of the streets that honored street capitalists for their prowess in gambling and their generosity toward the African American community as a whole. This distinction between those who contributed to the community and those who took from the community through their work formed the basis for who was a regular on the Avenue and who was a source of blight on the streets. The perception of vice also posed a problem for Pittsburgh's Black community as it opened up street spaces to increasingly violent police action. Many Hill residents named police brutality as a problem in their neighborhood, but working-class and middle-class Blacks differed on the solution. For middle-class African Americans, Black policemen were a solution to the twin problems of increasing vice and police brutality. Working-class African

Americans were more concerned about intermittent police suppression and violence against them on the streets. In this way, the conflict between street capitalists and divisions over the policing of the streets revealed increasing class tensions and a rift within the social networks of the Hill District.

Working-class Hill residents not only tolerated illegal laborers in their midst, they often cooperated with them. Street capitalists and laborers were kin to many within the working class and often invested their profits toward the advancement of the community. As the last hired, first fired, many working-class Blacks embraced illegal or quasi-legal labor as an alternative to labor insecurity. The streets of urban neighborhoods were spaces where men and women worked in both legal and illegal ways. Prostitutes and jitney drivers faced labor issues in their street work like competition, labor discipline, and encroachment. Residents of the Hill District also faced violence in the form of police brutality and increasing censure from middle-class reformers for increasing disreputable behavior on the streets. Street capitalists blurred the legal boundaries of labor while navigating class divisions within the African American community in unique ways. Middle-class African Americans expressed ambivalence, followed by growing hostility between legal and extralegal work. They struggled to deal with the most successful street capitalists, especially those who ascended into the ranks of the African American elite through combinations of illegal and legal labor. The relationships between these members of the working classes often shifted over time and through the social networks of the Lower Hill. Middle-class Hill residents defined night uses of street spaces as vice ridden, dangerous, and questionable. Many of the people working on the streets of the Hill District faced the possibility of association with illegal activity daily. The work of these street capitalists often faced similar issues of labor discipline and encroachment as legal businesses did, but they also had to deal with the prevalence of intermittent law enforcement, police violence, and public perception of their labor spaces. These class-inflected responses to street capitalism also influenced other uses of the streets. These labor issues reveal how working-class laborers, both legal and illegal, used street spaces as a conflicted capitalist space.

Jitneys (informal taxis) served African American neighborhoods and provided a needed service outside of the formal economy and transportation networks.[2] Jitneys were illegal but laws prohibiting their operation were seldom enforced. The complex interaction between street capitalists who operated in conjunction with jitney drivers and the intermittent enforcement of hackney licensing created tension between middle-class ideals of respectability and service to the community. Jitney drivers could work part time on the streets of the Hill District using a personal car or sharing a car between a group of drivers to earn money on the side. Jitney drivers often looked for work in legitimate cab companies, but restrictions on African American drivers in mainstream cab companies limited their opportunities to transform their skill into legal employment in a satisfactory way. Street corner shops along major thoroughfares served as jitney stations in the Hill. These same locations often served multiple purposes, both legal and illegal. Street corner shops like George Harris's confectionary and Gus Greenlee's Crawford Grill No. One often gained the ire of the elite African American community because of the late-night mixing of men, women, and children around their stores. While both locations served legal purposes within the community, they also served the illegal underground economy of the Hill District. The visible presence of illegal activities on the streets of the Hill District as well as the visible presence of women and girls on the streets at after-hours entertainment venues lessened the respectability of these establishments.

Jitneys held a complicated reputation on the Avenue; they were both necessary and potentially evil. These unlicensed taxi services were a hallmark of African American neighborhoods in Pittsburgh. In 1953, John L. Clark suggested, "On Jitney Drivers, a late report charges these fellows or some of them with transporting dope, 'pretty girls' to out of town joints and illegal sale of whiskey."[3] In 1954, a new city ordinance raised the fine for jitney driving but also caused confusion when the magistrates did not know who was responsible for its enforcement. In March of 1954, the police arrested forty-eight suspects for jitney driving and then arrested nineteen more the following week.[4] These arrests came in waves that often coincided with political appointments or campaigns. Avenue regulars and street capitalists argued that policing of jitney drivers often had little to do with their illegal enterprise and instead was a visible manifestation of vice on the streets of the Hill District.

Street capitalists and regulars often praised jitney drivers for their service to the community. Because of that service, the community tolerated their presence on the streets of the Hill District. One jitney driver and reader of the *Courier* commented on the illegality of jitneys in the Hill, saying, "It don't take 'em long to forget when colored people couldn't get a cab to or in the Hill District!" The same reader also commented, "Why pick on us when there are after-hour joints, numbers stations and prostitution houses operating right under the noses of the police?"[5] Another jitney driver suggested the main reason many operated illegal jitneys hinged on the availability of "better paying jobs" for African Americans. Access to better paying legal jobs would allow working-class Blacks to move away from street capitalism toward more acceptable forms of labor for those in the middle class.

In 1957, trolley and bus workers in Pittsburgh went on strike. Clark wrote in "Wylie Ave.," "Every now and then something happens to make working people come to the defense of 'jitneys.' Now, licensed trolley and buses are striking for more money than the Pittsburgh Railways Company wants to pay, and the people who supply revenue for the Railways Company, and salaries for its workers, must walk to their jobs, or hire cabs and 'jitneys.'"[6] According to Clark, jitneys had access to hackney licenses, but the large cab companies had monopolized cab service operations. Even the smaller start-up cab companies supported the prohibition of jitney licensing. He chastised his readers, "Under those conditions, and when strikes by trolley and bus operators take place, those 'lawbreaking jitneys' come to the rescue of people who don't own automobiles or live too far from their jobs to reach them by walking."[7] This unlicensed business not only assisted the community in the face of a transportation strike, but it also clearly operated at other times as well. Marcia Donnell, a long-time resident of the Hill District, recalled the role of jitneys in the Hill District, saying, "Another main source of transportation we had in the Hill District was Jitneys. And the reason for that was that Yellow Cabs did not want to come to the Hill District. . . . They were respectable as far as maybe that was so and so's uncle or a relative or you didn't even know them. All you just didn't want them to be was drunk."[8] The jitney stations were gathering places for the community and a place where illegal labor and legal labor collided. Jitney driving functioned out of the social networks that linked Hill District residents on the streets of their neighborhood.

Marcia Donnell also recalled that her husband, who worked in the construction trades, would also work as a jitney driver during the slow season or when the work was slim. She said, "When my husband was laid off from construction he would Jitney, he made good money. He would waste money, they would waste money, gamble a bit and drink a bit, but in those days a Jitney driver could make good money."[9] LeRoy also recalled the jitney stations in the Hill District and their role in the community, saying: "In the Jitney station they'd come in and sit down and there was a pay phone. Everybody knew the pay phone number. . . . While they waited for a call the drivers would be playing cards. It was just like the barbershop, you heard all the gossip there. You also made extra income because you didn't pay no taxes on what you earned. You could also play your numbers there. A bookie would come to the Jitney station and if you hit he'd bring your money to the Jitney station."[10] Marcia Donnell and Sarah Tomlin both recalled seeing young men congregating around the jitney station. They remembered seeing gambling going on but generally the jitney station was a place where the neighborhood gathered to meet a transportation need and as a hub of information, both formal and informal, for working-class African Americans in the Hill District.[11] While both middle-class and working-class African Americans used the services of jitney drivers, the working-class presence on the streets of the Hill District and their transportation needs led them to a greater dependence on the jitney system.

Many in the middle class commended the African American–owned Owl Taxi Cab Company in Pittsburgh for its service to the race and to the community as a whole. The Owl Taxi Cab Company exemplified approved African American business uses of street space. Reformers held up the activities of the Owl Company as a benchmark for other African American–owned businesses using street spaces. Jeanne Scott, the general secretary of the NAACP took credit for expediting access to licensure for the Owl Taxi Cab Company, saying, "The branch was in a large measure responsible for the breaking of the monopoly of the Yellow Cab in the city of Pittsburgh. Through the chairman of our legal committee, Atty. Paul F. Jones, the Owl Taxi Cab Company was granted a franchise for operation of 25 cabs. It is expected that the Public Utilities Commission will grant the request for increase of this number to 75."[12] For many, the option of an African American–owned cab company was sufficient, but for others, access to jobs within the large cab companies was the goal.

In another case, drivers for the Owl Taxi Cab Company protested in defense of a driver who was hit in the head with a blackjack by a plainclothes cop. The drivers described the incident as part of the "long-time continued harassment of their drivers by city police."[13] The officer in question claimed that the driver of the cab was driving recklessly and at excessive speeds and that, "Adams knocked him down with his cab after resisting arrest." Adams stated that he "did not know whether he was a cop or not."[14] The members of Transport Workers Local Union 62 supported Adams and stated they were trying to make a living and did not appreciate being "unjustly jeopardized by police officers."[15] The conflicts between African Americans and police often centered around a perception of unjust policing of their neighborhood.

Licensed cabs also had a reputation for bad behavior in the community. In an earlier column, John L. Clark railed against cabbies from the cab companies in the Hill, saying, "The Eyewitnesses say that drivers for the two companies will carry junkies to their 'pads,' haul thieves to safety and out of the reach of the police, make regular trips to pick up and return women who are unfaithful to their husbands and unmindful of small children left at home. But they refuse to give a lift in an emergency when a life could have been saved."[16] In the above case, a "skilled Northside worker" drove the two victims of a stabbing on Fullerton Street to the hospital. Some residents of the Hill believed the unlicensed jitney drivers were more dedicated to the community than the cab drivers working for the big cab companies.

Once both parties settled the streetcar strike, Black Pittsburghers still faced transportation issues in the city. Clark suggested automobile ownership increased among those who could afford it while those who depended on public transit would face higher fares. He wrote, "The street car strike has been settled and many people are happy because they no longer must move about in 'courtesy cars,' jitneys, taxicabs, or by foot. Automobile owners were the gainers during the 56-day strike, and will gain more since the stoppage has been removed. But those who ride the trolleys are still penalized."[17] Working-class African Americans in the Hill depended on public transportation, jitneys, and walking to get to their workplaces. Marcia Donnell recalled, "Now nobody had a car. My dad had a car and the insurance man had one, people like that, but very few had a car."[18] Those in the middle class who could afford a car did not have to face the same transportation difficulties that those in the working class faced during the streetcar strike, but few African Americans had cars in the Hill District. The streetcar strike forced many African Americans to use their social networks to get to work. Clark suggested, "But the penalty of being poor and being forced to pay more so that trolley car operators can live better has not prevented these poor people from rejoicing because the strike has been settled."[19] The streets of the Hill carried many working African Americans to and from their jobs. Social networks that were primarily operating through connections on the streets faced the common association of vice and illegality. Middle-class African Americans who were increasingly gaining access to more formal mechanisms of power used their social networks to determine which areas were respectable and which areas were "blighted."

Professional and elite residents defined street spaces as vice ridden and unsafe. One phenomenon leading middle-class African Americans to define the street as dangerous was the increase in knife carrying and other violent street crimes. Young men were the prominent offenders in violent crime on the streets. John L. Clark discussed the "history" of knife carrying in his "Wylie Ave." column, saying, "In the past twenty years, it has been the custom for youngsters even in the grades to 'wear' a switchblade knife to mimic the dress standards set by their parents."[20] This statement suggests that many Hill residents blamed the decline of their streets on migration and a lax style of parenting that created violent juvenile delinquency. Middle-class residents questioned the safety of the streets, especially at night. Many reformers, however, blamed inadequate and ineffective police presence for a rise in street violence.

John L. Clark recognized the role of policemen and women in his column, but he often called on them to increase their diligence on the streets. Clark commended police officers for their crackdown on drugs on the Avenue. Street spaces free of drugs and those selling them were inherently safer and more respectable than the usual condition of street spaces in the Lower Hill District. In one case, Clark tells of a raid on a speakeasy, but this speakeasy was "one of the quietest speakeasies in the country. It is more like a neighborhood hangout." The raid was the result of a tip from a "dope addict" and Clark was concerned the "county detectives made no effort to arrest the addict, and she was reported to be bragging about the damage she had caused."[21] This intermittent enforcement of law led to a perception that many police officers were, at best, disinterested in criminal activity in the Hill, and at worst, on the take. For small-time street capitalists, police presented an imminent threat to their livelihood and to their customers while larger-scale street capitalists faced little potential interaction with the police.

Clark also expressed concerns over the perceived brutality of police officers on the streets of the Hill District. In "Wylie Ave." he commented, "Complaints as usual, centered on brutality of police, gambling house privileges, wide open 'speakeasies' and opportunities for 'pretty girls' to sell their beauty so that 'pretty boys' would have more money to spend on the 'squares.'"[22] Clark's concern about police brutality echoed the concerns of many Hill residents. An editorial in the *Courier* claimed:

> It cannot be too often noted that congested Negro districts in urban centers, North and South, offer two temptations to police: the first and worst is traffic in vice. These congested areas would not be contaminated with so many different and vicious forms of vice if the existence of vice did not have significant value to some police officers. The other temptations, as bad in the North as in the South, is to be brutal in dealing with residents of these congested districts. . . . The fully armed policemen who took part in this sadistic orgy were members of the James squad. . . . These are the men who mercilessly beat, cuffed,

and pounded a 122 pound man. . . . Let us concede that the victim had committed a crime. Does that justify mayhem on the part of seven policemen? What did the policeman mean who yelled to the victim: 'We ought to lynch you' . . . This type of beating is not practiced against any but unprotected and defenseless elements in the community. No such beatings are meted out to racketeers and gangsters, or even to sex offenders if they are white.[23]

The brutality of police officers toward African American residents of the Hill District and the perception that the Hill District was "targeted" by raiders more than other neighborhoods in Pittsburgh led many African Americans to question the motives of the police force. A 1954 *Courier* article on police brutality detailed multiple cases of civil rights abuse in cities across the North. This article reminded readers of their rights and implored readers to obtain badge numbers for police officers who executed illegal searches or arrests.[24] Once arrested, Black Pittsburghers faced beatings while in police custody and "head whipping" in the cells of the Centre Avenue station house.[25] Violence toward African Americans on the streets of Pittsburgh from those enforcing the law raised another concern over the safety of street spaces for the working class. Conservative African Americans like columnist George S. Schuyler expressed different views of police conduct on the streets of the Hill District. Schuyler chastised Hill residents for their complaints of police brutality, which he claimed were "as phony as a three dollar bill."[26]

The police had a mixed reputation on Wylie Avenue and other streets of the Hill District. In 1956, Mrs. I. L. Kirkley, of 4639 Chance Street, complained to the NAACP that, "her grandson, Robert Lee Felder was beaten by police. Later arrested, and the family was not informed where he was being detained." The NAACP's records regarding the case "revealed that he was taken to Shadyside Hospital for treatment. Further investigation disclosed that he is now being held in Allegheny County Jail. Case will be referred to Legal Redress Committee."[27] Police brutality was a genuine concern on the streets of African American neighborhoods. As a solution, many middle-class African Americans argued for Black police officers to be assigned to African American neighborhoods.

In addition to questions of police brutality on the streets of the Hill District and other African American neighborhoods of Pittsburgh, city police also faced accusations of corruption and racial discrimination. Clark reported a rumor on the Avenue about an organized crime group forming in African American neighborhoods taking over the numbers rackets. According to the rumor, this organization operated with the full knowledge and protection of both government officials and the police. Clark stated, "The numbers racket provides substantial incomes for officials in each of Pittsburgh's thirty-two wards. And no downtown city official is big enough to reduce or cut off this revenue without serious and damaging political reaction."[28] The concerns over corruption in the police force led many middle-class African Americans to decry the state of the streets and label them as dangerous to good people. Clark described some of the concerns over the state of the streets in the Hill, saying: "These people take the position that hoodlums are running wild, robbing, injuring, and otherwise threatening the lives of people but in the meanwhile, the Police Department is busy arresting small fry numbers writers. They say that numbers writers can be arrested any time, but it requires a concentrated and continuous drive to stop the prevalent thuggery, and that the entire police force should be assigned to this type of crime."[29] While small numbers writers were nuisances but were not dangerous, the perceived violent elements of the streets were a larger threat. LeRoy recalled the encroachment of white numbers men into the Pittsburgh market. He stated, "We had the numbers up here, black people started it in Pittsburgh and then the Italians came in when they saw we were making money."[30] For many working-class African Americans, the numbers were a way to risk a small amount and potentially gain a large return. But at its core, the numbers were illegal.

To many middle-class African Americans, the police were not directing their efforts toward the real threats to respectability and safety on the streets of the Hill District. Some believed that the increased raids in the Hill District may have "tightened up" the "racket element" in the Hill but "confidence games" took their place.[31] Within a decade of World War II, African Americans in the Hill District lost interest in the numbers runners to focus on more pressing problems of increasing violence and drugs on the streets. The police force, however, seemed slow to shift focus to the issues that concerned middle-class African Americans in the Hill District.

Frank E. Bolden portrayed the middle-class vision of the positive aspects of policing in the Hill District. In a series entitled "Heroes in Blue," Bolden profiled policemen and women and their service to the city. The editor of the *Courier* wrote a note in preface to the first installment of the series, saying, "Good policemen, or policewomen, are more than rough tough guys. They are better than rough, tough guys. Even though the price of prudence and restraint, of intelligence and daring, may cost an officer his life, he must be equipped with the foregoing and with many other attributes gained only through experience. The good policeman is neither white nor colored. He is both. He is the good man."[32] Bolden stressed that the professionalization of the police force was more important than their race. In his view, having good cops patrol the streets of the Hill District was more important than having Black officers alone. Bolden suggested that Black officers may have struggles between neighborhood social network ties and their duty. For Bolden, the professionalization of the police force allowed younger men, and importantly, Black men, to participate in a profession where they could receive promotion based on merit rather than perceived graft or patronage as the reason for promotion.

Although they often faced discrimination in promotion, Bolden stridently argued that African American police officers should receive promotions based on their merit. Bolden focused his series on African American police officers, but he downplayed any idea that African American police officers were more trustworthy than their white colleagues. Bolden diminished concerns over police brutality and corruption within the police force. Instead, his series emphasized merit-based promotions throughout the series. He demonstrated many cases of African American police officers who had *retired* from the police force because they were consistently passed over for promotion.[33]

In another article, Ralph E. Koger outlined a number of distinguished African American police officers who, in his opinion, deserved promotion to detective. Koger's article argued that the number of "full-fledged city detectives" who were African American had fallen to its lowest level and that "Director Rosenberg" had an opportunity to promote African Americans to detective based on merit.[34] Koger then went on to imply that Director Rosenberg had used the "merit-grade detective gimmick" to promote white officers while passing over equally qualified African American officers.[35] Both Koger and Bolden suggested that qualified African Americans in the police force were not getting fair representation. Although there were many commendable officers in the police force, Koger also referenced officers in the "James Squad" as officers who "reportedly 'almost lynched' a Negro, later ruled innocent by a jury, in a case which occurred in the Hill District." These officers operated with little apparent oversight and typified African American concerns about the police in the Hill District. For many middle-class and elite African Americans the solution to the problem of unethical and brutal police in the Hill was to promote and recruit African American police officers.

Police raids played an integral role in "cleaning up the Hill." Police raids varied in their effectiveness. "Wylie Ave." often commented on possible payoffs and other political reasons police raided certain establishments and avoided others. Some questioned the efficacy of police officers when they were quick to arrest African Americans and slow to arrest whites breaking the law. An editorial in the *Courier* commented: "Leniency on the part of police and others have allowed vice dens to exist in the Hill District which serve as irresistible lures to sex-minded whites. These whites invade the Hill District and they don't draw any color line. Their nocturnal visits are for pleasure and in open defiance of the law. The first job of Rookie Rollason should have been to arrest these white men and the taxi driver who had come to the Hill District with the intention of violating the law through traffic with women."[36] Through the 1950s, middle-class African Americans shifted their concerns to crime in the Hill District as a marker of what the city called blight. The *Pittsburgh Courier* showed an increase in articles addressing drugs and vice in the Hill District. Reports of blight coincided with reports of drugs and prostitution. John L. Clark accused Hill police of shielding vice peddlers and being "in the know" about where all the best numbers joints were and when raids would take place.[37] The common perception of police complicity in vice activities in the Hill strengthened middle-class calls for Black officers and for increased police focus on vice in the Hill. In 1951, Pittsburgh city and Allegheny County formed a collective vice squad focused on cases of prostitution and narcotics primarily in the Hill District. This squad raided "sin dens" throughout the Hill District to such a degree that some complained that the Hill District was a convenient target for raids when other areas of the city suffered from increased vice and drug problems.

In the Lower Hill District and among the working class, vice often was a part of social networks on the streets. The *Courier* interviewed a Pittsburgh police inspector who stated that he had "started a campaign to keep people, who throng the streets during the wee hours of the morning in search of such devilment, off the streets. And that includes persons suspected of loitering to contact dope pushers or addicts."[38] Hill residents on the streets after hours could be arrested for loitering or suspicion of vice-related crimes. In 1956, vice squads in the Hill arrested "30 persons for loitering in the Lower Hill District and later discharged them after investigations for suspected connection with narcotics, gambling, illegal liquor or prostitution traffic."[39] Suspicion of illegal activity was sufficient to remove people from the streets of the Lower Hill. Many of the people working on the streets of the Hill District faced the possibility of association with illegal activity daily.

In the postwar period, drug use became a pressing concern on the Avenue. One raid uncovered a large marijuana-growing operation and two dealers were arrested. During the course of the raid, one dealer confessed that "'he went on the weed' when 18, while a GI serving in Europe. He returned to Pittsburgh and planted three patches of marihuana, and has manufactured reefers ever since."[40] Police also discovered heroin on the two men as well as paraphernalia for injection of heroin. Drug use and dealing seemed most prominent among younger African Americans in the Hill District. Middle-class African Americans expressed concern over the number of teenagers using drugs on the streets of the Hill District. In 1951, the Irene Kaufmann Settlement House sponsored a forum on the topic of "The Dope Habit Among Teen-Agers."[41] This forum addressed a growing problem on the streets of the Hill District. Speakers included "a social worker, a police inspector, a physician, and a local teen-ager."[42] Later in the year, police raided a "teen-age den" where they found thirty-three teenagers "from 13–19 years old." Police arrested them for smoking marijuana and drinking "whisky, beer, moonshine, and wine."[43] Both boys and girls faced sentences in the morals court for their actions. Police eventually arrested an adult male on charges of running a house of prostitution. The police also found a number of switchblades in the club after they "cleaned the place out."[44] The *Courier* reported this raid and claimed that the tip came from neighbors after much speculation over the location of claimed teenage dens.

The rise of dope in the Hill District also revealed new characters on the streets of the Hill. These men were not the street capitalists of the earlier era. The influence of drugs and the decline of the system of reciprocity common before the emphasis on destroying vice in the Hill District had transformed street capitalists from urban Robin Hoods to celebrity crooks and conmen. LeRoy recalled the exploits of one of his relatives who was a major player in the dope scene in the Hill District, King Count Frank, who spoke to *Courier* reporter Frank Bolden from Allegheny County Jail on Frank's "fight with the Devil" of heroin.[45] In 1951 police arrested Mary Lee Suber of 309 Dinwiddie Street for shoplifting in a downtown department store. She blamed her fall from grace on a narcotics addiction and her boyfriend, King Count Frank. The *Courier* article states, "Then under threat of halting her supply of the harmful drugs, Miss Suber said her boyfriend forced her to steal."[46] The *Courier* report described Mary Lee Suber as a "harmless, scared, Hill District Girl," and placed all the blame on Frank and his influence over her.[47] This description emphasized the prescribed nature of women on the streets. For many, women were not rational actors on street spaces; they were under the influence of men if they did not ascribe to respectable behavior patterns assigned to women. Suber was not the only woman associated with King Count Frank and his narcotics operation. Later the same year, King Count Frank described a woman he called "Miss Kicks" who he called his girlfriend and who shared many similar characteristics with Miss Suber including being sent to Kentucky for rehabilitation.

Frank E. Bolden interviewed King Count Frank for a series in the *Courier* to describe how he came to be the lead drug pusher in the Hill District and to reveal to the community the dangers of narcotics use. In the first installment, Count Frank, recovering from a near overdose, responded to Bolden, saying, "You want the story of my life? . . . It's too weird . . . too fantastic . . . no one would believe it."[48] The *Courier* described the scene of Frank's arrest where police officers found King Count Frank unconscious with a syringe in his arm on the floor of the bathroom. As a result, Count Frank agreed to tell his story to *Courier* readers so that, "his life story might save other youth from a similar fate."[49] Frank recalled a life that solidified many middle-class African Americans' fears of children on the streets, saying, "I was sort of a dead-end kid from the start. Home didn't mean too much to me. I spent lots of time on the streets with my gang. I was in Juvenile Court six times before I was 14. The first time for loitering on the streets after midnight."[50] King Count Frank further recalled many exploits as a "king of the Fullerton Street gang" where he honed his skills on the streets with petty crimes like loitering and theft. Count Frank then went on to describe his "descent into h—" where he became addicted to marijuana.[51] Through his association with the narcotics scene on the streets of the Hill District he became involved with a "Miss Kicks," also called "Vicki," who he moved in with in his new "crib."[52] He recalled, "in order to pay expenses at my crib, I made money by pushing reefers, and 'Vicki' would cruise a bit [prostitution]."[53] As Count Frank got hooked on a drug called paregoric or PG he recalled, "Me and [relative's name deleted] would lay up in the crib coolin' and turnin' each other on with paregoric, while our ribs [women in the drug scene] would go down around Fullerton and Clark Streets to 'kick mud' [form of prostitution] with passing motorists in order to get money for me and [relative's name deleted] and themselves to buy PG with."[54] While Frank's crimes escalated to armed robbery of a numbers station to pay for morphine, he also got into increasing trouble with the police.

King Count Frank recalled a time when police officers beat him and a member of his crew, saying, "I'll never forget that d—d ole lieutenant [name deleted] at Number Two [Centre Avenue Police Station]. He and some other 'killjoys' beat the livin' h—out o' us. He and the rest beat us with their fists and a rubber hose, and then kicked us with their feet and stomped us after we had been knocked down and tried to get up. . . . Those dogs beat us worse than any Nazi or Jap would a prisoner."[55] In addition to the beating, Count Frank stated that police officers contacted family and friends to try to coerce a confession to other robberies in the Hill District that he claimed to have nothing to do with. The linkage of drug use with prostitution was not the only way that young Black women descended into the sex trade. The area around Wylie Ave. was no stranger to prostitution and related vices.

Sex work flourished along the Ave and other streets in the Lower Hill District. The "Wylie Ave." column suggested sex work did not always violate the morals of the working class, but there were those in the middle class who disapproved. The streets of the Lower Hill had been a haven for sex workers and other illicit professions for many years. The efforts of city officials to address blight and vice by promoting aggressive redevelopment efforts in the downtown "Golden Triangle" area and in the Lower Hill threatened street spaces for sex work. Sex workers used street spaces in the Lower Hill district to conduct their business. Private homes and businesses also played a role in the sex trade in the Hill District. Marcia Donnell recalled prostitution on her street as a child, saying, "Everybody knew everybody. Prostitution was out there but it wasn't like they stood on the corner, we just knew certain houses where people went."[56] King Count Frank recalled the overlap between the drug scene and sex work when one of his girlfriends "Roxie" became a sex worker. Count Frank recalled, "So I moved Roxie from New Kensington back here and put her in [name deleted] house on Logan Street. Later Roxie's sister [name deleted] who was working in a house at _____ and _____ Streets [name of streets deleted] got Roxie on the line there. At this house the girls had punch cards on which they kept a record of their customers, but Roxie always held out between $16–$18 for ole Count."[57] Sex workers organized their work through punch cards and by using their feet to move to conditions more to their liking.

In the 1950s, sex work moved outdoors and onto the streets. Side streets and alleys off Wylie Avenue functioned as meeting places for sex workers and their clients as well as business places. LeRoy recalled how sex work operated on the streets of the Hill District, saying, "Pimps would use their cars to move women around. They would drop them off at a corner and leave them to walk the corner. If the pimp trusted the girl, he would let her go all night but if he didn't he might pull around the corner to make sure she delivered the money to him."[58] Legitimate businesses also acted as fronts for both sex workers and numbers activities in the Hill District. One prominent example of this overlap between legal and illegal businesses occurred in the Crawford Grill No. One owned by noted numbers man Gus Greenlee. His bar and grill hosted some of the greatest jazz players in the era and served great food and drink, but alongside his legitimate business interests he operated a thriving numbers game and allowed pimps like Pigmeat to operate their business within his walls.[59]

The Crawford Grill also held a reputation as both a legitimate business and a hub of both numbers and sex work. The surrounding area remained a popular location for parlor- and street-based sex work well into the period of urban redevelopment. "Pretty Girls" occasionally wrote in to the "Wylie Ave." column to set the record straight on their activities on the Ave. Whether in salons or on the streets these women worked in an area under increasing police scrutiny. In 1953, police arrested seven women on prostitution charges. Police arrested these women for soliciting on the streets of the Hill District.[60] While some sex workers operated out of brothels, increasingly, more prostitutes operated out of private homes while a majority moved onto the streets and alleys in the postwar period. By the period of urban renewal, women who used the streets as a workplace faced increasing encroachment from developers and others trying to eradicate perceived blighted areas in the city. Clark quoted a "veteran Pretty Girl" who wrote into the column, saying, "Between the city police and the Urban Redevelopment Authority, she claims 'Pretty Girls' can no longer 'model' in an area close to the Golden Triangle. The one remaining short street where 'pretty models' are still working is due to be closed early next year."[61] The Urban Redevelopment Authority and other progressive institutions in the city targeted the streets where these women worked as signs of urban decay and blight. Women involved in illegal labor on the streets resisted the encroachment of redevelopers into their streets. Redevelopers often listed prostitution as one of the reasons for defining a space as blighted. The "Pretty Girls" faced removal from the streets as a part of redevelopment.

Later in 1957, Clark wrote, "Tearing down the Lower Hill has not caused the veteran 'pretty girls' to retire, according to our night reporter. He says the same 'beauties' of 20 years ago can be found 'modeling' at Townsend and Epiphany, Townsend and Hazel Sts., and on Colwell St., and at least one reports for midnight duty out of Whitcomb St."[62] Map 5.1 illustrates the

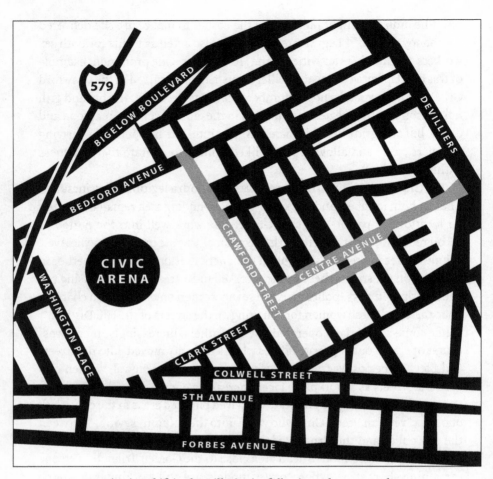

MAP 5.1 Prostitution shift in the Hill District following urban renewal.
Jason Klanderud, Altair Media Design, Designer.

movement of prostitution away from the Lower Hill renewal area and into space within the borders of the Upper Hill. The marked streets reveal the shifting locations for street-based sex work under the influence of urban renewal. Women practicing sex work on the streets of the Lower Hill District did not end their work; instead, they shifted the location of the streets they used for their work out of the path of urban renewal. Sex workers on the streets faced a forced eviction from the street spaces as urban renewal destroyed where they worked.[63]

Urban renewal affected female sex workers as well as other street labor-ers. Clark detailed the difficulties "pretty girls" faced in the path of urban renewal, saying: "According to police circles, a double campaign is being conducted by the 'pretty girls,' and it is centered in the Third Ward. These opinions disclose that the once fabulous 'salons' on Elm, Epiphany, Fuller-ton, Colwell, Hazel, and Whitcomb Sts. are losing patronage because the younger and 'beauteous models' have other plans. The 'newer and pretty girls' are getting established on Centre Ave. from Crawford to Fullerton Sts., sometimes on down to Clark St. — the course to be taken by the 'redevelop-ment' shift."[64] Over time, the association of the streets with crime and blight drove middle-class African Americans away from street spaces.

The *Courier*, on the other hand, discussed "pretty boys" and other men in-volved in the sex trade. In one case, police charged four men with moral charges, primarily forcing their wives into sex work.[65] The *Courier* often discussed men in gambling and drug-related vices rather than in the sex trade, but they did appear albeit infrequently. Sex workers migrated with legal businesses and African American residents into the Upper Hill and other African American neighborhoods where Lower Hill residents relocated. Clark reported, "Latest information on the 'pretty girls' is hard to believe. From one close to the picture, the column is told that between eight to ten of these 'beauties' who took the oath 'never to be a square' thirty-five and forty years ago, are looking about for new locations to 'work.'"[66] These "girls" var-ied in age including into their fifties and sixties. Women were not the only workers in this type of enterprise.

The women engaged in sex work did not often mention men, either as clients or as pimps. In one case, a former "pretty girl" wrote in to "Wylie Ave." explaining her return to Pittsburgh after some time in another city, saying, "I got out of the racket, went back home and stayed for two years. But now that I am back I have to make new friends. All the chicks and pimps are either using dope or selling it."[67] The rising prevalence of dope and drug use in the Hill District changed the nature of the streets for African Ameri-cans involved in illegal labor. In one reported incident, one woman claimed she shot her "boss" because "he wanted her to use dope and also to be a prostitute for him."[68] In this case, the man flagged down a patrol car while injured and then he led the policemen to the location of the female shooter. When police arrested the woman, she admitted that the man she had shot was her pimp. She faced a firearms violation, and the police held the man on pandering charges. Only the man faced charges related to the sex trade.

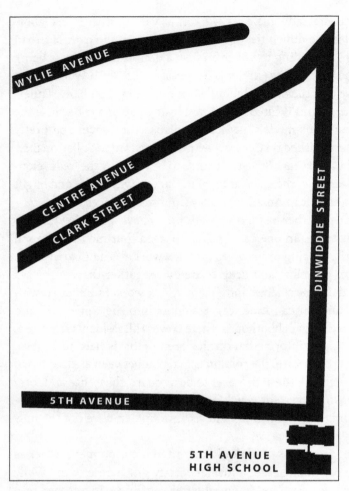

MAP 5.2 5th Avenue High School and Dinwiddie Street.
Jason Klanderud, Altair Media Design, Designer.

Undercover vice officers posed an added threat to working "pretty girls," whether in private clubs or on the streets. LeRoy recalled walking to school at Fifth Avenue High School along Dinwiddie Street where many pimps lived. He stated, "Most of the pimps lived on Dinwiddie Street. I would walk past their houses on my way to high-school and you'd see all their Cadillacs parked and sometimes you'd see them on their porches dressed nice and you'd think that's what I want to do when I'm older."[69] Map 5.2 shows the location of Dinwiddie Street in relation to Centre Avenue and Wylie Avenue and the location of Fifth Avenue High School.[70]

LeRoy suggested that many in the working class did not question the presence of sex workers on the streets of the Hill District, saying, "People didn't really care about pimps and prostitution. It was a hustle. You had to make money somehow. Everyone wanted to be a pimp; they drove a Cadillac and dressed nice."[71] The idea of a hustle permeated working-class African American culture. For many working-class Blacks the goal of making enough money to support your family took precedence over the legality of the enterprise.

The business owners of these illicit businesses, like numbers saloons and prostitution houses, faced the prospect of raids, but it does not appear that they faced significant pressure from the community to close. In 1957, police raided thirteen establishments and arrested people "on a variety of charges which ran the gamut from writing numbers, selling beverages illegally (in some cases moonshine), or visiting the places where such whims may be indulged."[72] In the many reported raids, police often arrested men for gambling and women for illegal liquor sales and prostitution-related offences. Many of the women and men arrested for one illegal activity were also charged with others. Clark suggested, "Men and women who are bent on making a livelihood by operating speakeasies, gambling houses and 'pretty girl salons' will be forced to close down these rackets unless they stop 'snitching' on each other."[73] The article insinuated the people registering these complaints were often engaged in the same activities they were reporting. African Americans involved in both legal and illegal labor often worked on the streets of the Lower Hill together. Additionally, many of the businesses operated by street capitalists often faced questionable enforcement from the police and questionable respectability from those in the middle class.

"Wylie Ave." did not censure those African Americans working in less respectable lines of work, although the *Pittsburgh Courier* did in other columns. Police raids and other crackdowns on illegal labor occurred throughout the period, but the *Courier* suggested the raids were ineffectual in preventing vice in the Hill District. Working-class and working-poor African Americans in the Hill District seemed less sure of their stance on vice in their neighborhood. The connections between political powers, street capitalists, illegal laborers, and legitimate businessmen remained tight, making any outright disavowal unlikely.

Working-class African Americans did not hold uncontested opinions of the interrelation between legal and illegal businesses. This tension between middle-class notions of respectability and daily working life on the streets of the Hill played out in the pages of the *Pittsburgh Courier*. Society pages, gossip columns, and other recurring features emphasized the behaviors of African American elites. Other columns, like "Wylie Ave." and "Deep Wylie" focused on the social network of "regulars" on the Avenue and disdained the lifestyle of African American elites. This contradiction illustrates some of the tensions within the African American community in the Hill District.

In 1962, a reporter for the *Pittsburgh Courier* declared Wylie Avenue "Dead." He recounted the characters of the street and the businesses he remembered. In his opinion, urban redevelopment destroyed the nature of Wylie Avenue, the romantic world of the street capitalists, and the neighborhood as a whole.[74] The construction of the Civic Arena and the displacement of over 8,000 low-income residents of the Lower Hill transformed the nature of the Hill District. Businesses relocated from Wylie Ave to other neighborhoods, and residents moved out of the Hill District to other areas of the city. These changes to the streets of the Hill District, and primarily Wylie Avenue, transformed African American Pittsburgh. The displacement and relocation of so many African Americans from the neighborhood stretched the social networks of the Hill. African Americans of all classes would rebuild their cultures in other areas of the city, but other neighborhoods would not be the same as the heart of the Hill District. Middle-class African Americans and their working-class brothers and sisters viewed life on the streets of the Hill differently. For middle-class and elite African Americans, the streets of the Hill became a liability that exposed them to the hardships of relocation and urban renewal. Working-class Blacks faced the destruction of their workplaces and the classification of their streets as dangerous and deviant. The ethos of street capitalists that prioritized service to the community declined in favor of a new vision of celebrity criminals who were under no reciprocal obligation to the neighborhood. Developing problems of drug use and the delegitimization of street capitalism coincided with the rise of Black policing in the Hill District which solidified the efforts of the Black middle class to emphasize respectable forms of labor and approved uses of street space. Urban redevelopment revealed the class-based tensions within the African American community. Urban redevelopment transformed more than just the streets of the Hill district. It challenged the system of neighborhood cohesion and reciprocity provided by street capitalists while also solidifying a break between the middle class and their working-class neighbors. The death of Wylie Ave. signaled the end of street capitalists as romantic characters on the streets of the Hill, but the middle class was not free of its ethos of community redistribution of wealth and informal power. Instead, the memory of reciprocity lingered in the working class and traveled through the streets of Pittsburgh where it followed displaced residents to Homewood, East Liberty, and the Northside.

CHAPTER SIX

Centre Avenue

Freedom Corner and the Modern Black Freedom
Movement, 1945–1968

Alma "Speed" Fox is by turns described as a fiery capital "L" Lady who was impeccably dressed, the picture of African American womanhood, and as the "Civil Rights Mother" of the movement in Pittsburgh for full political, social, and economic equality. She worked as a professional in the Department of the Interior in the Bureau of Mines and as the head of the National Association for the Advancement of Colored People (NAACP) Women's Auxiliary before becoming the executive secretary of the Pittsburgh branch of the NAACP in 1967 alongside Byrd Brown as president.[1] Fox organized protest marches against institutions like Duquesne Light, Mine Safety Appliances, Sears and Roebuck, Kaufmann's Department Store, Hornes, Gimbels, the Board of Education, and the University of Pittsburgh to shame them into integrating their workforces and accepting African Americans into skilled positions. Fox recalled a time when it seemed "there was some picket line to get on every single solitary week."[2] She also recalled the importance of Centre Avenue and Crawford Street, otherwise known as Freedom Corner: "every time the NAACP planned a demonstration, we would start at the corner of Centre and Crawford. . . . So the NAACP named that Freedom Corner."[3] This location was a visible reminder of the destruction of the Lower Hill District and was also the "the logical place to start a demonstration." Fox recalled, "Yes, and most of our demonstrations, we had something, we were walking down to the City Council Building to have a demonstration, or we were walking down to Point Park to have a demonstration. So that was the logical place for everybody to start there." Freedom Corner became a central location for protest action originating in the Hill District and moving into the streets of downtown Pittsburgh. This street corner formed a hub of information and activism in the social networks of African American Pittsburgh.

Many of the men in the civil rights movement in Pittsburgh claim Speed as the driving force behind their introduction to activism in the city, though she originally claimed that she feared that activism was unladylike. Fox recalled her first participation in a demonstration thinking, "Hmm, they don't represent me. Then I heard myself say aloud that I did know who did represent me. I picked my daughter up and, with her in my arms, I joined my first demonstration."[4] Alma S. Fox organized the movement for full rights for all African Americans and stressed the importance of women's participation in the freedom struggle as well as in the feminist movement. Fox recalled, "You have to be willing to give your all, because freedom is not free. Everybody put their necks on the line for the movement. We get no more than we demand!"[5] Her adept planning and provisioning of street protests and her sharp understanding of where and how to make street protests effective by mobilizing social networks pushed the struggle for the streets of Pittsburgh and for the full equality of African Americans into the center of political, social, and economic life in the Steel City.

After World War II, African Americans in Pittsburgh intensified their fight for political and economic equality. Organizational policy from professional African American organizations like the NAACP and the Urban League stressed programs aimed at gaining access to formal power through political and social rights. During the post–World War II period, African American professional leaders focused their efforts on equal access to skilled industry positions and in housing, while working-class African Americans used their social networks to open industries to fair employment practices and to remove quota placements on public housing. African Americans used their neighborhood-based social networks to forge an alliance of informal and formal power between working-class laborers and the middle, professional class that produced many gains for social and economic rights. Black Pittsburghers struggled to juggle their responsibility to provide for their families with the expectations of organizations that used their growing consumer power to encourage businesses to hire African Americans. They faced dilemmas and limits on their ability to participate in street protests because of a desire to retain their employment and fulfill the work hours required to make a living.

The community supported the efforts of the NAACP, Urban League, and affiliated organizations, but participation was often intermittent. Street spaces became a theater of protest for all African Americans as they used every available space to make their desire for equal rights and equal access a reality. Men, women, and children attended political street rallies and used the public space of the streets as political space to express their vision of social, political, and economic equality. In figure 6.1, Teenie Harris photographed women, including Marva Jo Hord (Harris), outside of Woolworth's lunch counter downtown protesting their segregation policies in the South. Protests like this one were targeted at businesses who did not hire Black

FIGURE 6.1 Women, including Marva Jo Hord (Harris), protesting outside of Woolworth's carrying signs reading "A protest against this co. policy in the south," "Chatham students protest civil rights violation," and "Chatham students protest Woolworth lunch counter segregation," Smithfield Street and Sixth Avenue, Downtown, 1960. Charles "Teenie" Harris (American, 1908–98), black-and-white: Kodak safety film, H: 4 in. × W: 5 in. (10.20 × 12.70 cm), Carnegie Museum of Art, Pittsburgh: Heinz Family Fund, 2001.35.15700, © Carnegie Museum of Art, Charles "Teenie" Harris Archive.

employees or who discriminated against Black customers. African Americans leveraged their social networks to push for better paying jobs in both existing and emerging industries. Fair employment legislation gave African Americans some legal standing to protest discriminatory hiring practices, but African American organizations also used street protest and picket lines to shame employers into breaking the color line in their businesses. African American organizations spanned the interests of both middle-class and working-class employees, but they had the most success placing professionally trained middle-class African Americans in newly opened skilled positions. These successes encouraged African Americans of all classes in a continued struggle for equal access to meaningful labor.

The push to integrate public accommodations included many African Americans from the Hill District. The locations where they pushed for access included some emerging Black neighborhoods outside of the Hill District. For many African Americans in Pittsburgh, the Hill District was the center of their social networks in the city, but East Liberty and Homewood also boasted increasing African American populations following urban renewal. The social networks that connected Black Pittsburgh stretched and flowed into emerging neighborhoods. For many African Americans, East Liberty had the potential to become the "Black Squirrel Hill" of Pittsburgh. Black families slowly made inroads into East Liberty as they moved out from the Hill District. Conflicts between white residents of East Liberty and Lawrenceville and incoming African American residents escalated and coalesced around use of the Highland Park Pool. Pennsylvania passed equal accommodation laws in 1939, but enforcement was uneven and significant discrimination and segregation continued well into the 1950s. The Civic Unity Council, which was an organization founded in 1946, stated, "Pittsburghers, it seems, experience their strongest feelings of racial dissimilitude in those circumstances which require physical contact with strangers on a plane of social equality. Dance halls, bars, skating rinks, and pools are outstanding examples."[6] Discrimination in public accommodations continued, especially in areas of physical contact or where the potential to meet a romantic partner might exist. Among these spaces, public swimming pools were often the most visibly segregated. In the neighborhood of East Liberty, the city of Pittsburgh operated at least two public pools including the Klein Pool and the newly built Highland Park Pool.

The Klein Pool predated the Highland Park Pool, but white swimmers largely abandoned Klein Pool when the city built Highland Park Pool. This segregated pool system existed for many years, to which the Civic Unity Council stated, "The custom thus established has been condoned by most residents of the area (including members of both races), has been vigorously supported by many, and has been physically defended by a few. This custom, this segregated use pattern so clearly at variance with democratic principles and state laws, —is the problem."[7] Entrenched racism made the process of integrating the Highland Park Pool and other public accommodations difficult as incoming residents clashed with longtime white residents of emerging Black neighborhoods.

African Americans risked violence from street gangs and white residents of East Liberty and Lawrenceville as they walked to the park and pool from their homes in an attempt to integrate the pool. Street gangs of white young men threatened the safety of African American swimmers. The racial animosity over the integration of the pool escalated as African Americans pushed for full access to the Highland Park Pool instead of the city pools normally reserved for segregated African American use. The *Pittsburgh Post-Gazette* often described the violence in the pool grounds and on the streets of East Liberty as riots. These racially motivated incidents emphasized the violence that spilled out of the pool area onto the street nearby. The *Post-Gazette* reported, "A second riot broke out late last night when a score of Negroes marched from Penn township to Lincoln and Lemington avenues, and after tearing palings from a fence began attacking a dozen white youths."[8] According to the report, a majority of the "disorder" came from African American bathers against white citizens of the neighborhood. The article goes on to list those arrested in the disturbances, but only two of those arrested were white while the other seven youth arrested were African American. The *Post-Gazette* focused on what they described as intense violence between white and Black bathers. They did not acknowledge any right of African American bathers to use the pool. Incidents between pool goers continued each summer in the East Liberty neighborhood. African American and progressive organizations pushed for the integration of pool facilities through formal social networks, public protests, and legal measures as well.

An NAACP report on the Highland Park Pool described the conditions of African Americans in the East End by saying: "The Y.M.C.A. is an exception along with the Salvation Army, a newly reorganized Community Council, and, to a lesser extent, the schools. These agencies have not yet succeeded in making much of an impression on the community pattern. The Y.M.C.A. has been unable to gain admittances to any of the roller skating rinks for its group of Negro and white girls. Business establishments generally, particularly restaurants and bars, exclude Negroes. Churches are segregated. The Y.M.C.A. has very few Negro patrons, and their activities are very limited."[9] A local attorney, Richard Jones, believed if African American adults could use the pool without fear for their safety and without reprisals from local agitators, then the lawsuit from the NAACP would not be necessary. Roy Wilkins, the executive secretary of the NAACP, endorsed the action of the Pittsburgh branch toward integrating the Highland Park Pool. He also admitted, "We have made significant gains in race relations in the last ten years, but the warning signs of Cicero was to be found among them, in the bombings in Southern cities, in the successful race hate campaigns waged by several Southern senatorial candidates, the alliance between Dixiecrats and some elements of the Republican Party."[10] The NAACP recommended that African American adults attend Highland Park Pool daily to continue the push to integrate the pool.[11] National leaders of the NAACP viewed the Highland Park Pool case as one of many important battlefields toward full citizenship for African Americans. This was not strictly a local fight; African Americans in Pittsburgh were fighting for equal access to city-owned accommodations all over the country and the Pittsburgh case could establish a legal precedent.

The Civic Unity Council, an interracial group of young activists in Pittsburgh that developed out of the NAACP, prepared several reports describing the racial conditions of the East Liberty neighborhood and the progress toward integrating the Highland Park Pool. The Highland Park Pool was one of the newest and best-maintained public pools in the city. African Americans moving into East Liberty faced off with their new neighbors over public accommodations and the streets of the new neighborhood as they integrated the East End of the city. Pittsburgh police considered East Liberty "the toughest section of Pittsburgh" for interracial relations.[12] Police often blamed the "Larimer Avenue" gang for a number of racially motivated beatings on the streets of East Liberty.[13] Although there were many organizations promoting positive interracial relations by 1948, they had "not yet succeeded in making much of an impression on the community pattern."[14] Interracial organizations like the "Young Progressives" and the "Youth for Wallace" pushed for integration of public spaces and greater access for African Americans to public venues.

The Civic Unity Council suggested, "There is a general impression among pool personnel that the militant 'White Supremacy Lads' are mostly Larimer Avenue people supported, to a limited extent, by a group of veterans from Lawrenceville."[15] East Liberty had a "rather large and scattered" African American population in the mid-1940s, but these African Americans faced discrimination and segregation in their daily lives. It was in this climate of discrimination in public accommodations that a group calling themselves "Youth for [Henry A.] Wallace" began their campaign to integrate the pool. On July 18, pool employees refused admittance to a group of young people because some of them were African Americans. These young people wrote a letter to Mayor David Lawrence describing their treatment at the pool and listing the descriptions of all the employees at the pool as well as the badge numbers of the police officers who watched what was "most certainly a violation of the Equal Rights Law of the Commonwealth of Pennsylvania."

These youth sent a list of demands to the mayor's office. The group demanded police protection for all African American swimmers and a face-to-face meeting with the mayor. The mayor responded to their charge of discrimination at the pool with assurances of his cooperation and adherence to the public accommodations law while adding, "In this policy our Director of Parks and Recreation actively concurs, and it will be enforced all the way down the line."[16] Young adults from the Youth for Wallace used and repeated this statement from the mayor to leverage perceived access to formal social power in their call for integration of the pool. In a subsequent letter, Ms. Esther Bliss wrote to Mr. Howard B. Stewart, the director of Parks and Recreation, quoting the statement from the mayor and then adding, "In view of this clear statement by the Mayor, a group of white and Negro young people from our organization are returning to Highland Park Pool this coming Sunday, August 8th. We expect that there will be adequate police protection to guarantee the safety of our group from attacks by hoodlums."[17] The Young Progressives of America used a police escort to enforce their admittance into the pool while also inviting members of the press to observe their pool visits to shame those who opposed integration. Frequently, however, the white press focused on incidents of street violence.

In 1948, the *Pittsburgh Post-Gazette* reported on "disorders" at the pool between members of the Young Progressive Party and the local white youth. The *Post-Gazette* described those pushing for integration as troublemakers and communists, while also emphasizing their ties to organized labor. The article stressed the idea that organizers of the protest knew there would be disorder and strongly suggested that the protestors intensified the "riot" and the street violence that spilled out of the pool area onto neighboring streets. The *Post-Gazette* article mentioned an incident of "hoodlums" following a few young women members of the Young Progressive Party who threw stones at them as they waited at a trolley stand.[18] The risk for African American bathers and their white allies intensified after they left the somewhat protected spaces of the pool and headed home on the streets.

In 1950, the *Post-Gazette* reported Nathan Albert's conviction in a plot to incite a riot at the Highland Park Pool. Albert, a secretary of the Squirrel Hill Communist Club, allegedly incited a race riot at the Highland Park Pool. According to the *Post-Gazette*, an FBI informant "testified Albert was 'instructed' at a meeting prior to the racial disturbance at the pool—to take some Negroes there with him."[19] The prosecution argued that the riot precipitated from the action of bringing African Americans to the pool. The police officer injured in a related incident on the streets after the African

American bathers left the pool admitted, "he didn't see any disturbance," and he could not remember if the person who stabbed him was a member of the Young Progressives or "a Larimer Ave. hoodlum," as the defense suggested.[20] In all, the case seemed to focus on Albert's communist leanings rather than any concrete evidence against him for the disorders at the pool and on the streets of East Liberty. Later, the state superior court denied Albert's request for a retrial.[21] In the descriptions of violence at the pool and on the surrounding streets, both the African American and white press focused on the agitation of youth. This emphasis on street violence focused on youth gangs and retaliation from groups of young people. African American organizations wanted to change the focus away from youthful outbursts of violence developing out of informal social networks toward respectable adult interactions through formal networks of power between other patrons of the pool.

African American youths and adults faced the threat of violence when they used the Highland Park Pool. A gang of young men called the "Larimer Avenue Gang" beat and injured two young African American men after they swam at the pool. White police arrested three members of the gang and later released them from the juvenile detention center on their own recognizance. The NAACP filed a complaint with the police charging aggravated assault and battery.[22] This incident was not the only case of local gangs violently objecting to the presence of African American swimmers at the Highland Park Pool. The Larimer Avenue Gang often appeared in accounts of violence against African American swimmers and in the few accounts of "riots" over African American swimming at the pool.

Many civil rights organizations pressed for greater rights for African Americans in Pittsburgh, but they did not all have a similar vision for Pittsburgh's African American community. The United Negro Protest Committee (UNPC) and the Leadership Action Committee on Civil Rights (LACCR) established an annual picnic to "discuss plans for closer cooperation in promoting the cause of civil rights in Pittsburgh." A spokesman for the event stated, "If we can picnic together we can work together."[23] Leaders held the picnic in Highland Park, the site of many picnics and gatherings for elite and middle-class African Americans. Public gatherings like picnics provided an arena for African Americans to gather and put together a plan for pursuing civil rights on the streets of Pittsburgh. The gathering of multiple civil rights organizations to discuss how better to work together raises the question of why such a meeting was necessary. The organizations represented used the picnic to declare a truce of sorts and to reaffirm their intention to work together in the future. This meeting also solidified informal social networks in the neighborhood in the form of interorganization cooperation through formalized social networks.

Marcia Donnell, a middle-class African American woman born in the Hill District, recalled how informal social networks leveraged their limited access to formal power through politics when she was a young adult, saying, "So when it came time to vote we weren't voting for president or vice president, we were voting for committee people. And they did things for the community. Like, you would have a Christmas tree in the middle of your street because of your committee people."[24] She also recalled an incident when she was campaigning for a local committee person on the streets of the Hill District, and a neighbor approached her and informed her that she could be in danger of losing her job with the state for political campaigning. She was very thankful to that neighbor because she did not want to lose her job. She said from that point on she remembered to vote but made sure she followed the rules for political participation on the streets.[25] These rules limited African American political uses of street spaces, and many people feared losing hard-won jobs due to an unfavorable opinion from employers. The informal social networking in the neighborhood allowed residents to ebb and flow with their political participation while maintaining their growing access to formal power.

Sala Udin, a local working-class civil rights activist and resident of the Hill District, also recalled the importance of street spaces in the protests of the 1960s. He revealed the origin of the spot called Freedom Corner, the corner of Centre Avenue and Crawford Street, where African Americans in the Hill District defied city planners and their agenda to move urban renewal programs into the Upper Hill District. This intersection was a site where the informal social networks of the street overlapped with the power of a coalition of African Americans who were developing access to formal networks of power. Centre Avenue and Crawford Street became the gathering place for street-based protests in the Hill District.[26] Parades and picket lines to protest hiring discrimination likely gathered at Freedom Corner before commencing their protest of the Civic Arena project. The *Courier* reported, "Following the expose by the *Courier*, several weeks ago, and a mass parade and picket line, last Saturday, around the Civic Auditorium, the latter authorities announced this week that more Negroes would be hired, and in jobs other than those in the menial category."[27] In 1962, residents of the Hill District also implemented a selective buying campaign to pressure companies to hire African Americans in nonmenial jobs. The *Courier* reported the selective buying campaign was "almost 100 per cent effective during the

FIGURE 6.2 Protest march with women and men holding signs for equal rights and CORE, heading toward Downtown on Centre Avenue with Epiphany Church in background, c. 1960–1968. Charles "Teenie" Harris (American, 1908–98), black-and-white: Kodak safety film, H: 4 in. × W: 5 in. (10.20 × 12.70 cm), Carnegie Museum of Art, Pittsburgh: Heinz Family Fund, 2001.35.3059, © Carnegie Museum of Art, Charles "Teenie" Harris Archive.

height of the job drive."[28] African Americans in the Hill District and other areas of the city boycotted the products of companies that refused to hire Blacks to skilled positions within their company. This tactic yielded new jobs for professional and skilled African Americans.

Street protests, as shown in figure 6.2, a photograph by Teenie Harris, targeted businesses who refused to hire African American laborers. These protests also encouraged Black Pittsburghers to decide which businesses they would patronize and leverage their informal power of the purse. Campaigns in the *Courier* and through the NAACP and the Urban League encouraged African Americans to spend their hard-earned money carefully to support businesses that hired African Americans if they could not support Black-owned businesses.[29] Harris took that photo in the same year as K. Leroy Irvis's drive to create additional employment opportunities for African Americans in Pittsburgh. Unlike previous drives by the Urban League of Pittsburgh and the UNPC, this campaign was successful, but at the cost of Irvis's position with the Urban League. The protest "embarrassed" white donors to the coffers of the Urban League and R. Maurice Moss fired Irvis.[30] By the 1950s, picketing became a popular device to promote changes in employment discrimination.

The UNPC pushed for skilled jobs within the city bureaucracy and other areas of formal power as well. The UNPC scheduled a planning meeting with Cornelius J. Daly, the regional coordinator of the President's Committee on Equal Opportunity, to discuss "the Pittsburgh scene from a federal funds discrimination standpoint," and address the issue of hiring African Americans as skilled laborers in "several of the city's bureaus which presently do not have any colored employees."[31] While the city stressed there were no African Americans on the civil service lists, the UNPC countered with examples of African American men who had passed the civil service exam and were not appointed to positions.

The UNPC also addressed hiring issues in other stores. The supermarket chain A&P faced protests designed to pressure them into hiring African Americans in their stores. Charles "Teenie" Harris was both the spokesperson and a member of the delegation of the UNPC meeting with the A&P delegation. The A&P delegation agreed with the UNPC delegation, "a substantial percentage of the Negro community patronizes the A&P stores in the tri-state area and this should be taken into consideration when the hiring comes."[32] The UNPC's threats succeeded in persuading A&P to hire African Americans. Originally, A&P suggested "there were 28 job openings in which Negroes would be welcomed if they applied."[33] African Americans applied for the positions and they took positions in both full-time and skilled employment. The UNPC pledged to tackle African American employment at the other grocery stores "one at a time" to focus their energies on achieving jobs for African Americans. The UNPC also discussed an "on-the-job training program" for African American hires in A&P. African Americans wanted access to jobs as truck drivers and in the refrigeration department.[34] These positions were semiskilled and paid significantly better than positions previously available to African Americans. The UNPC pushed diligently for jobs that moved African Americans into positions beyond manual labor, into positions that developed formal power.

African Americans looking for skilled work faced a difficult battle against unions and their discriminatory practices. Police frequently arrested street demonstrators from the Committee of Racial Equality (CORE) and UNPC in their efforts to peacefully persuade the electrical union to accept African American members to their organization. Members picketed on the streets surrounding construction sites at Chatham Center and other sites for refusing to hire African American contractors and laborers.[35] The push to integrate labor unions and grant African Americans greater access to skilled positions continued as a major component of the UNPC's mission. While this push to integrate the unions may appear beneficial to the working classes at large, the major thrust of the push for integration benefited the middle-class or *skilled* laborers rather than those members of the working classes considered *unskilled*.[36] These pushes for equality in the arena of jobs and hiring benefited African Americans with greater education and access to training than African American day laborers or others in more precarious labor positions.

In 1966, the UNPC protested the lack of African American hires in the truck driving and delivery and warehouse departments. The UNPC expressed concern over the lack of supervisory and managerial positions available for African Americans. These positions were fundamentally middle class rather than working class.[37] Kaufmann's department store did not immediately acquiesce to the demands of the UNPC. The UNPC threatened a selective buying campaign and street picketing if Kaufmann's did not provide a "clear picture, by Friday, of the Negro job situation."[38] The UNPC successfully used selective buying campaigns and picketing on the streets to integrate the workforces of several companies so this was not an empty threat to the ownership of Kaufmann's. The Hill District Board of Trade joined the Business and Professional Association (BPA) in their protest claiming, "So great, however, has been the decline in revenues of Hill District businesses since the new direct-to-downtown via Webster Ave. bus route has been in operation that the whole program of the new Hill District Board of Trade is being sabotaged."[39] The Port Authority also faced pressure from the UNPC to hire African Americans as drivers as they transitioned to a bus-based system. The UNPC stated, "The United Negro Protest will ever be at PAT's back with an implicit threat of demonstration, boycott and massive jitney car pool."[40]

In 1952 the CORE formed a local chapter in Pittsburgh which became "quite active with its program of non-violence in local racial situations."[41] The local branch of CORE met at the Irene Kauffman Settlement House in the Hill District where they coordinated their nonviolent efforts throughout the city.[42] By the end of the 1950s, African American civil rights agitation through CORE and other organizations shifted from a focus on gaining access to public accommodations and discrimination in social life to a strong push to integrate the workforce, especially in skilled positions. This movement forged an alliance between middle-class African Americans and their working-class neighbors as both pushed for greater access to economic freedom and equality through formal power.

In 1961, Hill District ministers held a "Civil Rights Leadership Training Institute" for lay leaders in the participating churches. The training certified them as "human relations consultants" for "their respective congregations."[43] Church leaders, civic leaders, and labor organizations joined forces to protest discriminatory hiring practices by those building the Civic Arena. The protestors made the case that the removal of African American families from the Lower Hill entitled them to representative hiring in the project that paved over the streets of their neighborhood. The protestors and the NAACP felt the hiring of eight African Americans was insufficient compared to the numbers of African Americans in the Pittsburgh population as a whole and especially the disproportionately African American population of displaced residents from the arena area.[44] The protestors gathered for the march in the Hill District and from there, marched "through the streets of Homewood, East Liberty, and the Hill District." The protest gained a few jobs for African Americans in the Civic Arena as guards, engineers, and electricians as well as a new African American receptionist.[45]

The UNPC focused much of its effort and protests on gaining access to trade unions for African American men. In February 1952, the Courier reported the UNPC's "almost daily" protests and demonstrations "which resulted in some 22 arrests during the past week, 19 magistrate court fines and subsequent appeals, and civil disobedience and the picketing of various types of employers."[46] At the same time, Herbert Hill of the national branch of the NAACP pursued cases against Pittsburgh's construction industry in Washington, D.C. in front of the U.S. Civil Service Commission. The UNPC used demonstrations and peaceful protests to push for their vision of civil rights in Pittsburgh. In 1963, the *Rome* (Georgia) *News Tribune* carried an article by then Mayor David Lawrence who quoted an unnamed African American source who stated, "Don't be fooled by all the talk about social equality. We really don't want it. But what we do want is economic opportunity for the Negro—and you can't have that with millions of persons unemployed."[47] The goal of economic equality and access to better-paying employment for African Americans drove much of the civil rights activity within Pittsburgh.

In the mid-1960s, reformers targeted the streets themselves for cleanup and renewal drives. The Citizens Committee for Hill District Renewal

(CCHDR) sponsored a street cleanup drive in the Hill District, aimed at African Americans. They stated, "One of the goals of the CCHDR and other civic and civil rights groups is a cleaner community, unmarred by carelessly strewn litter, dirt and debris. With the help and support of a majority of citizens in the Negro communities, this goal can be reached."[48] While this goal had the support of "a majority of citizens in the Negro Communities," it clearly did not have full support. Inspector John Kelly instituted a series of cleanup drives in conjunction with middle-class African American leadership designed to clean up the Hill. Inspector Kelly asked "for the support of the Negro community in the area's drive to clean up the Negro ghettoes morally as well as of physical debris."[49] Ralph Koger also stated that African American leadership quickly pointed out "gambling, bawdy house, and alcoholic beverage rackets operating in their communities."[50] Middle-class organizations defined African Americans working as illegal laborers as a menace and a risk to public health. Working-class African Americans often appreciated a hustle. As LeRoy, a young working-class Black man at the time recalled, "everyone had a hustle, pimping was the main hustle until dope came along."[51] Like jitney drivers, those working in sex work and numbers were related to those who only pursued legal enterprise, so few members of the working classes complained about illegal labor as long as those practicing illegal labor kept their connection to the community through informal social networks.[52]

The UNPC used the might of the city health inspector's office to expand a "filth drive" in the Hill District. Nominally, the drive focused on dilapidated structures and public health concerns, but in practice the drive focused on areas of perceived blight on the streets of the Hill District, including numbers operations and areas where sex workers worked in the Hill. The way those involved with the drive spoke of those working in illegal occupations changed from earlier descriptions of "pretty girls" to "whores" and from "sporting men" to "muggers, dope pushers, junkies, and other characters."[53] The UNPC stressed the importance of sanitary conditions and that they would no longer tolerate "filth."[54] This emphasis on eradicating filth implied that unsanitary conditions extended further than the physical building but also included the character and actions of individuals that frequented the unsanitary establishments.

Pittsburgh's middle-class and elite African Americans also distanced themselves from African Americans of the working classes through their vision for civil rights. The *Pittsburgh Courier* posted their revised views on the purpose of editorial columns, saying, "Such a broadened policy is the only way the *Courier* can keep pace with the activities of a small but growing number of the so-called 'New Look' Negroes who are making their mark in personal achievements and community-wide leadership not as Negroes — but as professional men and women, politicians, parents and civic-minded taxpayers who happen to be Negroes."[55] This change in editorial policy defined a self-aware group of middle-class professional African Americans who separated themselves from the informal social networks of the neighborhood by diminishing their emphasis on race and racial issues and by increasing their focus on markers of professional status and formal power.

The UNPC met with the Port Authority Transit (PAT) officials to discuss hiring African Americans and routing issues specific to African American neighborhoods. These bus routes took many working-class African Americans to their jobs in other areas of the city. It was crucial to African American communities that their residents could get to their jobs.[56] Business owners also expressed their interest in the routes of public transit in African American neighborhoods. The BPA also announced a protest against PAT for changes to the Bedford Avenue route claiming route changes had decreased traffic to their businesses in the Hill District. In a previous transit strike, African Americans used jitneys, unlicensed taxis, to bypass the transit system so they could clearly execute a boycott of the transit authority. African American hires as drivers for the Port Authority were a top priority for the UNPC. The chairman of the UNPC, James McCoy, suggested, "if the PAT is slow in making progress in the employment of Negroes or in the improvement of transportation facilities then the UNPC has recourse to demonstration, the boycott of facilities owned and operated by PAT, and the creation of a jitney or car pool to service residents in Negro communities where PAT buses or trolleys operate."[57] Trolleys operated in most African American neighborhoods. Trolleys created "traffic hazards" on many of the main streets in the Hill District. African Americans wanted the PAT to replace the trolleys with busses, as they promised previously. Residents of the Hill District and Homewood expressed discontent with the scheduling of bus and trolley routes in their neighborhoods. African Americans complained that PAT used "obsolete buses" and others worthy of "the junkpile" in African American neighborhoods.[58]

In a subsequent article, the *Courier* suggested the UNPC succeeded in getting PAT to replace the trolleys on the Bedford Avenue line with buses and to look into the condition of the buses in Homewood.[59] This partial victory did not include additional jobs for African Americans, but the transition to buses alleviated some of the congestion on the streets of the Hill District and showed that the Port Authority responded to some of the demands made by the UNPC. PAT's response to the concerns of the BPA and other African American organizations, however, did not alleviate the objections of African Americans in the Hill District. In mid-1966, the BPA and leaders of several churches in the Hill District coordinated a protest against the Port Authority and their revised route along Webster Avenue. Although this protest occurred, other African American organizations were supportive of PAT's revisions, including the UNPC, Hill House Association, the Poverty Program, and other local book clubs and block organizations.[60] Teenie Harris photographed African Americans waiting for the Bedford Trolley in the Hill District (see figure 6.3). This bus line serviced the major thoroughfare in the Hill and allowed many residents to get to their jobs in other parts of the city. African Americans depended on the Bedford route. The path of the Bedford bus route through the Hill District determined the main artery of Hill District traffic patterns. African Americans in the Hill district protested route changes to the Bedford route because the proposed route added time to their commute.[61]

The street protests over PAT routes continued into the fall and incorporated agitation designed to improve the conditions of streets in African American neighborhoods. In negotiations with PAT, local African American groups faced a complicated mix of issues. When the Port Authority delayed replacing trolleys with buses, they stated poor road conditions as the primary obstacle, but the city's Department of Public Works had jurisdiction over the road conditions in African American neighborhoods. African American groups moved to pressure the city to clean the streets and restore the cleaning equipment previously moved to "unnamed areas, populated exclusively by white families."[62] The UNPC claimed streets in the Hill District had "not been washed for ten years."[63] The UNPC claimed previous requests to the city for street cleaning in the Hill went unheeded. The UNPC "blasted the indifference of city officialdom, arguing that sanitation takes a beating under such circumstances and that human health, morality rates and other factors enter the picture."[64] This linkage of street cleanliness and morality was common among African American groups, but it was also a technique used by African American organizations to advocate for city involvement. This technique also involved African American churches who often equated cleanliness to godliness.

In the mid-1960s, the UNPC and other African American organizations became polarized in their thinking, some focusing more on issues of economic justice and others focusing on social or political equality. The UNPC showed signs of addressing issues of poverty and other economic injustices

FIGURE 6.3 Men and women boarding the 85 Bedford trolley with billboard in background advertising Heinz green pea soup, Hill District, October 1946. Charles "Teenie" Harris (American, 1908–98), black-and-white: Ansco safety film, H: 4 in. × W: 5 in. (10.20 × 12.70 cm), Carnegie Museum of Art, Pittsburgh: Heinz Family Fund, 2001.35.6700, © Carnegie Museum of Art, Charles "Teenie" Harris Archive.

within the African American community. The UNPC solidified its relationship with other antipoverty programming for African Americans. The *Courier* reported on this renewed alliance, saying, "The venture is designed to cement better relationship between the city and county poverty programs of Pittsburgh and UNPC, according to the General UNPC Chairman James McCoy Jr."[65] The UNPC, among other African American organizations working with and within the working class, slowly invested more of its time and resources in economic justice initiatives.

In discussion with John W. Dameron, executive director of the Port Authority, the chairman of the UNPC James McCoy revealed an important area of disagreement. Dameron told McCoy, "I have a Negro boy working in my office doing some investigating work." To which McCoy replied, "How old is he?" When Dameron replied with the man's age of twenty-four, McCoy responded, "How long does it take a Negro to become a man?"[66] This discussion developed into a "feud" between the leadership of the two organizations when Dameron could not provide figures for how many African Americans worked for the Port Authority. This discussion between McCoy and Dameron also revealed a new thrust within the UNPC and other African American organizations working with and within the working classes.

The UNPC leveraged both formal and informal networks of power to benefit African Americans in Pennsylvania. They developed the idea behind a civil rights bill in the Pennsylvania legislature that established neighborhood-centered poverty agencies to deal with slumlords and poor housing conditions. In 1965, the *Pittsburgh Press* reported on a protest march designed to pressure Pennsylvania legislators to strengthen the bill. In the *Press*'s report, over 500 members from both Pittsburgh and Philadelphia gathered on the steps of the Capitol.[67] The proposed legislation would create centers to help working-class and poor African Americans directly address some of the most pressing civil rights issues in their neighborhoods.[68] The UNPC also protested frequently for greater access to skilled and professional jobs for middle-class and elite African Americans.

African American organizations from the working classes expressed greater degrees of discontent and a stronger language against economic and social oppression in Pittsburgh. Street-based protests included several racial incidents that spilled from indoor venues onto the streets of the Northside and the Hill District. In 1967, a series of racial incidents broke out in Oliver High School on the North side. The Northside of Pittsburgh contained a group of neighborhoods containing the major African American neighborhoods of Manchester and other smaller neighborhoods as well as many white neighborhoods whose residents resented the possibility of African American "encroachment." In the 1950s, residents of the Northside used street protests and public write-in campaigns to block a proposed public housing project. Racial tensions had not diminished much by 1967, and if anything, race relations on the Northside turned more militant in the areas where African Americans and white residents interacted and spilled out onto the streets of surrounding neighborhoods. In a comment in the *Courier*, Carl Morris, referenced the incident, arguing that outside militant agitators alone did not spur violence at Oliver High School, but that the real agitators "are better neighborhoods, better jobs, a better way of living."[69] Morris is one of many African Americans who noted the rise of militancy among working-class African American youth, suggesting a departure from other African American groups he associated with middle-class concerns. He described these organizations as "responsible," but he characterized them as out of touch or unaware of the issues concerning working-class African American youth.[70] In this way, African American organizations focused their efforts on accessing formal networks of power within the city government. African American youth instead leveraged their informal social networks for access to power in increasingly violent and militant expressions of discontent over the state of their civil rights. Morris also linked the explanations given by middle-class leadership for the violence at Oliver High School to similar explanations for the "summer riots" in cities across the country.[71] Black militancy established a stronger foothold within the African American working class as the issues of the African American working class diverged from those of the middle class.

In 1965, the poet Langston Hughes wrote an allegorical discussion published in the *Courier* arguing that the methods of the middle class had lost their appeal to African American youth who were embracing militancy, saying, "Speech making is not enough. Marching is not enough. Martin Luther King is not enough. The young Negro is impatient."[72] The older methods of street protests and marches no longer met the needs of African American youth. Hughes also foreshadowed much of the agitation against the Vietnam draft and other issues of special concern to the African American working classes and especially the young within those classes. Baseball legend Jackie Robinson spoke to the concerns of the "New Negro," especially those of the young working classes, saying, "The grass roots Negro in many communities, the individual we call the man on the street, is no longer excited or soothed because Mr. Big Negro Leader is welcomed to City Hall. He is no longer excited about a few big jobs being passed around. . . . The civil rights leadership will have to learn how to communicate with him better and they can start by learning how to communicate with each other better."[73] This "New Negro" moved away from the tactics of previous generations and focused on a grassroots policy based in the working classes and focused on informal power.

By the mid-1960s many African American workers recognized that civil rights gains were mostly isolated to the middle class. An article in the *Courier* stated, "In spite of the fact that so many Negroes are being appointed to high positions, today the position of the Negro masses is still very bad. There's a vast amount of poverty. And the attention of civil rights leaders should be centered on that."[74] In fact, working-class African Americans focused much of their street protests on opposing the draft and pushing for American troops to come home. Working-class African Americans also expressed some solidarity with other nations including Africans in Rhodesia and South Africa.[75] For many in the working class, civil rights at home were insufficient when faced with a lack of rights for colored people around the globe.

In August of 1967, the Southern Christian Leadership Conference or SCLC, officially supported the views of Dr. King against the Vietnam War and pledged to work toward ending poverty.[76] As a part of this push to end poverty, SCLC also advocated a community-based program to promote Black unity. This program focused on "development of economic and political power and by constant emphasis on Negroes owning and controlling their own communities."[77] This emphasis echoed many of the demands emerging out of informal social networks in African Americans neighborhoods such as the Hill District and Manchester.

The 1960s brought a divergence between the informal social networks of the African American working classes and the formalizing networks of the middle class. In the early years of the Modern Black Freedom Movement, African American middle-class leadership in Pittsburgh worked alongside and within the social networks of the working class. But as African Americans gained access to formal power through legal civil rights in the mid-1960s, the goals and aims of the social networks split from each other. This split became more evident as Vietnam protests and antipoverty programs gained priority within the African American working class. While middle-class African Americans questioned the motives of the African American working class, the working classes developed their own program for Black liberation. This program, organized through informal networks of power, addressed more than skilled labor and access to recreation. It also addressed economic injustice and expressed solidarity with people of color in other countries. The rising tide of street violence and working classes acceptance of any method to break the hold of the middle classes confused African American middle-class leadership within traditional organizations like the NAACP and the Urban League. Street violence and street protests transformed working-class politics in the late 1960s, but these transformations were not the *death of civil rights*; they were a continuation of the informal street politics of the African American working classes.

CHAPTER SEVEN

Crawford Street

Street Democracy, Violence, and Retreat
from the Streets, 1965–1970

As the movement for full equality for African American Pittsburghers shifted from one based in organizations to one based in street-level social networks of the working class, new voices emerged. In 1965, Frederick August Kittel Jr., who had grown up among the books in the Carnegie Library on Wylie Avenue before traveling across the country, returned to a boarding house room on Crawford Street in the Hill District. To earn extra cash, he wrote papers for his oldest sister, who was a student at Fordham University in New York. With the $20 she sent him for his essay titled "Two Violent Poets: Robert Frost and Carl Sandburg," he traveled to McFerran's type-writer store in downtown Pittsburgh and purchased a Royal Standard typewriter. Once he was back in his room, he worked out his new pen name by combining his middle name with his mother's maiden name.[1] August Wilson, the bard of the streets, was born. Wilson wrote of the neighborhood, the characters on Wylie Avenue and Crawford Street, the stories of the world around him, a world disrupted by urban renewal, and promises from the city to the residents of the Hill that remained broken. The people of the neighborhood who Wilson observed were not the Black elite of Sugar Top, the neighborhood that emerged at the top of the Hill that the Hill District was named for, but the working-class men and women who also took a collection of odd jobs to make ends meet. Men like the jitney drivers who "spent as much time telling tall tales and ribbing one another over games of checkers as they did answering the phone on the station wall." These men and women formed the characters of his major work, a series of plays that dramatized the people he knew from his neighborhood, a century of Black life in Pittsburgh. For Wilson, the story of the Hill District was one of social networks and struggle. Wilson's Hill District reflected back the sounds of the street, the music of the language of the working class. For Wilson, those African Americans who allied themselves with formal power through embracing their status as elite or even middle-class Black *leadership* had lost their connection to the neighborhood and to the culture. He told literary scholar Bonnie Lyons, "they are no longer the same people. . . . They are clothed in different manners and ways of life, different thoughts and ideas. They've acculturated and adopted white values."[2] This division between the working-class residents of the Hill District and all other residents of Black Pittsburgh solidified as the middle class and elite pursued formal mechanisms of power that did not rely on social networks and street connections, while the working class remained closely tied to their systems of reciprocity on the streets. All the while, the streets of Black neighborhoods were becoming increasingly violent as the working class sought tools to address systemic police brutality, economic injustice, and their outrage over the assassination of Dr. Martin Luther King Jr.

As African Americans in Pittsburgh made some gains in the struggle for formal political, social, and economic power, rising militancy within the working classes strained the alliance with the middle class. Militancy was not a sudden development after the assassination of Dr. Martin Luther King Jr. in 1968. Instead, most working-class African Americans advocated for economic equality through their social networks' push for social and political equality. As the alliance between African Americans across social networks stretched to the breaking point in the middle of the 1960s, some in the African American working classes expressed a vision for street spaces that included violence as a tool for street democracy which transformed the future of African Americans in Pittsburgh and across the United States.

This fractured alliance between formal and informal social networks increased the tensions within the African American community. Informal grassroots organizing focused on issues of social justice and economic equality. Working-class community organizers challenged middle-class leadership and nonviolent direct-action modes of social struggle. These tensions played out on the streets as working-class African Americans called for a return to the systems of reciprocity that governed interactions in their neighborhood. While elite and middle-class Blacks gained increasing access to formal power through integrated suburban communities and higher-paying professional and skilled jobs, municipal and street-level informal politics reflected the growing influence of poor and working-class Blacks. Conflicts intensified on the streets as increasing numbers of Blacks expressed a willingness to employ violence as a mode of political struggle and as a way of enforcing compliance from those who violated neighborhood systems of reciprocity.

In the spring of 1968, following Dr. Martin Luther King Jr.'s assassination, some primarily young working-class African American men used street spaces to express their discontent and disillusionment over the death of Dr. King and over the failures of the Modern Black Freedom Movement to address issues of economic equality. These men faced violence from police and military attempts to squash the street rebellions. While the "riot" in Pittsburgh was small by the standards of other northern cities, the continued use of force to contain the threat of violence closed streets for many African Americans in the working class. These incidents of street violence transformed the Hill District forever.

The split between middle-class visions of civil rights and working-class ideas of social equality developed within the traditional civil rights movement and on the streets of African American neighborhoods in Pittsburgh. For those in the working classes, the idea of "Black Power" was not a departure from a push for civil rights, but instead a logical continuation of their demands for social and economic equality. An editor in the *New Pittsburgh Courier* decried the "crisis" of street violence caused by the "black power cries of a few misguided, youthful, firebrands" and the resulting "white backlash."[3] This author urged African Americans to vote in upcoming elections and fundamentally to stick to the methodology of street-based protests that resulted in civil rights gains. Black Power adherents were "moving too fast" and placed all African Americans in danger of losing their white allies, both in higher education and in labor.[4] Another author argued that the rising tide of street violence in northern cities came from "resentment over insufferable economic and social conditions that have remained too long unattended."[5] He went on to say, "But Black Power or no, white backlash or no, riots, violence and looting will occur again and again until slums and associated poverty are wiped from the American scene."[6] Clearly, African Americans held differing opinions on the methods of Black Power. The rising tide of street violence confused many in the middle class, but those in the working class perceived tensions within African American communities long before violence erupted on the streets.

African American middle-class leadership came of age within the early pushes for civil rights in the Modern Black Freedom Movement, but as their children came of age in the era of legislative victories their priorities changed. Middle-class African Americans often associated Black Power with youth, and by association, with unsophisticated attempts to push too far or move too fast. Additionally, Black Power combined the two dissenting groups within the African American community, the working classes and the young. African American working-class youth pressed their middle-class elders for answers, which were often unsatisfactory. In a letter to the editor, Tom Williams attributed street violence to youth, both Black and white, saying: "The present under 25 generation are 'war humans,' just as canines trained for war are 'war dogs.' They were born during World War II or after that. During their whole lives, they moved from that war into the Korean War and then into the Vietnam War with barely a moment of peace. . . . Should we be surprised? No wonder the younger generation doesn't want to listen to anything we have to tell them. No wonder they want to be entirely different in what they do for recreation. No wonder there is rioting."[7] Older African Americans often expressed confusion and disdain for the younger generation of African Americans. Alfred Duckett also commented on his understanding of the feelings of the younger generation of African Americans and their just cause for discontent, but he also decried their violent methods, saying, "We cannot win with them riots and them rocks and them firebombs. All we doing is creating a little more misery and most of it going to be our misery."[8] This struggle between working-class youth and the supposed leadership in the middle class exacerbated tensions within the African American community.

Community groups of African American youth planned a protest in Pittsburgh in the fall of 1967. The *Courier* reported on a protest of 250 "militants" on the steps of City Hall in downtown Pittsburgh. The march assembled at Freedom Corner in the Hill District and marched downtown with over 250 members "mostly under 25 years of age with a liberal saturation of beards, mini-skirts, and fishnet and colored stockings. Some children less than 10 years old were in the crowd."[9] None of the major middle-class African American organizations took part in this protest. Community organizers like Charles "Bouie" Hayden organized the protest against the "problems of unemployment of Negro youth, recreation, housing, police indignities and police pay raises"[10] at home while the government still placed an unfair burden on African American youth with drafted service in Vietnam. The protests by African American working-class youth confounded the expectations of the African American middle class.

In Pittsburgh, the summer of 1967 foreshadowed the street violence that developed as the city ignored the conditions of working-class African Americans. The *New Pittsburgh Courier* reported that a tip from an informer had averted a planned riot on the streets of African American Pittsburgh. The informer reported: "The riot agitators were to use rented buses, possibly school buses to get to the scene of the violence. High-powered rifles and snipers were to be dispatched to fan the riot flames once the breaking, burning, and looting was in motion." The informer was quoted as saying, "Youths from McKeesport, Braddock, Hill District, Northside, Homewood, and other parts of the city were said to have been solicited to aid in getting the action started with the two slogans or passwords, 'Bring Matches' and 'Black is Back.'"[11] Both the reporter and the informer suggested that local residents "ignored the call for rioting and arson," but the article created the specter of a tragedy barely averted.[12] Pittsburgh's more militant African American organizations used violence or the threat of violence as a common approach to achieve their goals. The United Movement for Progress (UMP), a grassroots organization led by Bouie Haden, used threats of political and physical violence to protest Mayor Barr's choice to lead the housing court.[13] These public actions differed from previous methods of protest in that they explicitly used the threat of street violence as a tool to gain their goals. These new African American activists, affiliated primarily with the working class, did not abdicate to the traditional power structure within African American organizations. Instead, working-class activists gained authority from alliances with other organizations rooted in the informal social networks of the African American working class. The Urban League of Pittsburgh maintained a firmly conservative reputation while simultaneously working with more militant organizations within the working class to push an agenda of economic justice. Historian Ralph Proctor described the relationship between the ULP, militant Black Power organizations, and corporate leaders in the city as walking "a tightrope between young, militant Black people and conservative corporate leaders who always seemed poised to take away their financial support should the Urban League become too 'militant.'"[14] The ULP had a reputation that was rooted in middle-class values and distanced from civil rights protests in the neighborhoods. Proctor described the reputation of the ULP as "a middle class group that did not work with poor people." They did not consider themselves a civil rights organization but a social service organization instead. This distinction is important as they also prohibited their officers from engaging in demonstrations, boycotts, or "other tactics used by civil rights organizations."[15]

In the fall of 1967, Mrs. Alice Nixon, Bouie Haden, the UMP, and many other activists attended a full day of hearings sponsored by the Committee Against Inadequate Relief (CAIR). CAIR organized around protesting a reform bill that had passed the House and was heading to the Senate floor. These hearings took place in Bidwell Presbyterian Church on the Northside. Bidwell Presbyterian Church was home to one of many African American faith communities that acted within the community to address injustice. Mothers on relief, activists, and those concerned with economic equality attended to protest and air their grievances over the "coercive, punitive, and inflammatory features of the bill."[16] Bouie Haden stated that this bill showed "the promise to relieve the condition of Negroes [was a] contrived farce to keep Negroes chained to poverty and suggested that 'bombs, guns, and killing' may be the only answer."[17] The *Courier* reported:

> Most of the speakers were convinced that the destructively bad points of the bill included a provision that mothers, teen-agers and all adults, whether afflicted or not, be forced to engage in any work or training programs offered: provision that mothers be forced into family planning and contraceptive programs: provisions which force the states to use these tactics through the threat of financial sanctions: and provisions which are an attempt to "save" money by cutting welfare costs: provisions which promote foster care as a better method of raising the children of the poor than in their own homes under their own mother's care: and provisions which force fathers to leave their homes and families so that the family can qualify for welfare.[18]

Reverend Alex Seabrook argued that Congress was "so worried about passing anti-riot legislation" that they then resorted "to passage of legislation barring decent living grants and normal family life, the very things which are bound to promote riots."[19] The activists present at this gathering connected street conditions to the prevalence of violence within the community. Street conditions within African American neighborhoods worsened as their communities faced high population concentrations and a deteriorating housing stock. The conditions were ripe for street violence and many in the working class were losing faith in nonviolent measures to gain equality.

African American activists stressed economic justice and antipoverty programs to help the working class. Working-class activism, which had long coalesced around ideas of economic justice and empowerment, rose again on the streets as African Americans in Pittsburgh realized some political gains. Militancy and street violence rose as working-class African Americans expressed their frustration at the lack of support from middle-class African Americans and their formal organizations. Charles Evers warned attendees at a local NAACP conference, "Unless America grants the Negro full and first-class citizenship in all particulars in the near future and unless the middle-class Negro joins fully in securing freedom and opportunity for the poor, we are going to have a bloody struggle of white against black, poor against rich, and youngsters against their elders."[20] Ralph Koger reported that Evers's speech exemplified the mood of the conference, which he described as "full-spirited aggressiveness, militancy . . . and determination to overturn the causes of their troubles."[21] Evers also called on middle-class

African Americans to support antipoverty measures and peace in Vietnam. Additionally, he called on "ministers, teachers, business people and professionals to support the social and political interests of the mass of Negroes."[22] Members of the NAACP and others in the middle class seemed confused over the rise of militancy within the working classes on the streets in African American neighborhoods.

While some middle-class African Americans expressed concern over the "problem of the poor," most were more concerned over the possibility of racial or class-based violence in African American neighborhoods. In the spring of 1968, African American organizations on the left of the political spectrum also agreed to collaborate with those of the antiwar movement and Dr. King (in the days before his assassination) on his "Poor People's Lobby and March" planned for later in April.[23] This collaboration between African Americans on the left and those of the antiwar and antipoverty movements developed through working-class concerns over the problems of economic and social justice.

Professional African Americans like Dr. Benjamin Mays, longtime president of Morehouse College in Atlanta, advised middle-class African Americans to address the problems of poverty in urban neighborhoods, saying, "There may not be too much the individual can do. But those of us who are reasonably affluent must be bothered about the fact that there are 32 million Americans and a billion others who are poor. We should dedicate ourselves anew to a program to eliminate poverty, disease, war and prejudice."[24] The rising tide of discontent within the African American working class disturbed those African Americans in the middle class, but they expressed confusion over how to address the concerns of the poor. Middle-class African Americans feared the risk of street violence from the masses of poor African Americans in the "ghettos" of the urban North, and Pittsburgh was no exception. African Americans living in Pittsburgh's increasingly dilapidated neighborhoods faced little prospect of governmental support.

Unrest was growing within African American Pittsburgh and much of it was rooted within the streets of the Black neighborhoods of Pittsburgh. Sala Udin knew these streets by heart. As a resident of the Hill District from childhood, he had watched the development of the Modern Black Freedom Movement on the streets of the neighborhood. He recalled hearing "increased unrest, especially among young people, increased unemployment, increased confrontation between police and the black community."[25] These tensions grew and festered in the neighborhood as progress from formal organizations seemed too slow and proceeding by half measures. The streets of Black neighborhoods erupted in sporadic violence that echoed around the United States in the language of riot. Udin recalled that in the mid-1960s, folks in the neighborhood would laugh off the possibility of a riot in the city, saying, "No, man. You know Pittsburgh is backwards. We ain't even had a riot yet, man. Naw, we ain't had no riot."[26] The social networks in Black Pittsburgh pulled on a tradition of radical economic justice, self-defense, especially against police brutality, and an emphasis on international struggles against poverty, colonialism, and war that had been present in Pittsburgh since the end of World War II.[27] Sala Udin recalled that the assassination of Dr. King "tipped over what had been bubbling up for a very long time." Udin had recently returned from the movement in the South as a Freedom Rider. His work organizing in the South with the Student Non-violent Coordinating Committee (SNCC) gave him significant social capital in Pittsburgh as a native son who had been in the trenches and had returned to the Steel City. Many of the formal organizations in African American Pittsburgh sought his input, but he made his alliance with the working class and militant groups clear, saying, "So I understand power relationships. I understand institutions. I understand the role of the police. I understand the economy. I understand education and institutions like that. I understand the civil rights movement and the power structures within the civil rights movement and where I sit myself in that movement. I'm a Black Power guy and I'll work with you preachers and NAACP types, but be clear—I'm not one of you. I'm a Black Power militant."[28] By the time of the assassination of Dr. Martin Luther King Jr., the social networks within the African American neighborhoods of Pittsburgh had changed, as the roots of a expanding Black Power influence in the working class took priority in the struggle for the streets of Pittsburgh. This Black Power influence had an emphasis on economic justice and a commitment to self-defense through an ever looming possibility of street violence. This struggle for the neighborhood streets put organizations' formal power in opposition to working-class social networks and their position as both targets of state violence and militants ready to use violence for self-defense.

On April 4, 1968, James Earl Ray assassinated Dr. Martin Luther King Jr. in Memphis, Tennessee. This act of violence sparked street revolts in many urban cities in the North. Pittsburgh also experienced street violence in the aftermath of this act of racial terror. The definition of this street violence differed between the stakeholders describing it. Official sources, including the *Courier* and the *Post-Gazette*, referred to the eight-day period of street violence following King's assassination as "disorders."[29] This time of grief, outrage, and terror spilled onto the streets of African American neighborhoods in the city of Pittsburgh. To call it a disorder minimized the long roots of this street-based conflict and the tensions that played out in the period following Dr. King's assassination. In the days and weeks following the assassination, preexisting tensions erupted within African American communities in Pittsburgh and spilled onto the streets of the Hill District, Homewood-Brushton, and the Northside. African Americans in Pittsburgh defined these actions in different ways. Working-class African Americans described the street violence as both riots and retaliation for years of racial oppression. In the editorial section of the *Pittsburgh Courier*, Thomas Picou described the feelings of many working-class African Americans, saying, "The ghetto is a smoldering pot of frustration, bitterness, and poverty. There is no one reason for what happened last week. It's the result of years and years of anguish."[30] Working-class African Americans in Pittsburgh believed the conditions of urban neighborhoods caused the retaliations that occurred on the streets of Pittsburgh. The assassination of Dr. King was a contributing spark that escalated street violence, but it alone was not the only fuel.

Many white Pittsburghers expressed shock at the response of African Americans in their city. Experts had assured them that their city was not very likely to erupt into the street violence they heard about in cities like Los Angeles and Detroit. Overall, the *New Pittsburgh Courier* downplayed the street violence associated with the disorders. Their coverage focused instead on actions by middle-class African Americans to subdue unruly youth and street gangs in the Hill District and their peace marches into the downtown area. The *Post-Gazette*, on the other hand, described the violence as a riot and the violence perpetrated by rioters as an escalation of violence between protestors and the mechanisms of state power in the form of police and National Guard troops.[31] This discrepancy illustrated the difference between the Black press's coverage of racial disorder, which emphasized the role of middle-class leaders, and the white or mainstream press, which lumped many African American actors into the same group of perpetrators of street violence. Very little of the press coverage focused on the actions of working-class African Americans to aid those affected by street violence or to subdue violence on the streets of African American neighborhoods.

White Pittsburghers expressed shock and dismay that such racial street violence happened in their city. For many years, the *Pittsburgh Post-Gazette* had listed reasons Pittsburgh was unlikely to experience racially based street violence, saying, "Among major cities, Pittsburgh was lowest in terms of Southern-born Negroes, highest in Negro homeownership, and was a city where civic and political leaders seemed able to get things done on behalf of the black community."[32] Yet at the same time, "this city's Negro population veiled a long-standing suppressed hostility. It was angry about housing, about education, about the police, about a lack of action by government agencies and about the daily indignities suffered in contact with the white community."[33] As African American youth hit the streets, the compounding effect of their grief and the anger at conditions in central cities transformed street spaces in their neighborhoods into a theater of violent protest. While the street violence in Pittsburgh was significantly less destructive to human life than the violence in other northern urban cities, the presence of working-class street violence demonstrated resentment toward structural inequality in Pittsburgh and the United States as a whole.

The *Pittsburgh Courier* reported on Stokely Carmichael's call for African Americans to avenge King's death, saying, "When white America killed Dr. King, it declared war on us. We have to retaliate for the execution of Dr. King."[34] Carmichael then described the form retaliation would take, saying, "Our retaliation won't be in the courtroom, but in the streets of America."[35] Retaliation for Dr. King's assassination would take place on the streets of African American neighborhoods where the working classes ruled, rather than in the courtrooms where professional middle-class African Americans or the formal organizations of the African American community held sway. In cities all over the urban North, violence erupted on the streets in protest of the senseless killing of Dr. King; Pittsburgh was no exception.

On April 5th, one day after Dr. King's assassination, African American street protestors expressed their frustration at the compounded injustice of King's death and the persistent violence within the city of Pittsburgh toward Black people. Residents from all over Black Pittsburgh met at Ebenezer Baptist Church on Wylie Avenue in the Hill District to grieve together and plan a way forward. Ralph Proctor recalled that "for the first time, militant, conservative and middle of the road members of civil rights groups met at the same time, in the same place. There was no posturing, no one-upmanship, and no contentious conversations."[36] The anger and outrage, especially among younger Black residents, was clear. Proctor recalled a tense moment in the meeting where the assembled residents asked some of the men present to go ask the neighborhood state-owned liquor stores to close early. They also asked K. Leroy Irvis, who was a state representative, to ask the governor to force the state-owned stores to close as a preventative measure. Irvis had no success in his efforts. In his report to the group, Irvis stated that the lieutenant governor said that the stores would only close if there were trouble. A young man responded from the back of the gathering, "Shit, if that's all it takes to shut the mother-fucker down, they got that!" After which, a group of young men left the meeting, heading toward the liquor store, where they kicked in a plate glass window while the police watched.[37] The collected efforts of civil rights groups meeting at Ebenezer Baptist Church tried to enlist the help of the police at the Number Two police station in the Hill District, but to no effect. Many of the residents of the Hill District recall how the police watched but did not respond to looting and violence as long as it was contained to the neighborhood. As soon as violence threatened to leave the Hill District, that is when they would use violence to contain the "riot" to Black neighborhoods. In figure 7.1, Teenie Harris documented police officers pursuing young people in a gathered crowd during the street uprising. The collaboration between civil rights groups in the immediate aftermath of King's assassination would be short-lived. Protestors from the working classes filled the streets of the Hill and other African Americans neighborhoods in Pittsburgh. Protestors targeted white-owned businesses and others they defined as exploitative of the African American community.

The potential for violence on the streets was not limited to those who were using the theater of the streets to make their point. Troops directed violence toward *respectable* middle-class organizations as well. Byrd Brown and members of the NAACP, ULP, and other activists met at Freedom Corner with plans to march downtown to honor King and protest his murder. As the marchers proceeded from Freedom Corner, police troops in riot gear met them, ready for a confrontation. Byrd Brown recalled that the officers claimed the march could not proceed because of threats against Brown's life. Alma Fox recalled the repeated efforts of one white police officer to hit Brown with his riot stick. Officer Slaughter (a Black police officer) prevented the white officer from reaching Brown. Brown stated, "Since he couldn't hit me in the head, he kept moving until he could reach between the lines of police and poked me in the ribs." He continued, "We are going to march. Your attempt to stop us is illegal. . . . We have ten thousand people; you have 300 cops. You can't stop us."[38] In the midst of this tense situation a group of about twenty-five Black men rushed the police line, knocking Alma Fox to the ground. The riot police were standing in a ready stance where the officers' feet were touching the feet of the officers next to him. This caused their legs to be spread apart. Fox recalled, "I saw all this room and quickly crawled between one of the cop's legs. Once I got behind the police I stood up and yelled 'Come on, come on; I got through, so can you.'"[39] Police then grabbed Fox and placed

FIGURE 7.1 Police officers, including Sam Karam, in riot gear pursuing individuals in crowd near Perry High School, 1968. Charles "Teenie" Harris (American, 1908–98), black-and-white: Kodak safety film, H: 2¼ in. × W: 2¾ in. (5.71 × 6.99 cm), Carnegie Museum of Art, Pittsburgh: Heinz Family Fund, 2001.35.4644, © Carnegie Museum of Art, Charles "Teenie" Harris Archive.

her into a wagon. The crowd reacted to this move by demanding Fox's release. The public safety director, deciding that this situation was quickly getting out of control, asked Fox to leave the transport wagon, to which she refused, stating, "I'm not going anywhere, this is my wagon now! Your cops threw me in here and I am staying until we can march."[40] At which point, the public safety director gave permission for the march to continue. Fox recalled looking back up to the Hill District as they marched downtown and seeing clouds of black smoke billowing from the fires that had begun in the Hill District.

While authorities contained street violence within African American neighborhoods, primarily the Hill District and Homewood, neighboring areas feared looting and firebombing would spread. Pittsburgh city police and National Guard troops used visible force to contain violence within African American neighborhoods. The police moved into the Hill and tried to suppress the street violence, but their attempts were unsuccessful. Allen Rosensweet of the *Post-Gazette* commented, "By midnight the use of firebombs . . . had spread additional terror."[41] Firebombs were the most visibly violent act on the streets of the Hill District and Homewood. Liquor stores and readily available materials allowed easy access to the tools required for firebombs, and the resulting burning businesses and homes left visible scars of violence on the street spaces of African American neighborhoods. Through much of the street violence, city firefighters did nothing to suppress fires burning in the Hill District. Violence flowed through the arteries of African American neighborhoods as looting and firebombing manifested African American outrage and discontent with racial conditions in Pittsburgh. The aftermath of the fires in the Hill left buildings looking like burned-out shells. The *Pittsburgh Press* toured the riot zone with Pittsburgh police officers. A police lieutenant said, "Most of the damage has been confined to the commercial district along Centre Ave." Firefighters battled a suspected arson along Wylie Avenue.[42] Ralph Proctor and Carl Morris suspected that "a majority of the Black businesses burned were at the hands of rogue White cops."[43] The same street spaces African Americans used to promote civil rights advances became violent spaces during the unrest. According to the *Post-Gazette*, Sunday marked the "Longest Day" of the riots and also the most violent. The street rebellion also gained its first and only recorded fatality on Sunday: 70-year-old Mary Antlo, who died when rioters threw a firebomb into her home.[44] National Guardsmen arrived to suppress the violence on the streets of Black Pittsburgh and to prevent its spread into neighboring, predominantly white, areas. This use of federal troops instigated another form of street violence, namely state-sponsored violence to contain the disorder.

The presence of the federal troops to quell a street rebellion in Pittsburgh added potential violence to the actual violence of the streets.[45] Middle-class African Americans and white residents of Pittsburgh feared street violence would spread to neighboring areas of Oakland, downtown, or Squirrel Hill. National Guard troops occupied strategic positions at the boundaries between the Hill District and other more affluent neighborhoods like Oakland and Squirrel Hill to prevent street violence from spreading into those areas, but they did not prevent street violence from spreading into African American areas like the Northside and Homewood.

Middle-class African Americans in affected areas expressed their fear of street spaces. John Welch recalled his parents and local residents of Homewood preventing children from playing outside both during the uprising and in the days following. Welch did not recall ever feeling unsafe in his home or actually seeing or hearing any street violence near his home, but his parents worried about his safety on the streets of their neighborhood. Parents expressed fear of street spaces deemed unsafe for young children.[46] Odessa Wilson recalled her actions during the riots, saying, "When we had the riots, I just stayed in the house. I worked at West Penn Hospital; I had a cast on my leg. I worried that if I went out, I wouldn't be able to get back."[47] Helen Mendoza also recalled staying indoors during the street violence. Most women stayed away from street spaces which left men, mostly young, as the dominant actors on the streets. Middle-class parents kept their children close by as middle-class and working-class African American fought in the ideological spaces of the streets of Pittsburgh.

Class and age differences played out on the streets. Older African Americans derided younger African Americans and tried to downplay the anger of younger generations on the streets. LeRoy recalled his participation in the riots on the streets, saying: "Yeah, the riots were fun. MLK got killed on my birthday, April 4th. When the rioting broke out we went out to make money. We broke into the state [liquor] stores. We started taking cash registers, meat cleavers, liquor. We sold lots of it to a guy off rt. 51. We rioted to make money. We were young and we wanted to make money. Others were upset about Martin Luther King."[48]

LeRoy recalled going out with a crew during the riots and he also stated that he was not the only one. Groups of young men swarmed the streets with varying motives. Ralph Proctor pointed out some of the ways that systems of reciprocity worked during the riots. Proctor recalled:

Some of the looters did not profit individually from the loot. Much of the food from the grocery stores was distributed to known needy families. One enterprising young man set up an impromptu shoe store on one of the Hill corners. As people with families, young children, or older people came by, he would invite them to sit on a looted bench and try on shoes. He had the foresight to loot a shoe size measuring device. He accepted no pay for his illegal activities. I watched in utter amazement. When he had given away all of his looted shoes, I asked what he did for a living. He replied that he was unemployed.[49]

Some of the men on the streets expressed their discontent at perceived exploitation of the African American community and the perceived apathy from the larger white culture at the assassination of Dr. King. Arthur recalled some of the anger rioters directed at members of the surrounding white community, saying, "When you're angry you don't have time to consider the consequences. All we knew was that we had to show somebody something. It just showed how unfocused some people were."[50] The men on the streets wanted to lash out at the injustice of Dr. King's death and the social and political injustice that African Americans dealt with in their neighborhoods. During the riots, working-class African Americans used street spaces to vent their anger at injustices perpetrated on their community. Street spaces offered a venue for them to display their anger and frustration at a system that seemed biased against them. The actions of many of those participating in street violence targeted those that they viewed as extracting resources from the community: absentee landlords, businesses owned by outsiders, and those that were not connected to the social networks of the neighborhood.

While the police and National Guard troops formed a barrier around the Hill District and other Black neighborhoods, the street violence turned toward punishment of the people and businesses that were disconnected from the social networks of the neighborhood. Proctor described the mood of the rioters, saying, "The word was out. Take vengeance against those who'd cheated or harmed the Black community."[51] Proctor also recalled warning K. Leroy Irvis, a prominent state representative from Pittsburgh, that the paint store on Centre Avenue that he lived above was targeted for burning. Irvis was able to evacuate his home before the store was burned, but he recalled it as "a scary moment."[52] In an interview by Dr. Lawrence Glasco, Irvis recalled that "the mob was organized. It wasn't just a mob."[53] Rioters targeted other stores like the Mainway Supermarket and a meat market near Centre and Wyle Avenues that had a reputation of selling outdated meat that was rejected from butchers in Squirrel Hill and selling marked up horsemeat instead of beef.[54] These establishments and others were seen as taking advantage of the community. For many who turned to political violence on the streets of the Hill District, these actions were a way to establish an alternative framework of law and order that focused on upholding the community networks and systems of reciprocity. Those who contributed would be protected and those who were extractive would be removed from the social network.

As social networks fractured in the Hill District and within the African American community, the violence on the streets of the neighborhood took on the character of an outrage. While the working-class actors on the streets of the Hill District did not refer to their actions as an outrage, the concept of outrage comes from the characterizations of Irish agrarian riots. This concept focuses on an informal, community-developed, alternative framework of law and custom that includes violence in opposition to state-sponsored violence.[55] The actions of Hill District residents during the Pittsburgh *riots* demonstrate their use of an alternative framework of law and custom that developed within their own social networks and systems of reciprocity. The violence of the outrage was targeted toward those that were seen as extractive. Those who were not contributing to the local system of reciprocity, and this could and did include middle-class and elite African Americans who had separated themselves from the community, were often targets of the violence on the streets. These efforts transformed the nature of the neighborhood and cemented the view of some in the middle class that the streets were inherently dangerous and in need of increased police presence and suppression. The development of this outrage on the streets of the Hill District gave permission for the city to use increasingly militaristic suppression on those residents who sought to draw attention to poor housing conditions, a lack of jobs that paid a living wage, a growing gap between rich and poor even among their neighbors, and an increasingly brutal police force on the city streets. The *Pittsburgh Courier* stated the problem plainly in its editorial section, summarizing the findings of the National Advisory Commission on Civil Disorders saying, "The 1960's riots were a manifestation of race and racism in the United States, a reflection of the social problems of modern black ghettos, a protest against the essential conditions of life there and an indicator of the necessity for fundamental changes in American society."[56] The National Advisory Commission on Civil Disorder, also known as the Kerner Commission, came to the conclusion that "the nation was moving toward 'two societies, one black, one white, — separate and unequal' and that 'white racism' was largely to blame."[57] The Kerner Commission largely put to rest the idea that "riots" were caused by "outside agitators" rather than residents of the neighborhood who were invested in the conditions of their own communities. These outrages came from the streets of the neighborhood where the residents were deeply invested in their social networks. Their grief over the assassination of Dr. King was a symptom of their larger grief at persistent second-class status and the mounting violence they faced on the streets.

During the outrages following the assassination of Dr. Martin Luther King Jr., tensions grew as clashes with police in the Hill District and other

African American neighborhoods like East Liberty became more frequent. On the second day of the outrages, Governor Raymond Shafer called on the National Guard to curtail violence in the streets of Pittsburgh. The troops occupied Wylie Avenue near the site of the Civil Arena with fixed bayonets. The purpose of these troops was to "take care of property and keep people from burning down any more property."[58] The massive presence of militarized police and National Guard troops just above the Civic Arena, a section that residents of the Hill District described as a "no-man's zone" between the downtown businesses and the Lower Hill District, was a slap in the face. Proctor described the scene: "The huge figure of Saint Benedict the Moor faced the downtown areas, and gazed on the sad scene of an occupying military force right there in the land that residents felt had been stolen from them by the city fathers, who now rubbed their noses in the dirt by stationing an army of control there. Black folks were not happy. How would you feel, if you woke up one morning and found soldiers patrolling up and down your street? Insult was added to injury by the fact that most of the soldiers and the police were White."[59] The troops occupying and controlling the Hill District used military-grade equipment including "machine guns, bazookas and other heavy armament." Proctor recalled an experience of Dr. Lloyd Bell, one of the first Black administrators at the University of Pittsburgh, who discovered National Guard troops using the university's athletic complex to stage their occupation of the Hill District. He proceeded to storm into Chancellor Posvar's office where he confronted him, saying, "How could you let the army use this University to house troops that are to be sent against Black residents, who were unarmed. We are supposed to be about education, not death."[60] Posvar indicated that he did not feel like he had a choice in the matter as the order came directly from the governor's office. The level of militarization increased as both city police and National Guard troops poured into the spaces between African Americans and their white neighbors.

Helen Mendoza recalled the aftermath of the riots, saying, "After the riots, everything changed, half the stuff was burnt down, all the little stores and the little places they had here went down. And people didn't have any money to put 'um back up. I think they hurt themselves more than anything because that's when they started tearing down everything."[61] Mendoza was not the only longtime resident who recalled the riots as a turning point in the neighborhood. Arthur also recalled how the Hill District related to downtown prior to the riots, saying, "Prior to the riots, you only went downtown if you had to pay a bill or something. Most of the time you didn't need to go down there and the few times you did go down there it was to pick up a few things they didn't have in the Hill because they did have a better selection down there."[62] After the riots, African American residents of the Hill District had to leave the neighborhood to meet many of their basic needs when Hill District businesses were unable to rebuild.

The advent of street violence in the Hill frightened middle-class African Americans and pushed many of them away from street spaces. They feared for their businesses and other investments in African American neighborhoods. In the early stages of street violence, working-class agitators, described as young African American men, gathered to express their anger at businesses perceived as exploiting the African American community. The *Post-Gazette* reported "a gang of about 100 young Negroes gathered at a supermarket in the 1900 block of Centre Avenue in the Hill District. Surging toward the Lower Hill they smashed windows and looted stores. They advanced upon Fifth Avenue, Wylie Ave., DeVillers Street and others on the Hill."[63] Groups of African Americans traveled through the Hill District looting businesses and private homes. These acts of vandalism and violence spread fear through the Hill District and throughout white neighborhoods of Pittsburgh. Robert Vickers recalled the damage rioters on the streets did to businesses in the Hill District, saying:

> I thought it was a bad, bad idea the shops and businesses here that we had for our use were burnt out so that we lacked the things that we needed. So now we had to go out of the neighborhood to get the things that we needed. At that time each neighborhood supported themselves you had your own clothing and shoe stores and once they were destroyed you had to leave the neighborhood to get that. People didn't move out of the neighborhood then because they didn't have any place to go but you had to leave the neighborhood to get what you needed.[64]

Arthur also recalled the feeling of many of the rioters and the pervasive sense of injustice many of the residents of the Hill District felt at the time of the riots, saying, "Prior to '68 the Hill was a different place and after Martin Luther King was killed and the Kennedy boys got killed and all the negative behavior of our leaders after being treated so badly people decided that any businesses being run by folks that seemed to be taking money from the Hill, owners of the little stores and businesses, there was a price to be paid but not realizing that tearing them down would change it forever."[65] Many residents of the Hill District pointed to the riots as the time when the neighborhood changed forever. Marcia Donnell also recalled the change in the neighborhood after the riots and the burning, saying, "A lot of this ended when Martin Luther King was assassinated and they had the rioting and the burning. And that changed and it never really came back to the little businesses. Once they burned down, they were never reestablished."[66] Urban renewal may have changed the streets, but the expressions of the grief of working-class African Americans on the streets during the riots changed the neighborhood itself.

Working-class African American men did not retreat from the streets. Many working-class African American men remained on the streets in both violent and potentially violent ways. While some working-class African Americans participated in the disorders on the streets of Pittsburgh, other African Americans occupied street spaces to prevent violence. But their very presence on the streets put them into positions where they risked perpetrating violence or becoming victims themselves. In the *Post-Gazette*, Jack Ryan described gangs of African American men roaming the streets attempting to quell tensions and violence on the streets. These groups of African American men used connections with other working-class African Americans in their neighborhoods to limit expressions of street violence.[67]

The white press and other African American leaders associated this street violence with youth and other radical elements within the Hill District. Descriptions of gangs of African American youth roaming the streets of the Hill and inciting violence dominate the mainstream accounts. When it became clear that Pittsburgh police could not contain the street violence, Governor Shafer called in more than one thousand National Guardsmen to assist the police. Police brought their own types of violence to the streets of Pittsburgh. Police brutality was a consistent theme for African Americans in Pittsburgh and many African Americans felt the police unfairly targeted the neighborhoods of the Hill District and Homewood. Police in riot gear added to the air of unreality on the streets of Pittsburgh. Arthur recalled National Guard troops containing the violence within African American neighborhoods, saying: "If there's going to be anything done we should have gone downtown and tore up downtown or Oakland, or out Centre Avenue beyond the Hill where all the supermarkets and stores are and did it there. But they kept it all in the Hill the National guard came because it was easy for them to strategize to stop it or could limit it from traveling further all they had to do was block one set of streets here and one set of streets there and set up a curfew."[68] LeRoy also recalled the anger of the rioters and the presence of National Guard troops on the streets, saying, "White men surrounded our neighborhood. We were trying to get out to do damage where damage mattered. Once you got to Crawford and Centre you had to have a pass to get downtown. I got a degree in accounting and I worked at Pittsburgh National Bank so I had a pass to go downtown for work."[69] The National Guard troops used the threat of violence to contain rioters within African American neighborhoods, while working-class African American men looked for ways to direct their anger toward the neighborhoods they associated with injustice like downtown and Oakland.

Mayor Barr and others in power attempted to diminish the power of those on the streets by referring to them as children or youth in need of correction and discipline in the pages of the *Post-Gazette*. Those in power did not acknowledge the rioters' concerns and their organized use of street violence to make their point. One defining characteristic of the "disorders" was the organization of those participating in street violence. One characterization from the *Post-Gazette* described both confusion and order among the people on the streets, saying: "The gangs roamed in wild confusion, from street to street in the Hill District, through the Uptown area and lower Oakland and Soho. One gang vandalized stores in the 3400 block of Butler Street, Lawrenceville. The vandalism erupted about 9:30 p.m. At that time, a gang of about one hundred young Negroes gathered in the 1900 block of Centre Avenue at a supermarket. They started marching toward Downtown smashing windows and looking stores as they went."[70] White residents of the Hill District did not understand the street violence surrounding them, but they recognized the organization of the participants, saying, "But they expressed surprise when their stores were burned out and before the week was over it would appear that this had been a studied technique of ridding the Hill District of stores owned by white merchants."[71] Middle-class African Americans also expressed surprise that working-class African Americans would turn to street violence, but they also stated their understanding of why some would feel they had no other options.

Working-class African Americans used street violence as one method of airing their grievances with the city, but they also were the targets of street violence as police and National Guard troops were called in to suppress the actions of militant African American youth. The *Pittsburgh Post-Gazette* described the situation on the streets of the Hill District, saying, "Roving gangs of young Negroes in racial unrest wreaked destruction through the Hill District and other city sections last night."[72] Descriptions of the situation in the Hill emphasized the young nature of the rioters and their power to destroy while diminishing and elevating violence against the rioters. Working-class African American men also faced violence from mechanisms of the state while they participated in violent acts on the streets. Some middle-class African Americans pursued different strategies from those of the working classes in their grief over the death of Dr. King. Many of the middle-class residents of the Hill District relied on the methods of nonviolent civil disobedience to express their grief over the assassination of Dr. King.

Immediately, when word of Dr. King's assassination reached African Americans in Pittsburgh, NAACP leaders planned a street march from "Freedom Corner," Centre Avenue and Crawford Streets, to Point State Park downtown. Middle-class African Americans used the tools of nonviolent direct action, including marches, to distance themselves from those using street violence as a tool in African American neighborhoods. Marching from Freedom Corner to the halls of city government or to Point State Park commonly represented solidarity within Pittsburgh's African American community, but this march instead represented a conscious break with the actions of some within the African American community. The conscious use of nonviolent direct action contrasted with the eruption of street violence within the Hill District. Middle-class African Americans differentiated themselves by claiming the title of responsible citizens as opposed to the working-class "hooligans" on the streets. They linked disavowal of street violence with respectability and therefore linked violent street behavior with youth and the working class.[73] The police attempted to break up the march citing concerns over safety, but they were unable to deter those gathered to pay tribute to Dr. King. This contestation in definition extended to the description of the street violence as a whole.

Police and African American leaders contested descriptions of the "troubles" in the Hill, most refusing to term the racialized street violence as a "riot." Director Craig had described the troubles as a "riot," which he said occurs when local authorities can no longer stem the trouble and outside assistance, such as the National Guard, is required. This bristled police superintendent James W. Slusser, who called the trouble "disturbances" but not a "riot." A riot, by his definition, is a situation where a disturbance gets completely out of control of the law enforcement agencies. This Slusser said with a great deal of vigor, had not happened here.[74]

Police and city officials had a lot of investment in the definition of the disorders on the streets of Pittsburgh. Pennsylvania's governor, Raymond P. Shafer, also termed the disorders "not a riot, but a disaster," in his tour of the Hill District.[75] The *Pittsburgh Post-Gazette* also discussed the "dismay" of African American leaders over the street violence from what Slusser called "the criminal element, a small percentage of the population looking for an excuse to make trouble and thus further their own interests."[76] Slusser further "dismissed the idea of an organized disturbance and he said that no evidence had been uncovered that so-called 'outside agitators' from other cities had taken part in the disturbances."[77] Slusser vehemently denied any possible organization in the actions of the youth on the streets. He also admitted that burnings in the Hill appeared targeted toward white business owners in the Hill, but he diminished the importance of that by arguing that street gangs burnt some African American–owned businesses as well.[78] Slusser and other members of city government downplayed the class differences among African Americans in Pittsburgh and especially downplayed the role of working-class African American men and women in using street violence to display their discontent over the state of African American Pittsburgh.

Very few of the accounts of the violence on the streets of the Hill District and other African American neighborhoods in Pittsburgh mentioned the role of women among the agitators. The *Post-Gazette* did mention the need for police to establish a separate holding area for female participants arrested during the days of unrest.[79] This vision of women among the agitators on the streets directly contrasted the image portrayed by the city of African American male youth, potentially outsiders, and acting out of a mob mentality. Women as rioters did not fit the official vision of the city's self-promoted heroic role in squelching the violence on the streets of the Hill District. City officials seemed incapable of addressing the root issues that enraged those on the streets. Mayor Barr formed a task force to address the concerns of those in neighborhoods affected by street violence, but there were no representatives from those communities on the task force. Barr dismissed the concerns of residents by claiming, "the task force must be structured internally if we are to move promptly in attempting to deal effectively with the problems besetting central cities."[80] The task force and other methods the city used to address the concerns of those on the streets were not effective in diminishing the concerns of African Americans in Pittsburgh.

The white mainstream press created a mob of street agitators they could easily dismiss. In the view of the press, participants in street violence were either young African American men, without connection to any community, or outside agents from other areas. The African Americans on the streets of the Hill, Homewood-Brushton, the Northside, and Beltzhoover were members of the African American community expressing their discontent with the current racial situation in Pittsburgh in a viable way. The idea of a mob of unorganized youth comforted those in the elite and middle classes. In their view, young people did not have the experience to mount an organized and effective street protest; instead, they turned to disorganized mob activity and street violence. Nonetheless, these actions expressed rising discontent and militancy within the working classes of African American Pittsburgh.

The city looked to African American leadership to control the youths on the streets in Pittsburgh. In the African American neighborhood of Beltzhoover, Jack Ryan of the *Post-Gazette* credited African American leaders for quelling violence on the streets, saying: "It was a group of Big Daddies, men who cared, that kept the area of Beltzhoover and Knoxville quiet during the disorders earlier this week. With total community involvement and cooperation from the various state, county and city law enforcement agencies, a mixed and varied crowd of 100 men worked their regular jobs and then patrolled the streets to keep the area militants and youngsters in line."[81] Other African American neighborhoods also used local residents to control street violence. In these cases, working-class African Americans patrolled the streets in red vests instead of police officers and used their connections within the social networks of the community to diffuse street violence in Homewood-Brushton. Working-class African Americans in Homewood did not trust in the police. Internal suppression stood a greater chance of ending the street violence than any state-sponsored attempt to end street violence in African American neighborhoods like Homewood or the Hill District. Working-class African Americans did not trust police power to protect them. In the *Pittsburgh Courier*, an anonymous writer stated: "Martin Luther King is dead. No single black voice has risen since his death to complete his unfinished task and challenge those who are bent on making a mockery of American democracy. Today, we have no effective independent, self-less black leadership. All of our militant voices have either been jailed, killed, or frightened into silence. But somehow a new leadership must come and it will not come from the talented tenth, not from the heads of foundation-subsidized black organizations, but from the ranks of the agonizing poor."[82] Pittsburgh's African American workers called for new leadership that would reflect their concerns rather than those from the "talented tenth." In Homewood, "20 young volunteers roamed Homewood-Brushton, not to plunder or burn, but to urge their peers to cool things. They wore red vests, or smocks, carried city identification cards, and let it be known that 'Operation Red Shirt' as it was called, was strictly an idea that had emerged from the Negro ghetto."[83] The most successful techniques to suppress street violence came from those African Americans most intimately connected to the concerns of the working class in urban neighborhoods. Those in middle-class leadership who had separated themselves from working-class African Americans in the city center did not have as much power to speak to the concerns of the African American working class. The streets of African American neighborhoods were the location of the "disorders" and the location where tensions between middle-class African American leadership, working-class African Americans, and the city government played out.

The city turned to working-class African American leaders like William "Bouie" Haden and Byrd Brown to convince African American youths to "cool it." As many as 3,500 marchers, both Black and white, "marched, chanted, and sang, stopped at the New Federal Building, the proceeding to Gateway Center." It was at Gateway Center, the result of a contested urban renewal project, where Byrd Brown spoke to the marchers, telling them that the city had asked him "to tell the Negroes in Pittsburgh to cool it." He responded, "I will not ask the people to cool it. I did not cause the situation that exists today and I accept none of the responsibility for it."[84] African American working-class youth were the only effective agents at containing and clarifying the concerns of African Americans on the streets. African American youth took to the streets to express their discontent with the racial and economic situation in Pittsburgh and in the United States as a whole. Haden and Brown did not always have the support of the city government or the majority of African American middle-class leadership. Their grassroots organizing of the working classes of African American Pittsburgh often placed them at odds with other African Americans in leadership. Additionally, Haden's outspoken criticism of African American middle-class and elite organizations did not earn him many friends among those in power, and his agitation for working-class issues reinforced tensions between working-class and elite African Americans.

The disorders on the streets of Pittsburgh were not the result of working-class agitation for equality. African American militancy developed over the postwar period and it exploded into street violence after the assassination of Dr. King. While some middle-class African Americans viewed the rhetoric of Black militants with hostility or suspicion, working-class African Americans defended the aims of Black Power, saying, "The idea of 'black power' merely emphasizes the need to augment Negro influence by developing separatist institutions, ranging from economic enterprise to political organization. Older civil rights organizations take umbrage at the separatist impulse because it appears to repudiate the principle of integration. Considering that ethnic labor unions, ethnic political machines and other ethnic institutions have been essential to the rise of various minorities, it is puzzling to hear it said that Negroes must restrain themselves from following the same course."[85] For this author, African Americans needed to develop their own institutions separate from those of white society. Other ethnic groups used separate institutions to consolidate their power in their own communities. This allowed them to make gains toward equality. Black Power advocates wanted to focus African American efforts on community building at a local level rather than pursuing integration as a strategy for economic advancement. The author also believed integration worked against the organizational interests of African Americans. He argued, "Those institutions in the black community which are 'integrated'- whether political organizations, the rackets, or social welfare agencies—actually contribute to black impotence, for they are integrated only in the sense that they are dominated by whites and serve white interests."[86] The writer argued that once African Americans organized in separatist ways, allies would seek them out by making "genuine concessions" that served both parties equally.

Jerry Dorsch wrote into the *Courier* expressing concerns over the lack of equality African Americans experienced in the city. Dorsch argued that while Americans fought communism in Vietnam, the ideas of communism made inroads in America's African American communities. Dorsch stated,

> We should stop running from the truth and prove to the world that we are not paper tigers. This country is the prime target for the communists and they someday will bring war to our own back yards. Many of us refuse to believe this and say they would not dare. The truth is that they are here now and are putting their plans to work. The weapons they are using is propaganda. Our own Government will not admit how much influence the communist propaganda has on our own people. We should face the fact that we have a job to do if we want this country to stay free and safe. We are all sitting back and letting the communist inspire the Negro people to riot and burn and they tell them that this is the only way you can get Civil Rights. They, the communists could care less about the Negro or his civil rights, and yet we all share the blame for letting many of the Negro people fall into the leadership of the communist. The Negro does not want our sympathy, he only wants an opportunity to be recognized as an equal American citizen.[87]

Working-class African Americans faced the double burden of racial and economic inequality, so they fought for economic justice in addition to political rights and skilled jobs. The lack of economic equality caused stresses to develop within the African American community. The tensions between working-class and middle-class African Americans expanded as the middle class gained access to more skilled positions and the trappings of wealth. The additional stresses of an unpopular war in Vietnam and the assassination of Dr. King caused many African Americans to question why they were not enjoying full equality from civil rights gains.

Alfred Duckett wrote a commentary column for the *Courier* entitled "Big Mouth." In his column, Duckett discussed the Vietnam War and the prevalence of prejudice against African Americans at home, saying, "We live in a crazy world. We got black kids fighting brown kids and when they get through, if they ever get through, the coming home to a white world of prejudice and white niggerness and jimcrow homes and jobs and graves. We explain they is so many black marching feet because black kids glad to escape into a army where there is a little more democracy than in they hometown. We admit that and ain't even ashamed how naked we are — naked down to our bare skin."[88] Many African Americans argued that the funds the government spent on the war and on space exploration could easily deal with the pervasive problems of poverty in central cities nationwide. One writer in the *Courier* argued: "Further, the cost of the war is always used as an excuse to pay off costly programs like housing construction. Some people want more cuts like those already being made in anti-poverty programs, but don't want to cut back on luxuries like supersonic planes and the race to the moon. Putting a man on the moon by 1970 will cost more than putting the poor in decent homes. Since astronomers assure us that the moon will still be up there past 1970, what's the rush?"[89] The problems of poor housing conditions, economic inequality, and cultural and residential separation of working-class African Americans from middle-class African Americans led to increased tensions between the two groups as their visions for African American Pittsburgh diverged. Those African Americans who focused on the problems of poverty and residential segregation did not always win favor from the traditional middle-class leadership within the African American community.

Incidents of violence on the streets, such as arson and vandalism, increased in Homewood and other African American neighborhoods in the late 1960s. These increased incidents of street "disorder" manifested in areas where conflict between middle-class African Americans, working-class African Americans, and whites escalated over issues like community control of schools, access to jobs, and race relations.[90]

The struggles between African American elites and those in the working classes coalesced around opposition or support for Black militancy. Many of the criticisms of Bouie Haden came from members of the African American elite, and while Haden did not claim to speak for all African American working classes, he did express his support for their views. Morris and others critical of Haden derided Haden's views and accused him of undermining racial harmony and increasing tensions within the African American community of Pittsburgh. William Robinson compared the political maneuvering of African American elites to boxers when he commended Larry Huff's work in Homewood, saying: "Feinting and jabbing, Larry first took on the more 'militant' brothers in his own backyard (Homewood-Brushton). He sparred with Bouie Haden and even developed a small following. Relying upon his strong ties with City Hall, Huff countered the Hayden contingent with a request for more constables to 'clean up' Homewood-Brushton and skillfully utilized white media to protect his image and concern for the community. Still maneuvering, Huff used some fancy footwork and moved to the forefront of the Pittsburgh Southern Christian Leadership Conference—more specifically the Poor Peoples March."[91] Robinson credited Huff with taking Haden down as the presumed leader of working-class militant African Americans in Homewood. Huff's connections with powerful allies in the mayor's office differed from Haden's community-organizing methodology. Working-class community organizing focused on issues outside of the political arena. Middle-class African Americans in organizations like the Urban League and the NAACP used formal political connections with allies in city government to push their vision for African American Pittsburgh. Some working-class African Americans accused middle-class African Americans of living as if civil rights reforms were complete and of not caring about issues of economic equality that were important to members of the African American working classes.

Outrage on neighborhood streets emphasized tensions between middle-class and working-class African Americans. The theater of the street demonstrated these tensions in the period from the mid-1960s through the end of the decade. The street violence that occurred after the assassination of Dr. Martin Luther King Jr. was only one expression of the discontent present among the African American working classes in Pittsburgh. Some middle-class African Americans withdrew from the fight for economic justice to focus instead on the rewards they could reap from the civil rights movement in the areas of political rights and increased access to jobs. The late 1960s showed a rising tide of militancy developing within the working classes in urban areas. This militancy did not always express itself only in violence but also in the threat of street violence.

Conflicts within African American neighborhoods centered on different interpretations of equality. For many middle-class African Americans, access to professional jobs, suburban homes, and participation in the political process marked success and at least marginal steps toward equality with white society. Working-class African Americans did not always measure equality the same way. Street democracy allowed working-class African Americans to express their vision of community through grassroots organizing. As African Americans redefined street spaces through class interactions, street democracy developed out of the interactions between the working class and the working poor. On the streets, African Americans in the working classes worked together in basic equality whether they worked in legal or illegal labor. Often the lines separating working-class African Americans from the working poor blurred significantly. Militancy developed on the streets as working-class African Americans expressed their discontent on the streets in both violent and nonviolent ways.

Issues of family, work, and community control galvanized *militant* African Americans. While these issues were important to some in the African American middle class, local control was the primary concern for those in the working class. Middle-class African Americans often denigrated those in the working classes by defining them as youth or focusing on their perceived lack of sophistication in their organization or agitation for equality. The cleavage between the classes played out on the streets of Homewood-Brushton and the Hill District through the theater of street violence and protest. Middle-class African Americans gradually withdrew from the streets to focus their continued efforts to gain full racial equality on defined street-based protests, professional positions, homes in the emerging suburbs, and in the political arena. Street democracy fell primarily to those in the working classes of African Americans in Pittsburgh. The split between African American elites and the working class appeared most strongly in the days following the assassination of Dr. Martin Luther King Jr. African Americans had warned the city's civic, social, and political leadership of the risk of street violence if conditions in urban African American neighborhoods did not improve. The violence on the streets of Pittsburgh was not the disorganized mob violence portrayed by the mainstream press. Instead, it was an expression of racial and economic outrage born of the oppression of the African American working class within the central city.

Epilogue

Whose Streets? Our Streets!

The chant "Whose Streets? Our Streets!" has been heard frequently in street-based protests and outrages as a part of the Black Lives Matter Movement and Movement for Black Lives. It emerged in the days following the murder of Michael Brown in Ferguson, Missouri, on August 9, 2014, by police officer Daren Wilson. In the hours after the murder, Michael Brown's lifeless body was left in the middle of Canfield Avenue, in his neighborhood, as crowds gathered and news of the latest murder spread by cell phone, texts, and Twitter. Historian Barbara Ransby described the scene on the streets of the neighborhood, saying, "After the shooting, neighbors initially stood around in disgust, witnessing the grizzly spectacle and demanding answers. After the coroner removed Brown's body, protests and vigils sprang up spontaneously. Neighborhood residents set up a memorial with flowers, photos, and stuffed animals at the site of the shooting. A police car reportedly drove over the makeshift memorial and destroyed it, which many saw as another gesture of callous disregard for Black suffering and mourning. The second night, hundreds of Ferguson residents poured into the streets. They marched, chanted, sang, and refused to disperse when police demanded that they do so."[1] The outrage in Ferguson developed on the streets of the neighborhood, and the social networks of the residents created and sustained the outrage of poor and working-class people against the pervasive violence of the police department.

The words "Whose Streets? Our Streets!" make a claim that centers street space as a site of presence and belonging within a community. Tamar Carroll, an associate professor of history at Rochester Institute of Technology, defines the slogan this way, "It's about asserting one's claim to public space. Protesters have used it to say, 'We're gathered here. We're significant by virtue of being here expressing our viewpoints. And we matter as inhabitants of this space.'"[2] Social networks connect us to those in our community. These connections reinforce our common humanity. The Black Lives Matter Movement is fundamentally a humanizing movement designed to promote the dignity of all people. "In addition to being distinct in its inclusivity, this new movement is defined by action—street protests, uprisings, and various forms of direct action—and it is at its heart a visionary movement, calling not only for reforms but for systemic and fundamental change."[3] Ransby also centers the importance of Black feminist traditions of organizing, saying, "This movement has also patently rejected the hierarchical and hetero patriarchal politics of respectability. Organizers have eschewed values that privilege the so-called best and brightest, emphasizing the needs of the most marginal and often maligned sectors of the black community: those who bear the brunt of state violence, from police bullets and batons to neoliberal policies of abandonment and incarceration. Black feminist politics and sensibilities have been the intellectual lifeblood of this movement and its practices."[4] Like the social networks in the Hill District, often created and maintained by women in the working class, the modern Black Lives Matter Movement is a multifaceted effort that struggles against the violence, oppression, and exploitation of poor and working-class Black people.

Like Pittsburgh, Ferguson is a Rust Belt city where Black residents continue to suffer from the fallout of deindustrialization and the twin violence from the state, both in overpolicing and negligence. The Department of Justice found that in Ferguson, the "police department and court operated not as independent bodies but as a single money making venture." According to Ransby, "Investigators found that officers stopped and arrested people without cause and used excessive force almost exclusively against African Americans." The police department used fines from misdemeanor violations and traffic offenses to fill municipal coffers at the expense of Black citizens. "The majority-Black population of Ferguson felt under siege from a callous group of white cops and city officials, who saw them all as a resource to be ruthlessly exploited, as well as being some version of Michael Brown—that is, less than human."[5] The economic decline of Rust Belt cities was felt first in a loss of jobs and housing. Predominantly Black communities like the Hill District in Pittsburgh suffered through decades of high unemployment, crumbling infrastructure, and punitive policing, including stop-and-frisk type programs meant to root out crime before it could occur. This characterization of the neighborhood defines the streets as inherently violent and crime-ridden. It ultimately places the blame for violence on the behavior of the residents rather than on structural forces that penalize poverty.

Social networks in the neighborhoods of Pittsburgh created space for people to grieve, to come together, to create an idea of community, to create an idea of what community-oriented policing could and should look like, and to push back against unfair housing and policies that diminish the humanity of the neighbors in their area. The continuation of housing segregation in

Black neighborhoods, alongside definitions of those neighborhoods as violent and unsafe, created a process by which more and more Black people were pushed into smaller and smaller areas that were experiencing rapid deindustrialization and deskilling and neglect. These forces led to an era of increased police presence and militarization of police by emphasizing law-and-order tactics for policing in neighborhoods. All of these factors were not unique to Pittsburgh. Instead, these themes of deindustrialization and law-and-order policing swept the country as liberals backed away from their support for civil rights and the humanization of Black people on the streets of their neighborhoods. Like the streets of the Hill District, the streets of Canfield Drive and West Florissant Road became the space where outrage erupted over more than the murder of Michael Brown. The streets of Ferguson, Missouri, also became theaters of warfare as the neighborhood pushed back against a longstanding practice of racially biased policing and state-sponsored violence on the streets. Ransby situates the uprising in Ferguson as a part of the struggle against the violence of the state, saying,

> The Ferguson uprising, an organic mass rebellion sparked by Brown's death at the hands of a member of a notoriously racist local police force, was a defining moment for the early twenty-first-century Black Freedom struggle. Hundreds of people took to the streets and made them their own. They defied state power and exposed what many outside the Black community would rather ignore—the violent underbelly of racial capitalism and systemic racism. And the police did indeed show their true colors by firing teargas and rubber bullets and rough-handling peaceful demonstrators. In the summer and fall of 2014, Ferguson became the epicenter of not only Black resistance but resistance to the neoliberal state and its violent tactics of suppression and control. It was evident that, while Brown's killing was the catalyst, the Black working class of Ferguson was angry about much more, and their anger resonated and reverberated around the country and beyond.[6]

Ferguson residents came together to push back against a system of state authority that did not derive from the consent of the governed. Instead, they upheld their own law and custom in the face of multifaceted exploitation against them because they were primarily Black and poor. Activists created their own systems of reciprocity, their own law and custom, to support and sustain their movement, to humanize their neighborhood, and to give Michael Brown dignity in death.

The outrages on the streets of the United States following the extrajudicial murder of Black men and women by officers who were sworn to serve and protect in the twenty-first century often echoes the patterns of working-class outrage that developed on the streets of the Hill District, and many Black neighborhoods in the United States, following Dr. King's assassination. It is critical to understand the role of social networks, both physical and digital, in creating an alternative framework of law and custom that operates in an informal community. This alternative framework of law and custom comes out of a system of social networks through systems of reciprocity on the streets. The actions of residents of the Hill District during the Pittsburgh "riots" and in the current Black Lives Matter protests demonstrate their use of an alternative framework of law and custom that developed within their social networks and systems of reciprocity. Like the violence in Ferguson, community members targeted the violence on the streets toward those seen as extractive.

Similar to the outrages in the late 1960s, outrages in the twenty-first century encompass multiple dimensions of violence. Barbara Ransby discusses the two sides of the violence against the neighborhood poor and the use of looting in Ferguson, saying, "The injustice of police violence against Black bodies is seen as contiguous with the everyday threat of violence that prevents the working poor, unemployed, and underemployed from having food, clothes, or even small luxury items that are dangled in front of them every day by the multi-billion-dollar advertising industry. Looting, in some people's minds, may at least temporarily jettison that unjust arrangement."[7] The development of outrage on the streets of the Hill District permitted the city to use increasingly militaristic suppression on those residents who sought to draw attention to poor housing conditions, a lack of jobs that paid a living wage, a growing gap between rich and poor even among their neighbors, and an increasingly brutal police force on the city streets. Activists in the twenty-first century relied on their conception of intersectional solidarity to create social networks rather than a perceived notion of the politics of respectability to inform who could lead a movement.

Social networks are not the sole purview of technology or the internet. The social networks formed on the streets of the neighborhood emerge from person-to-person connections, both the physical streets and on the digital streets of social media. Social media has formed in the twenty-first century as a powerful tool both for connection and isolation. Yet while hashtags have proved critical for raising awareness, disseminating evidence from the perspective of those targeted by police violence, and coordinating street-based direct action, it is also possible to be performative in one's support. Social networks imply the interpersonal connectivity that occurs through our relationships with one another; what makes the connection personal and substantial is its physical counterpart, when online connections push people to organize and act together offline in solidarity.

From the earliest days of the Black Lives Matter Movement, social media has been a critical organizing tool that has connected the streets of desperate neighborhoods to the world. Black Twitter has had a direct role in organizing both in the digital streets and on the ground in places like Pittsburgh and Ferguson. Kimberly McNair defines Black Twitter as a neighborhood that exists in both offline and online forms, saying, "To this extent, the 'Black' in Black Twitter extends past the online neighborhoods that are interconnected by signifying cultural knowledge and practices and addresses the offline reality of blackness born out of continued subjugation."[8] From its origin, the Black Lives Matter Movement has deftly used social media to cultivate solidarity nationally and globally. Social media became a new digital tool to cultivate new social networks across larger spaces and a way to create a digital neighborhood of care and mutual support.

During the Ferguson uprising, activists in the neighborhood received social media messages of support from occupied Palestinians and other movements to resist oppression globally. Activists in Ferguson used social media to call for support from outside their physical neighborhood through a social media campaign called #FergusonOctober. This campaign asked supporters to come to Ferguson to protest with them. Jelani Cobb described the reach of the social media campaign, saying, "Ferguson October drew supporters from New York, Georgia, New Jersey, Chicago, and California. At least one activist had come from Hawaii to participate in the weekend of civil disobedience."[9] Marches in solidarity with Ferguson took place in communities all over the country and even the world, even as other shooting deaths of unarmed Black people, including twelve-year-old Tamir Rice in the Rust Belt city of Cleveland, Ohio, spurred activists to consider Ferguson as a part of a significant movement against state-sponsored violence against Black people.

This reemergence of a sustained movement against state-sponsored violence sparked after a period not of erasure but of inattention. In 2010, prior to the onset of Black Lives Matter, Pittsburgh erupted in protest following the beating of teenager Jordan Miles as he was walking in the African American neighborhood of Homewood. While walking to his grandmother's house from his mother's home at night, three plainclothes officers accosted

Jordan Miles as they were cruising Homewood in an unmarked police car. Miles ran, fearing they were trying to rob him. Miles was injured in the violent struggle that ensued but was still charged with a felony. The officers contend they saw Jordan behaving suspiciously and that he exhibited signs that he was armed, but they never found a gun on the young man or anywhere near the arrest site. Miles claimed that the officers never identified themselves and started yelling at him, "where is your money? Where is your gun? Where is the drugs?"[10] The beating and arrest of Miles sparked demonstrations across the city that foreshadowed Black Lives Matter protests that would develop later in the decade.

The *Pittsburgh City Paper* investigated a pattern of previous grievances against the three Pittsburgh plainclothes officers who were a part of a specialized unit called a ninety-nine unit. These units utilized plainclothes officers to patrol neighborhoods that seemed to have high crime rates. Nineteen days before the altercation with Jordan Miles, the same three officers accosted Lamar Johnson over the scent of marijuana in the air. Like Miles, they wrestled him to the ground suspecting that he had a gun and that he might be attempting to swallow narcotics. No drugs or weapons were discovered, and Johnson was released without being charged. This information was not admissible in the civil lawsuit against the officers in federal court because a judge ruled that the evidence was prejudicial. Carrie Lewis, an attorney representing Miles, said, "the Lamar Johnson case is almost exactly the same. . . . Three weeks before they jump out of a car and throw Johnson to the ground that indicated to me that that's their style."[11] The jury found a mixed award in the civil trial following Miles's arrest. They claimed that Miles was falsely arrested but that the officers did not use excessive force, and they awarded Miles $119,000 in a civil rights suit.

Much of the police efforts to justify the use of force against Miles hinged on the description of Homewood as a violent and crime-ridden neighborhood, a claim that residents contested. In 2014, the *Pittsburgh City Paper* interviewed residents of Homewood who fought back against the characterization of their community as the "home of the drive-by," saying, "Numbers don't tell the whole story. To hear the way the defense would portray Homewood through statistics, and through the lens of the police, was discordant to me, because I live in Homewood. . . . It's not a war zone. I was sitting with my neighbors, and we know what living there is like as opposed to the caricature they painted."[12] This description of Homewood also played into racially motivated stereotyping and systemic bias within the city of Pittsburgh police department.

In 2021, the *Associated Press* and the *Hill* investigated a private Facebook group called "Pittsburgh Area Police Breakroom," where officers posted comments that were "openly hostile and sometimes racist towards protesters who rallied in the city following the death of Antwon Rose, an unarmed Black teenager who was killed while running from police."[13] This use of social media by police officers using racist and dehumanizing language is common. The *Associated Press* reported on the Plain View Project, which published a database of similar posts from eight police departments that did not include Pittsburgh area police departments. Professor David Harris of the University of Pittsburgh School of Law discussed the implications of racial bias within the police department in his book *A City Divided*, which examines the 2010 beating of Jordan Miles and the subsequent protests. In interviewing Harris, Bill O'Driscoll of the *Pittsburgh Post-Gazette* states, "Racism only adds to the trouble caused by how officers are trained, socialized and deployed. Mr. Harris contends that in recent decades, police have been taught a 'warrior' mentality that frames every encounter with a citizen as potentially deadly. Police, Mr. Harris reports, routinely trade videos of civilians killing cops—just one of the things that convinces them the job is more dangerous than statistics show, and further justification for acting like an occupying army in neighborhoods they are sworn to protect."[14] This warrior mentality helps explain the reaction of police to the circumstances surrounding the murder of Antwon Rose in 2018.

On June 19, 2018, Antwon Rose II, an honor student and an active volunteer at afterschool programs, was shot and murdered in East Pittsburgh, Pennsylvania, by Officer Michael Rosfeld. Officer Rosfeld was previously employed as a university police officer at the University of Pittsburgh. During his time as a university cop, there had been claims that Officer Rosfeld used his power to perform false arrests, assault individuals, and falsify records. The University of Pittsburgh had released Officer Michael Rosfeld from duty to avoid any potential red flags on his service record. He had only been sworn into the East Pittsburgh police department hours prior to killing Rose. Rosfeld's trial started on March 19, 2019, and ended on March 22nd, 2019. The video footage of Rose running from the car and being shot three times in the back received a vast amount of social media coverage. The coverage of Rose's murder was contentious because many Pittsburghers, both Black and white, believed the official story that Rose and Hester had been involved in a drive-by shooting before the traffic stop. Others stressed that Rose was unarmed at the time of his murder and as a critical view of the Black Lives Matter Movement, one did not have to be blameless or respectable to deserve human dignity and abide by the rule of law. The court selected jurors from Harrisburg rather than from the Pittsburgh area to ensure a fair trial. On the first day of the trial, Rosfeld testified that he saw a gun being aimed at him but was unsure if it was Rose or Hester, so he shot after the boys in self-defense. The jury finalized their verdict in less than three hours and found Rosfeld not guilty. The community of East Pittsburgh and the city of Pittsburgh reacted to Antwon Rose's murder by creating and participating in many protests that physically occupied the streets.

Protests began almost immediately after the verdict and took place outside of the East Pittsburgh Police Department and on the parkway east freeway.[15] This use of streets and blocking traffic was a tactic used by other Black Lives Matter protests, including the protests in Ferguson, Missouri. Local Ferguson activist David Whitt defined his reasoning for occupying the streets of his neighborhood during the Ferguson uprising, saying, "Hell no, we ain't going nowhere. You know, we was occupying the streets that we paid for."[16] Blocking traffic and occupying the space maintained by tax dollars is a clear nonviolent, direct-action strategy focusing on disrupting movement and commerce in a city. It is also a method police have most targeted as an unlawful protest. In 2021, thirty-four states introduced eighty-one bills purportedly aimed at preventing riots. These bills often absolved individuals who hit protestors occupying the streets with their cars of any wrongdoing.[17] In a social media post, Pittsburgh area police advocated the use of lethal force against protestors who occupied a highway while protesting Antwon Rose's murder, saying, "In another post, a now-retired Pittsburgh police officer talked about being stuck in traffic for hours in June 2018 after protesters commandeered a highway days after a former East Pittsburgh police officer shot and killed 17-year-old Antwon Rose as he ran from a traffic stop. After the officer mentioned having his service weapon in the trunk, other officers said he shouldn't hesitate to use lethal force because he'd be protecting himself, while others said police should use dogs and water cannons to clear the demonstrators, a reference to police tactics during civil rights protests in the '60s."[18] This connection to the use of force dogs, water cannons, and the oppressive tactics of police under the likes of Birmingham's Eugene "Bull" Connor demonstrates the intent to keep the racial status quo and to keep Black residents of Pittsburgh "in their place."

The cultivation of street space in Black neighborhoods as a type of Black-controlled public space where residents can work out their view of democracy that may be an alternative framework of law and custom is not a new concept. The work of activists in the twenty-first century to use streets to build spaces of humanity and dignity for all people through the connecting work of the Black working class connects back to similar efforts to build and sustain social networks in the Hill District after World War I and through the 1960s. These social networks developed from an ethic of connection and care. Ferguson activist Kayla Reed described her understanding of what they were working toward in Ferguson by linking their struggle to the streets and to an ethos of love, saying, "What started in the streets of Ferguson has inspired people around the world. . . . The reality is that these are our streets. They were built on the backs of our ancestors. So we are going to claim them as long as we want to. We will stay in the streets until we are equal citizens, period. We don't do this because we hate the police; we do this because we love each other. This movement was born in love, and love always wins."[19] This struggle for the street and for the full dignity and humanity of all Black people continues in the neighborhood, on the corner, and in the digital streets until we all get free.

Acknowledgments

I would like to thank my family, first and foremost, who made this book possible. Context is always important, but in this case, I came from a family of rebels, pacifists, protestors, sharecroppers, and peacemakers. Thank you to my late father, Daniel Barber, for always believing that I could do anything I set my mind to and for taking me to Mississippi to meet my great grandmother, Mama Shook—Minerva Rollins, who ignited the questions in my mind over what life was like for a Black woman in the South. Thank you to my chosen family and extended family, great aunts and uncles, aunts, uncles, and cousins—first, second, and otherwise—for their commitment to social justice and for showing me the power of community. Thank you for teaching me that the right words can make a difference and that listening to other people's stories has the power to change the world. Thank you to my mother, Renee Black, for putting up with me, believing in me, and helping me through in ways too innumerable to count. You are still the only person who can call this "our book." I will count myself blessed if I become half the woman you are.

I also want to extol the support of my husband and partner, Jason Klanderud. If life is an adventure, I'm thankful to have you by my side. You are an excellent father to our two children, Noah and Lana, who have grown up with this project, and your constant reminders to them that their mom is a scholar makes everything I do feel that much more important. Thank you for seeing what I do as an art and a science and for being there to juggle the craziness that is the life of a scholar, artist, and parent with me. This book would look significantly different without your astute observations and keen insight. Thank you for being the cornerstone of my community. Your support and love help me persevere through the tough times, and having you with me makes the celebrations that much better.

It is difficult to produce anything of quality without accumulating many debts of gratitude. Creating this book required collaboration, imagination, and perseverance from all involved. I wish to gratefully acknowledge my scholarly community—Joe W. Trotter Jr., Scott Sandage, Lisa Tetrault, and Edda Fields-Black—all scholars I admire and whose work and scholarship have influenced my thinking. I sincerely appreciate the ways you have all supported my work, even when you questioned whether I would uncover the stories I was searching for and moved with me from being my teachers to being colleagues in the work of scholarship. I have deeply appreciated the scholarly community I have cultivated outside of my graduate program, including Tiffany Gill, Erica Armstrong Dunbar, Clarence Lang, Sherika Crawford, and Cornelius Bynum. Thank you for your mentorship and support as I navigated the early years of scholarship, teaching, and service.

The Center for Africanamerican Urban Studies and the Economy or CAUSE at Carnegie Mellon University also provided regular scholarly fuel for my thinking on

African American history and how to connect scholarly work to broader community work. I've also benefitted significantly from conversations with CAUSE postdoctoral fellows, including Millington Bergeson-Lockwood, G. Derek Musgrove, and Luther Adams. I was also honored to participate in CAUSE's Remembering African American Pittsburgh Oral History Project documenting African American life in Pittsburgh after World War II. Working on this project introduced me to oral history methodology under the excellent tutelage of Benjamin Houston. Through my engagement with CAUSE and their anniversary conference, "Perspectives on African Americans in Pittsburgh: Twenty Years Later," I had the rich opportunity to present my work on the Hill District to the residents of the neighborhood. It remains vital to me that my work faithfully represents the stories and ethos of the neighborhood. To that end, this book would not be possible without the stories of Marcia Donnell, Barbara Gaston, Helen Mendoza, Sarah Tomlin, Robert Vickers, Odessa Wilson, Dewayne Ketchum, "Arthur," and "Leroy." Thank you for sharing your understanding of your neighborhood and for trusting me not to take your story and make it unrecognizable like others from the universities had. The engagement from the community as a part of CAUSE events profoundly shaped this book, and I cannot overstate how much it means to have the residents of the Hill District see their community reflected in this work.

A special thank you to the staff at Carnegie Mellon's Hunt Library, especially Sue Collins and the interlibrary loan department. I would also like to thank the staff at the Archives Services Center at the University of Pittsburgh for their assistance in wading through the local collections for the National Association for the Advancement of Colored People (NAACP) and the Urban League of Pittsburgh (ULP). I would also like to thank the staff at the Library of Congress for their help hunting down local branch information in the national collections for the NAACP and Urban League. Thank you all for your professionalism and perseverance in finding the difficult sources I was looking for and closing the gaps. My sincerest thank you to Charlene Foggie-Barnett, the Teenie Harris community archivist at the Carnegie Museum of Art, for her deep knowledge of and care for the Teenie Harris Archive. It is a treasure that was invaluable for this book. Thank you to Brandon Proia from the University of North Carolina Press, Justice, Power, and Politics Series, and series editors Rhonda Y. Williams and Heather Ann Thompson for believing in this project from the beginning. Your encouragement and patience kept me working on it when doubts crept in. Thank you for always seeing the power and politics of social networks on the streets.

In closing, thank you to the intellectual community of the Association of Black Women Historians (ABWH) and the Association for the Study of African American Life and History (ASALH) for creating a community for scholars who deeply engage with Black women's history and the full range of Black life. Presenting these ideas in these organizations' nurturing spaces helped refine my thinking and connected me to a social network of scholars who genuinely value Black life. Thank you for being my scholarly neighborhood. I look forward to continuing to work in these streets.

Notes

Introduction

1. August Wilson, *Fences: A Play* (New York: New American Library, 1986), xvii.

2. Nancy Isenberg, *White Trash: The 400-Year Untold History of Class in America* (New York: Penguin Books, 2017). Isenberg argues that the concept of waste developed a specific English meaning that implied both idleness and potential not yet realized.

3. Robin D. G. Kelley, "Congested Terrain: Resistance on Public Transportation" in *Race Rebels: Culture, Politics, and the Black Working Class* (New York: The Free Press, 1994).

4. Kelley "Congested Terrain," xii.

5. St. Clair Drake and Horace R. Cayton, *Black Metropolis: A Study of Negro Life in a Northern City* (Chicago: University of Chicago Press, 1993).

6. Kelley, "Congested Terrain," xii.

7. Lance Freeman, *A Haven and a Hell: The Ghetto in Black America* (New York: Columbia University Press, 2019), 44–45.

8. J. Trent Alexander, "The Great Migration in Comparative Perspective: Interpreting the Urban Origins of Southern Black Migrants to Depression-Era Pittsburgh," *Social Science History* 22, no. 3 (1998): 349–76; James R. Grossman, *Land of Hope: Chicago, Black Southerners, and the Great Migration* (Chicago: University of Chicago Press, 1989); Steven Hahn, *A Nation under Our Feet: Black Political Struggles in the Rural South from Slavery to the Great Migration* (Cambridge, Mass.: The Belknap Press, 2004); Darlene Clark Hine, "Black Migration and the Urban Midwest: The Gender Dimension, 1915–1945," in *The Great Migration in Historical Perspective: New Dimensions of Race, Class, and Gender*, ed. Joe William Trotter Jr. (Bloomington: Indiana University Press, 1991), 128–46; Townsand Price-Spratlen, "Urban Destination Selection among African Americans during the 1950s Great Migration," *Social Science History* 32, no. 3 (2008): 437–69; Joe William Trotter Jr., *Pittsburgh and the Urban League Movement: A Century of Social Service and Activism* (Lexington: University Press of Kentucky, 2020).

9. Peter Gottlieb, "Rethinking the Great Migration: A Perspective from Pittsburgh," in *The Great Migration in Historical Perspective: New Dimensions of Race, Class, and Gender*, ed. Joe William Trotter Jr., (Bloomington: Indiana University Press, 1991), 73–74.

10. Joe William Trotter Jr., "Race, Class, and Industrial Change: Black Migration to Southern West Virginia, 1915–1932," in *The Great Migration in Historical Perspective: New Dimensions of Race, Class, and Gender*, ed. Joe William Trotter Jr. (Bloomington: Indiana University Press, 1991), 46; Joe William Trotter Jr., *Workers on Arrival: Black Labor in the Making of America* (Berkeley: University of California Press, 2019), 110; Karida L. Brown, *Gone Home: Race and Roots through Appalachia* (Chapel Hill: University of North Carolina Press, 2018), 41–44.

11. Gottlieb, "Rethinking the Great Migration," 72.

12. Mark Whitaker, *Smoketown: The Untold Story of the Other Great Black Renaissance* (New York: Simon and Schuster, 2018), 67–68.

13. Gottlieb, "Rethinking the Great Migration," 73.

14. Peter Gottlieb, *Making Their Own Way: Southern Blacks' Migration to Pittsburgh, 1916–30* (Urbana: University of Illinois Press, 1987), 185.

15. Trotter, *Pittsburgh and the Urban League Movement*, 28–29.

16. Trotter, *Pittsburgh and the Urban League Movement*, 29.

17. Trotter, *Pittsburgh and the Urban League Movement*, 39.

18. Trotter, *Pittsburgh and the Urban League Movement*, 60.

19. Trotter, *Pittsburgh and the Urban League Movement*, 60; quote from "Report from Home Economics Worker," February 1919, box 1, file folders 1, 20; box 3, file folders 87, 88,96, 115, 137; box 5, file folders 237, 238, Urban League of Pittsburgh Papers, Archives Services Center, University of Pittsburgh.

20. Gottlieb, *Making Their Own Way*, 187; quote from Home Economics Worker's Report, August 1919, Administration File, "Miscellaneous," Urban League of Pittsburgh Records, Archives of Industrial Society, Hillman Library, University of Pittsburgh.

21. Gottlieb, *Making Their Own Way*, 187; quote from Pennsylvania Department of Welfare, *Negro Survey of Pennsylvania* (Harrisburg, Pa.: 1928), 10.

22. Gottlieb, *Making Their Own Way*, 196.

23. Laurence Glasco, "Double Burden: The Black Experience in Pittsburgh," in *City at the Point: Essays on the Social History of Pittsburgh*, ed. Samuel P. Hays, Pittsburgh Series in Social and Labor History, 70. (Pittsburgh, Pa.: University of Pittsburgh Press, 1989).

24. For insight into the development of African American Urban History, see Adam Green, *Selling the Race: Culture, Community, and Black Chicago, 1940–1955* (Chicago: University of Chicago Press, 2007); Wallace D. Best, *Passionately Human, No Less Divine: Religion and Culture in Black Chicago, 1915–1952* (Princeton, N.J.: Princeton University Press, 2005); Alice O'Connor, "Race and Class in Chicago-School Sociology: The Underclass Concept in Historical Perspective," in *The African American Urban Experience: Perspectives from the Colonial Period to the Present*, ed. Joe William Trotter, Earl Lewis, and Tera W. Hunter (New York: Palgrave Macmillan, 2004); Robert O. Self, *American Babylon: Race, Power, and the Struggle for the Postwar City in California* (Princeton, N.J.: Princeton University Press, 2003); Wendell E. Pritchett, *Brownsville, Brooklyn: Blacks, Jews, and the Changing Face of the Ghetto* (Chicago: University of Chicago Press, 2002); Heather Ann Thompson, *Whose Detroit?: Politics, Labor, and Race in a Modern American City* (Ithaca, N.Y.: Cornell University Press, 2001); Kimberley L. Phillips, *AlabamaNorth: African-American Migrants, Community, and Working-Class Activism in Cleveland, 1915–45* (Urbana: University of Illinois Press, 1999); Lillian Serece Williams, *Strangers in the Land of Paradise: The Creation of an African American Community, Buffalo, New York, 1900–1940* (Bloomington: Indiana University Press, 1999); Arnold R. Hirsch, *Making the Second Ghetto: Race and Housing in Chicago, 1940–1960* (Chicago: University of Chicago Press, 1998); Anthony P. Polednak, *Segregation, Poverty, and Mortality in Urban African Americans* (New York: Oxford University Press,

1997); Darlene Clark Hine, "Black Migration and the Urban Midwest: The Gender Dimension, 1915-1945," in *The Great Migration in Historical Perspective: New Dimensions of Race, Class, and Gender,* ed. Joe William Trotter (Bloomington: Indiana University Press, 1991); Gottlieb, *Making Their Own Way;* Joe William Trotter, *Black Milwaukee: The Making of an Industrial Proletariat, 1915-45* (Urbana: University of Illinois Press, 1985); Kenneth L. Kusmer, *A Ghetto Takes Shape: Black Cleveland, 1870-1930* (Urbana: University of Illinois Press, 1976); Allan H. Spear, *Black Chicago: The Making of a Negro Ghetto, 1890-1920* (Chicago: University of Chicago Press, 1967).

25. Drake and Cayton, *Black Metropolis: A Study of Negro Life in a Northern City,* 198-208.

26. Drake and Cayton, *Black Metropolis,* 272-74.

27. Thomas J. Sugrue, *Sweet Land of Liberty: The Forgotten Struggle for Civil Rights in the North* (New York: Random House, 2008), 38, 338-46.

28. Davarian L. Baldwin, *Chicago's New Negroes: Modernity, the Great Migration, and Black Urban Life* (Chapel Hill: University of North Carolina Press, 2007), 6-7.

29. Baldwin, *Chicago's New Negroes,* 8.

30. Baldwin, *Chicago's New Negroes,* 16.

31. Baldwin, *Chicago's New Negroes,* 16.

32. Baldwin, *Chicago's New Negroes,* 19.

33. Stephanie J. Shaw, *What a Woman Ought to Be and to Do: Black Professional Women Workers during the Jim Crow Era* (Chicago: University of Chicago Press, 1996), 5.

34. Kevin Kelly Gaines, *Uplifting the Race: Black Leadership, Politics, and Culture in the Twentieth Century* (Chapel Hill: University of North Carolina Press, 1996); Touré Reed, *Not Alms but Opportunity: The Urban League and The Politics of Racial Uplift* (Chapel Hill: University of North Carolina Press, 2009), 6-7.

35. Trotter, *Pittsburgh and the Urban League Movement,* 1.

36. Trotter, *Pittsburgh and the Urban League Movement,* 182.

Chapter One

1. Frank E. Bolden, "John L. Clark 'Covers' Beloved Beat Last Time . . . Down Wylie Ave. Area," *Pittsburgh Courier,* July 1, 1961.

2. Mark Whitaker, *Smoketown: The Untold Story of the Other Great Black Renaissance* (New York: Simon & Schuster, 2018), 67-68.

3. Peter Gottlieb, *Making Their Own Way: Southern Blacks' Migration to Pittsburgh, 1916-30* (Urbana: University of Illinois Press, 1987), 89-90.

4. J. Trent Alexander, "The Great Migration in Comparative Perspective: Interpreting the Urban Origins of Southern Black Migrants to Depression-Era Pittsburgh," *Social Science History* 22, no. 3 (1998); Dennis C. Dickerson, *Out of the Crucible: Black Steelworkers in Western Pennsylvania, 1875-1980* (Albany, N.Y.: SUNY Press, 1986); Darlene Clark Hine, "Black Migration and the Urban Midwest: The Gender Dimension, 1915-1945" in *The Great Migration in Historical Perspective: New Dimensions of Race, Class, and Gender,* ed. Joe William Trotter Jr. (Bloomington: Indiana University Press, 1991); Townsand Price-Spratlen, "Urban Destination Selection among African Americans during the 1950s Great Migration," *Social Science History* 32, no. 3 (2008): 427-69.

5. Gottlieb, *Making Their Own Way*, 7.

6. Joe William Trotter Jr. and Jared N. Day, *Race and Renaissance: African Americans in Pittsburgh since World War II* (Pittsburgh, Pa.: University of Pittsburgh Press, 2010), 9.

7. Lance Freeman, *A Haven and a Hell: The Ghetto in Black America* (New York: Columbia University Press, 2019), 44–45.

8. Laurence Glasco, "The Civil Rights Movement in Pittsburgh: To Make This City 'Some Place Special,'" unpublished scholarly article, University of Pittsburgh.

9. Freeman, *A Haven and a Hell*, 51–52.

10. Freeman, *A Haven and a Hell*, 53.

11. James Borchert, *Alley Life in Washington: Family, Community, Religion, and Folklife in the City, 1850–1970* (Urbana: University of Illinois Press, 1980); James R. Grossman, *Land of Hope: Chicago, Black Southerners, and the Great Migration* (Chicago: University of Chicago Press, 1989); Hine, "Black Migration and the Urban Midwest"; Kimberly L. Phillips, *Alabamanorth: African-American Migrants, Community, and Working-Class Activism in Cleveland, 1915–45* (Urbana: University of Illinois Press, 1999).

12. Gottlieb, *Making Their Own Way*, 197–98.

13. Mary Dudley (known as Mary Dee), an African American DJ for Pittsburgh radio station WHOD, coined this description for the corner of Wylie and Fullerton Avenues in the Hill District. From *Wylie Avenue Days*, directed by Doug Bolin and Christopher Moore (Pittsburgh, Pa., 2007), DVD.

14. John L. Clark, "Wylie Ave.," *Pittsburgh Courier*, February 24, 1962.

15. Chester L. Washington, "Walking Up Wylie," *Pittsburgh Courier*, January 30, 1932.

16. "Arthur" (name omitted at interviewee's request, alias chosen by interviewee), oral history interview by Jessica D. Klanderud, January 18, 2013, Personal Collection, Hill House Senior Services Center, 2038 Bedford Avenue, Pittsburgh, Pa.

17. Barbara Gaston, oral history interview by Jessica D. Klanderud, January 18, 2013, Personal Collection, Hill House Senior Services Center, 2038 Bedford Avenue, Pittsburgh, Pa.

18. Carol B. Stack, *All Our Kin: Strategies for Survival in a Black Community* (New York: Basic Books, 1975), 33–37.

19. "Frog Week Awaits the Happy Guests," *Pittsburgh Courier*, August 1, 1925.

20. "Society Dons Festive Gown for Eventful 'Frog Week,'" *Pittsburgh Courier*, August 4, 1923.

21. "Many Out-of-Town Guests Arrive for Frog Week," *Pittsburgh Courier*, August 6, 1932.

22. "Smart Society Women to Add Gayest Bit to the Ever-Colorful Frog Week," *Pittsburgh Courier*, July 8, 1933.

23. "Society Wore 'Em at Frogs' Annual Outing," *Pittsburgh Courier*, August 9, 1924.

24. Sala Udin, oral history interview by Johanna Hernandez and Benjamin Houston, July 23, 2007, Center for Africanamerican Urban Studies and the Economy: Remembering Africanamerican Pittsburgh Oral History Project, Carnegie Mellon University, Pittsburgh, Pa.

25. Udin, oral history interview.

26. "Now Society's Fancy Turns to Thoughts of 'Frog' Festivities," *Pittsburgh Courier*, July 25, 1925.

27. "Now Society's Fancy Turns to Thoughts of "Frog" Festivities."

28. "At Last Burrell 'Fesses up,' Girls," *Pittsburgh Courier*, July 17, 1926.

29. John L. Clark, "Wylie Ave.," *Pittsburgh Courier*, August 2, 1930.

30. "Society," *Pittsburgh Courier*, September 13, 1930.

31. "Local Merchants to Welcome Frog Visitors," *Pittsburgh Courier*, August 1, 1931.

32. Chester L. Washington, "Deep Wylie," *Pittsburgh Courier*, August 17, 1929.

33. "Local Merchants to Welcome Frog Visitors," *Pittsburgh Courier*, August 2, 1930.

34. "Local Merchants to Welcome Frog Visitors," 2.

35. "Urban League Holds Better Baby Contest," *Pittsburgh Courier*, June 14, 1924.

36. "Health Campaign Plans Progressing," *Pittsburgh Courier*, May 20, 1933.

37. "Health Week Begins May 20," *Pittsburgh Courier*, May 21, 1927.

38. "Urban League Holds Better Baby Contest," *Pittsburgh Courier*, June 14, 1924; Urban League Auxiliary, "Origin of the Girl's Auxiliary," Archives of Industrial Society, University of Pittsburgh, Urban League of Pittsburgh, 1916–1968, box 6, Folder 81 (1919):11; Ira De A. Reid, *Social Conditions of the Negro in the Hill District of Pittsburgh; Survey Conducted under the Direction of Ira De A. Reid, Director, Department of Research, the National Urban League*, University of Pittsburgh Digital Research Library, Pittsburgh, Pa., 1999, 1930.

39. "Urban League of Pittsburgh: Health and Welfare: National Health Survey," in *National Urban League* (Washington, D.C.: Library of Congress, 1963); "Leading 'Clean-up' Crusade," *Pittsburgh Courier*, May 2, 1925.

40. Elsie Witchen, *Tuberculosis and the Negro in Pittsburgh: A Report of the Negro Health Survey* (Tuberculosis League of Pittsburgh: Pittsburgh, Pa.,1934).

41. "Urban League Healthweek May 20–26," *Pittsburgh Courier*, May 19, 1928.

42. "Urban League Healthweek May 20–26."

43. Marcia Joyce Donnell, oral history interview by Jessica D. Klanderud, December 12, 2012, Personal Collection, Hill House Senior Services Center, 2038 Bedford Avenue, Pittsburgh, Pa.

44. Robert M. Vickers, oral history interview by Jessica D. Klanderud, January 11, 2013, Personal Collection, Hill House Senior Services Center, 2038 Bedford Avenue, Pittsburgh, Pa.

45. Sarah Tomlin, oral history interview by Jessica D. Klanderud, December 12, 2012, Personal Collection, Hill House Senior Services Center, 2038 Bedford Avenue, Pittsburgh, Pa.

46. St Clair Drake and Horace R. Cayton, *Black Metropolis: A Study of Negro Life in a Northern City* (Chicago: University of Chicago Press, 1993).

47. Tomlin, oral history interview.

48. Tomlin, oral history interview.

49. Urban League of Pittsburgh, "Recreation Department Minutes," in *Urban League of Pittsburgh, 1916–1968*, Archives Services Center, University of Pittsburgh, Pittsburgh, Pa., 1936; "Musical Pink Tea Sunday," *Pittsburgh Courier*, January 14, 1933; "Health Program Planned by Urban League May 20–25," *Pittsburgh Courier*, May 5, 1928.

50. "Society," *Pittsburgh Courier*, October 16, 1926; "Urban League of Pittsburgh: Administration Department, Affiliates File," in *National Urban League* (Washington, D.C.: Library of Congress); "NAACP Public Accommodations Committee: Public Accommodations Complaint," in *Pittsburgh Branch, National Association for the Advancement of Colored People (NAACP), 1940–1974*, Archives Services Center, University of Pittsburgh, Pittsburgh, Pa., 1958.

51. Reid, *Social Conditions of the Negro*; "An Act Discrimination on Account or Religion, Creed, or Nationality," in *P. L. 872 1201*(State of Pennsylvania, 1939); "Office Files, General, Complaints," in *Urban League of Pittsburgh Records 1916–1968*, Archives Services Center, University of Pittsburgh, Pittsburgh, Pa., 1933. The 1939 Pennsylvania Public Accommodations Act prohibited discrimination in public venues because of religion, creed, or nationality, but both the Urban League and the NAACP branches in Pittsburgh established committees to deal with infractions of the law. Many venues avoided some of the legal problems associated with violation by establishing special days or times for African American patrons to use public facilities and to retain segregation between whites and Blacks within the city. Complaints against venues consistently suggested public venues like restaurants and dance halls in the neighborhoods in and near the Hill District and practiced frequent discrimination against African American patrons. Over the interwar period, the NAACP took over legal challenges to violation of the 1939 public accommodations law while the Urban League attempted to ameliorate tensions by making agreements with venues to broaden their accessibility to African American clientele.

52. Lee K. Frank, "A Sociological Analysis of a Predominantly Negro Social Club in Pittsburgh Pennsylvania" (master's thesis, Indiana State College, 1965), 5.

53. "Society," *Pittsburgh Courier*, October 16, 1926; "Society," *Pittsburgh Courier*, September 13, 1930; "Now Society's Fancy Turns to Thoughts of 'Frog' Festivities," *Pittsburgh Courier*, July 25, 1925; "Society Dons Festive Gown for Eventful 'Frog Week,'" *Pittsburgh Courier*, August 4, 1923.

54. "Urban League of Pittsburgh: Health and Welfare: National Health Survey"; "Leading 'Clean-up' Crusade," *Pittsburgh Courier*, May 2, 1925; "Health Campaign Plans Progressing," *Pittsburgh Courier*, May 20, 1933.

55. "The Picnic Season Opens with Moonlight Affair at Linden Grove, July 3rd," *Pittsburgh Courier*, July 4, 1925; "Social Events," *Pittsburgh Courier*, May 17, 1930; "Big Fourth at Soho," *Pittsburgh Courier*, July 9, 1932; Ted Washington, "Soho Has Glorious Fourth," *Pittsburgh Courier*, July 9, 1932.

56. Donnell, oral history interview.

Chapter Two

1. Lance Freeman, *A Haven and a Hell: The Ghetto in Black America* (New York: Columbia University Press, 2019), 41–43.

2. Ira De A. Reid, *Social Conditions of the Negro in the Hill District of Pittsburgh; Survey Conducted under the Direction of Ira De A. Reid, Director, Department of Research, the National Urban League*, University of Pittsburgh Digital Research Library, Pittsburgh, Pa., 1999, 1930, 11.

3. Reid, *Social Conditions of the Negro*, 9.

4. Robert Ezra Park et al., *The City* (Chicago, Ill.: University of Chicago Press, 1925); Clifford Robe Shaw, Frederick McClure Zorbaugh, Henry Donald McKay, and Leonard S. Cottrell, *Delinquency Areas* (Chicago, Ill.: University of Chicago Press, 1929); Paul Goalby Cressey, *The Taxi-Dance Hall; a Sociological Study in Commercialized Recreation and City Life* (Chicago, Ill. University of Chicago Press, 1935).

5. Reid, *Social Conditions of the Negro*, 10.

6. Olga Verin Kreisberg, "Manifestations of Racial Conflict in Negro Clients of a Child Guidance Clinic: A Dissertation Based upon an Investigation at the Pittsburgh Child Guidance Center." (PhD diss., Smith College, 1944).

7. Kreisberg, "Manifestations of Racial Conflict in Negro Clients," 14.

8. Kreisberg, "Manifestations of Racial Conflict in Negro Clients," 4–7.

9. Robert Hamlett Bremner, *From the Depths; the Discovery of Poverty in the United States* (New York: New York University Press, 1956); Michael Harrington, *The Other America; Poverty in the United States* (New York: Macmillan, 1962).

10. Marcia Joyce Donnell, oral history interview by Jessica D. Klanderud, December 12, 2012, Personal Collection, Hill House Senior Services Center, 2038 Bedford Avenue, Pittsburgh, Pa.

11. Sophonisba Preston Breckinridge and Edith Abbott, *The Delinquent Child and the Home* (New York: Charities Publication Committee, 1912).

12. "Urban League of Pittsburgh: Health and Welfare: National Health Survey," in *National Urban League* (Washington, D.C.: Library of Congress, 1963); National Probation Association, "Delinquency Prevention through Coordination; "Office Files, General, Morals Court," *Urban League of Pittsburgh Records 1916–1968* (Pittsburgh, Pa.: Archives of Industrial Society, 1926); Archive Services Center, University of Pittsburgh, box 81: folder 11, no. ff 267 (1926); "Leading 'Clean-up' Crusade," *Pittsburgh Courier*, May 2, 1925; "'Healthier Babies — Stronger Mothers' Slogan of Urban League Health Week," *Pittsburgh Courier*, May 12, 1928.

13. "Healthier Babies — Stronger Mothers."

14. "Healthier Babies — Stronger Mothers."

15. Clifford Robe Shaw and Ernest Watson Burgess, *The Jack-Roller, a Delinquent Boy's Own Story* (Chicago: University of Chicago Press, 1930); "Inquisitive Visitor," *Pittsburgh Courier*, January 25, 1930; National Probation Association, "Delinquency Prevention through Coordination," in *Urban League of Pittsburgh Records* (Pittsburgh, Pa.: Archives of Industrial Society, 1936); "Office Files, General, Morals Court," in *Urban League of Pittsburgh Records 1916–1968*; Miss Carrie Starks, "Carrie's Corner," *Pittsburgh Courier*, May 23, 1925; Urban League of Pittsburgh, "Recreation Department Minutes," in *Urban League of Pittsburgh Records* (Pittsburgh, Pa.: Archives of Industrial Society, 1936); Renia Ehrenfeucht, "Constructing the Public in Urban Space: Streets, Sidewalks and Municipal Regulation in Los Angeles, 1880–1940" (PhD diss., University of California Los Angeles, 2006), 48. Ehrenfeucht documents the connections between the playground movement and organizational concerns over juvenile delinquency and unstructured play on the streets. Urban League records reveal a strong emphasis on recreation programs for African American children as an alternative to street play. Boy and Girl Scout troops, homemakers' clubs, basketball

leagues, and other recreational activities for African American children all occupied much of the Urban League's focus on African American children in the Hill District.

16. "Delinquency Prevention through Coordination."

17. "Urban League of Pittsburgh: Health and Welfare: National Health Survey"; "Delinquency Prevention through Coordination"; "Leading 'Clean-up' Crusade"; "Healthier Babies—Stronger Mothers."

18. Middle-class reform-minded African Americans often pursued higher education in the fields of social work and sociology at the University of Pittsburgh, and consequently embraced progressive reform platforms in their efforts to better the prospects for members of their race. Progressive reformers embraced the social sciences of sociology and psychology. Between 1925 and the end of World War II, a break occurred within Progressivism where reformers focused on social work and made that into a profession and continued its link to reform while others moved into academia, predominantly the Chicago School of Sociology. These academic sociologists subsequently distanced themselves from reform and focused instead on objective research.

19. "Language 'Clean-up' Campaign Is Urged by Local Citizens," *Pittsburgh Courier*, May 9, 1925, 6; "Leading 'Clean-up' Crusade"; "Delinquency Prevention through Coordination."

"Social disorganization" within the city was a major concern of scholars in sociology and reformers engaged in social work within cities focused on what they viewed as rapid change within the city of Pittsburgh. The influx of southern-born African Americans during the First World War dramatically changed Pittsburgh's African American communities, especially the streets of the Hill District. As a result, Urban League reformers perceived increases in juvenile delinquency, prostitution, crime, and general disavowal of socially approved behavior patterns on the streets of Hill District as evidence of increasing social disorganization. The Urban League tried to reform the streets by displaying proper behaviors in public venues and trying to show the greater white population that African Americans were capable of acceptable public behavior and internal morality.

20. Christine Stansell, *City of Women: Sex and Class in New York, 1789–1860* (Urbana: University of Illinois Press, 1987); Cary Goodman, *Choosing Sides: Playground and Street Life on the Lower East Side* (New York: Schocken Books, 1979); Reid, *Social Conditions of the Negro*.

21. Karl Marx, *Marx's Capital: A Student Edition*, ed. C. J. Arthur (London: Lawrence and Wishart, 1992).

22. Barbara Gaston, oral history interview by Jessica D. Klanderud, January 18, 2013, Personal Collection, Hill House Senior Services Center, 2038 Bedford Avenue, Pittsburgh, Pa.

23. "Delinquency Prevention through Coordination."

24. "Inquisitive Visitor," *Pittsburgh Courier*, January 25, 1930.

25. Gaston, oral history interview.

26. Odessa Wilson, oral history interview by Jessica D. Klanderud, January 11, 2013, Personal Collection, Hill House Senior Services Center, 2038 Bedford Avenue, Pittsburgh, Pa.; Donnell, oral history interview; Helen Mendoza, oral history interview by

Jessica D. Klanderud, January 11, 2013, Personal Collection, Hill House Senior Services Center, 2038 Bedford Avenue, Pittsburgh, Pa.

27. Robert M. Vickers, oral history interview by Jessica D. Klanderud, January 11, 2013, Personal Collection, Hill House Senior Services Center, 2038 Bedford Avenue, Pittsburgh, Pa.

28. Vickers, oral history interview.

29. Urban League of Pittsburgh, "Recreation Department Minutes"; "Delinquency Prevention through Coordination."

30. Ehrenfeucht, "Constructing the Public in Urban Space."

31. Reid, *Social Conditions of the Negro*, 14.

32. John L. Clark, "Wylie Ave.," *Pittsburgh Courier*, November 3, 1923.

33. William S. Howell, "The Kay Boys' Club: A Social Center for the Hill District. From the Program of Dedication, 10–17 September 1944, New Kay Boys' Club Building, Wylie Ave. And Green St., Pittsburgh, Pennsylvania. Essay by Director, Kay Boys' Club," 1944.

34. "Playground Has Formal Opening," *Pittsburgh Courier*, August 16, 1930.

35. "Where Do Your Children Play?," *Pittsburgh Courier*, June 25, 1938, emphasis in the original.

36. Wendell Smith, "Mayor Scully and the Recreation Problem: His Honor Ignores Appeals for Better Facilities in City Setup," *Pittsburgh Courier*, July 26, 1941.

37. Editorial, "They Need a Playground," *Pittsburgh Courier*, November 4, 1939.

38. Norine A. West, "Parents Responsible for Child Delinquency, Says Woman-Judge in Address," *Pittsburgh Courier*, March 26, 1932; "Delinquency Prevention through Coordination"; Shaw et al., *Delinquency Area*; "Office Files, General, Monthly Activities Report," in *Urban League of Pittsburgh, 1916–1968*, Archives Services Center, University of Pittsburgh, Pittsburgh, Pa., 1933.

39. "They Need a Playground."

40. "These Youths Will Lose out When WPA Cuts Curtail Supervised Play Here," *Pittsburgh Courier*, July 5, 1941.

41. M. E. Hubbard, "Crime and the Negro," *Pittsburgh Courier*, September 5, 1931.

42. Wilson, oral history interview. Squirrel Hill was (and is) a wealthy, primarily white and Jewish neighborhood where a number of African American domestic laborers worked.

43. Wilson, oral history interview.

44. Gaston, oral history interview.

45. Charlotte Boxley, oral history interview by Diana Rogers, April 25, 2008, Center for Africanamerican Urban Studies and the Economy: Remembering Africanamerican Pittsburgh Oral History Project, Carnegie Mellon University, Pittsburgh, Pa.

46. J. Warren Madden, "Correspondence: Madden to Hill District Community Council Miss Stella E. Hartman Field Secretary," in *Urban League of Pittsburgh, 1916–1968*, Archives Services Center, University of Pittsburgh, Pittsburgh, Pa., 1936.

47. John L. Clark, "Wylie Ave.," *Pittsburgh Courier*, February 25, 1956.

48. Urban League of Pittsburgh, Baby Show, Photograph, 8×10" Gelatin Silver Print, Urban League of Pittsburgh Records, 1915–1963, AIS 1981.11, Archives Service Center University of Pittsburgh, 1930–1940.

49. Breckinridge and Abbott, *The Delinquent Child and the Home*.

50. "Local Church Holding Vacation Bible School," *Pittsburgh Courier*, July 17, 1926; Chester L. Washington, "Deep Wylie," *Pittsburgh Courier*, February 23, 1929; Urban League of Pittsburgh, "Recreation Department Minutes," in Urban League of Pittsburgh Records, 1915–1963, AIS 1981.11, Archives Service Center University of Pittsburgh.

51. Elbert R. Grey Sr., oral history interview by Jessica D. Klanderud, June 25, 2008, Center for Africanamerican Urban Studies and the Economy: Remembering Africanamerican Pittsburgh Oral History Project, Carnegie Mellon University, Pittsburgh, Pa.

52. Donnell, oral history interview.

53. "What Does Your Boy Do after School?," *Pittsburgh Courier*, March 22, 1930.

54. "Courier Newsies Club Growing Rapidly," *Pittsburgh Courier*, February 22, 1930.

55. Cum Posey and John Clark, "Wylie Ave.," *Pittsburgh Courier*, February 15, 1941.

56. Grey, oral history interview.

57. Grey, oral history interview.

58. Shaw and Burgess, *The Jack-Roller*; "Juvenile Gangs Spread Havoc throughout City," *Pittsburgh Courier*, June 14, 1941.

59. "Juvenile Gangs Spread Havoc throughout City."

60. Reid, *Social Conditions of the Negro*, 71, 75, 76–78.

61. Donnell, oral history interview.

62. Wilson, oral history interview.

63. Mendoza, oral history interview.

64. "How's Your Neighborhood?," *Pittsburgh Courier*, July 26, 1947.

65. "How's Your Neighborhood?"

Chapter Three

1. Dewayne Ketchum, oral history phone interview by Jessica D. Klanderud, April 14, 2016, Personal Collection.

2. John L. Clark, "Wylie Ave.," *Pittsburgh Courier*, April 19, 1930.

3. John L. Clark, "Wylie Ave.," *Pittsburgh Courier*, April 12, 1930.

4. Charles "Teenie" Harris, *Dolores Stanton and Eleanor Hughes Griffin standing in front of George Harris' confectionery store, 2121 Wylie Avenue, Hill District, July 1937*, gelatin silver print, Carnegie Museum of Art, Pittsburgh, Charles "Teenie" Harris Archive.

5. Charles A. Harris, oral history interview by Jessica D. Klanderud, January 1, 2009, Center for Africanamerican Urban Studies and the Economy: Remembering Africanamerican Pittsburgh, Carnegie Mellon University, Pittsburgh, Pa.

6. Marcia Joyce Donnell, oral history interview by Jessica D. Klanderud, December 12, 2012, Personal Collection, Hill House Senior Services Center, 2038 Bedford Avenue, Pittsburgh, Pa.

7. Donnell, oral history interview.

8. Harris, oral history interview.

9. "Leroy Jones" (alias chosen by interviewee), oral history interview by Jessica D. Klanderud, January 18, 2013, Personal Collection, Hill House Senior Services Center, 2038 Bedford Avenue, Pittsburgh, Pa.

10. "Leroy Jones," oral history interview.

11. "Leroy Jones," oral history interview.

12. John L. Clark, "Wylie Ave.," *Pittsburgh Courier*, March 8, 1930.

13. "Frogs Announce 1930 Program of Brilliant Events," *Pittsburgh Courier*, June 21, 1930.

14. Jule Bumry, "Hoppin' with the Frogs," *Pittsburgh Courier*, August 20, 1932.

15. "Ducks' Dance and Coming of Collegians Attract," *Pittsburgh Courier*, March 26, 1932.

16. "Old Clothes, Vogue at Depression Dance," *Pittsburgh Courier*, March 19, 1932.

17. "Old Clothes, Vogue at Depression Dance."

18. "Old Clothes, Vogue at Depression Dance."

19. "Charming Matrons Plan Novelty 'Depression Dance,'" *Pittsburgh Courier*, March 12, 1932.

20. Editorial, "H-E-L-P-!," *Pittsburgh Courier*, November 22, 1930.

21. "H-E-L-P-!"

22. John L. Clark, "Burroughs and Powell Both Wrong," *Pittsburgh Courier*, January 24, 1931.

23. Clark, "Burroughs and Powell Both Wrong."

24. J. H. N. Waring Jr., "What Does the Depression Mean to Pa. Boys, Girls? Well-Known Educator Asks," *Pittsburgh Courier*, May 13, 1933.

25. "H-E-L-P-!"

26. "'New Radicalism among Negroes' Says Logan," *Pittsburgh Courier*, July 8, 1933.

27. "The Depression and the Negro," *Pittsburgh Courier*, October 18, 1930.

28. "Our Depression Largely Impression," *Pittsburgh Courier*, October 3, 1931.

29. "Negro's Economic Status Weighted by New Burdens," *Pittsburgh Courier*, December 12, 1931.

30. Algernon B. Jackson, "Week-End Mosaics," *Pittsburgh Courier*, December 31, 1932.

31. John L. Clark, "Wylie Avenue Pittsburgh," *Pittsburgh Courier*, December 17, 1932.

32. "Rum-Runners Get Very Low Salary of $25," *Pittsburgh Courier*, October 22, 1932.

33. It is difficult to estimate the number of sex workers working within the Hill District at any one time or where they conducted their business, but historians like Ruth Rosen and Timothy Gilfoyle suggested that house-based sex work was more normative from the 1880s–1920s, while street walking emerged later. This transition coincided with a move from female-dominated sex work to a male-dominated system where female sex workers operated their business under the supervision and domination of a male pimp. See also Ruth Rosen, *The Lost Sisterhood: Prostitution in America, 1900–1918* (Baltimore, Md.: Johns Hopkins University Press, 1994); Timothy Gilfoyle, *City of Eros: New York City, Prostitution, and the Commercialization of Sex, 1790–1920* (New York: W. W. Norton, 1992); and "Prostitutes in History: From Parables of Pornography to Metaphors of Modernity," *American Historical Review* 104, no. 1 (1999) 117–41; Kevin Mumford, *Interzones: Black/White Sex Districts in Chicago and New York in*

the Early Twentieth Century (New York: Columbia University Press, 1997); Cynthia M. Blair, *I've Got to Make My Livin': Black Women's Sex Work in Turn-of-the-Century Chicago* (Chicago: University of Chicago Press, 2010)

34. "Our Cabbie Tells How He Helped a Girl to 'Walk Straight' Again," *Pittsburgh Courier*, April 27, 1935.

35. "Our Cabbie Tells How He Helped a Girl to 'Walk Straight' Again."

36. "Our Cabbie Tells How He Helped a Girl to 'Walk Straight' Again."

37. John L. Clark, "Wylie Ave.," *Pittsburgh Courier*, April 5, 1930.

38. Clark, "Wylie Ave.," April 5, 1930.

39. Clark, "Wylie Ave.," April 5, 1930.

40. Harry B. Webber, "Few Race Leaders Attend Hill Vice Committee Meet," *Pittsburgh Courier*, August 14, 1926.

41. "Revoke License of Paramount 'Inn,'" *Pittsburgh Courier*, March 28, 1925.

42. "Revoke License of Paramount 'Inn.'"

43. "Language 'Clean-up' Campaign Is Urged by Local Citizens," *Pittsburgh Courier*, May 9, 1925.

44. Chester L. Washington, "Up and Down the Avenue," *Pittsburgh Courier*, December 2, 1939.

45. Ira De A. Reid, *Social Conditions of the Negro in the Hill District of Pittsburgh; Survey Conducted under the Direction of Ira De A. Reid, Director, Department of Research, the National Urban League*, University of Pittsburgh Digital Research Library, Pittsburgh, Pa., 1999, 1930, 60.

46. Reid, *Social Conditions of the Negro*, 63.

47. "Up and Down the Avenue," *Pittsburgh Courier*, July 20, 1940.

48. John L. Clark, "Wylie Ave.," *Pittsburgh Courier*, October 13, 1945.

49. Robin D. G. Kelley, "Congested Terrain: Resistance on Public Transportation," in *Race Rebels: Culture, Politics, and the Black Working Class* (New York: Free Press, 1996), 57–58. This concept of theaters of public space is crucial to understanding the nature of public space in Pittsburgh's African American community.

50. Jason Klanderud, Prostitution Areas as Noted by Ira De Reid in 1929 Survey. This is a map (3.1) created from the information in Reid's survey.

51. Charles Teenie Harris, *Brick-paved alley behind houses with dilapidated fence and debris*, black and white: Kodak Safety Film, 2001.35.7542, Carnegie Museum of Art, Pittsburgh, Pa., 1938–1950.

52. Kelley, "Congested Terrain," 64.

53. John L. Clark, "Close up Dives in Hill District, Police-Federal Officers Urged," *Pittsburgh Courier*, December 12, 1925; "Police Raid Six Places," *Pittsburgh Courier*, November 16, 1946.

54. John L. Clark, "Wylie Ave.," *Pittsburgh Courier*, July 2, 1927.

55. Clark, "Wylie Ave.," July 2, 1927.

Chapter Four

1. Dewayne Ketchum, oral history phone interview by Jessica D. Klanderud, April 14, 2016, Personal Collection.

2. Alexander, "The Great Migration in Comparative Perspective: Interpreting the Urban Origins of Southern Black Migrants to Depression-Era Pittsburgh," *Social Science History* 22, no. 3 (1998); Joe W. Trotter, Jr. and Jared Day, *Race and Renaissance: African Americans in Pittsburgh since World War II* (Pittsburgh, PA: University of Pittsburgh Press, 2010); Laurence Glasco, "Double Burden: The Black Experience in Pittsburgh," http://www.angelfire.com/jazz/larryglasco/H1669/Burden.pdf; John Bodnar, Roger Simon, and Michael P. Weber, *Lives of Their Own: Blacks, Italians, and Poles in Pittsburgh, 1900–1960* (Champaign, Ill.: University of Illinois Press, 1983); Frank E. Bolden, "My Fight with the Devil," *Pittsburgh Courier*, November 3, 1951.

3. Bessie Holloway, "The Convenient Accused," *Pittsburgh Courier*, January 9, 1943, emphasis in the original.

4. Marjorie McKenzie, "Pursuit of Democracy," *Pittsburgh Courier*, January 30, 1943.

5. Charles "Teenie" Harris, *Soldiers from 372nd Infantry marching in parade, Fifth Avenue, Downtown, July 1942*, gelatin silver print mounted on cardboard, Carnegie Museum of Art, Pittsburgh. Gift of the Estate of Charles "Teenie" Harris, 1996.69.137, Charles "Teenie" Harris Archive.

6. "Pythians to Invade City," *Pittsburgh Courier*, July 21, 1928; "State Elks Invade City," *Pittsburgh Courier*, June 22, 1935; "Urban League Holds Better Baby Contest," *Pittsburgh Courier*, June 14, 1924.

7. "Urban League Holds Better Baby Contest."

8. "Move Ahead with 'Trade Week' Plans," *Pittsburgh Courier*, August 26, 1939.

9. "Mammouth BPA Parade, Marked by Floats, Bands Marching Units Introduces Negro Trade Week to 'Smoky City'!," *Pittsburgh Courier*, September 13, 1941.

10. "Refused Permit, Protest, Jailed," *Pittsburgh Courier*, October 6, 1934; "Views of Other Editors," *Pittsburgh Courier*, June 4, 1927.

11. Marcia Joyce Donnell, oral history interview by Jessica D. Klanderud, December 12, 2012, Personal Collection, Hill House Senior Services Center, 2038 Bedford Avenue, Pittsburgh, Pa.

12. "Leroy Jones" (alias chosen by interviewee), oral history interview by Jessica D. Klanderud, January 18, 2013, Personal Collection, Hill House Senior Services Center, 2038 Bedford Avenue, Pittsburgh, Pa.

13. Barbara Gaston, oral history interview by Jessica D. Klanderud, January 18, 2013, *Personal* Collection, Hill House Senior Services Center, 2038 Bedford Avenue, Pittsburgh, Pa.

14. Odessa Wilson, oral history interview by Jessica D. Klanderud, January 11, 2013, Personal Collection, Hill House Senior Services Center, 2038 Bedford Avenue, Pittsburgh, Pa.

15. "Arthur" (name omitted at interviewee's request, alias chosen by interviewee), oral history interview by Jessica D. Klanderud, January 18, 2013, Personal Collection, Hill House Senior Services Center, 2038 Bedford Avenue, Pittsburgh, Pa.

16. Rev. John Welch, interview by Jessica D. Klanderud, July 14, 2008, Center for Africanamerican Urban Studies and the Economy: Remembering Africanamerican Pittsburgh Oral History Project, Carnegie Mellon University, Pittsburgh, Pa.

17. Ketchum, oral history phone interview.

18. "Police and Minority Groups," in *Fair Employment Practices Committee*, National Archives - Mid-Atlantic Region, Philadelphia, Pa., 1945, 1–2.

19. "Improvement of Deportment of Car-Riding Public," in *Fair Employment Practices Committee*, National Archives - Mid-Atlantic Region, Philadelphia, Pa., 1945.

20. Milo to Mr. G. James Fleming Many, Regional Director, "Memorandum: Re: Pittsburgh Railways Co. November 1, 1944," in *Fair Employment Practices Committee*, National Archives - Mid-Atlantic Region, Philadelphia, Pa., 1944.

21. Greater Pittsburgh Citizens' Coordinating Committee, "Report on the Pittsburgh Railways Company," in *Fair Employment Practices Committee*, National Archives - Mid-Atlantic Region, Philadelphia, Pa., 1945.

22. "Report on the Pittsburgh Railways Company," 2.

23. "Report on the Pittsburgh Railways Company," 4.

24. "Report on the Pittsburgh Railways Company," 5.

25. "Report on the Pittsburgh Railways Company," 5

26. Robin D. G. Kelley, "Congested Terrain: Resistance on Public Transportation," in *Race Rebels: Culture, Politics, and the Black Working Class* (New York: The Free Press, 1994), 56–57.

27. Paul L. Jones, "Facts and Figures on - City of Pittsburgh's Housing for Negroes," *Pittsburgh Courier*, April 29, 1950.

28. Jason Klanderud, "Lower Hill Street Layout." This is map 4.1, created for this chapter using a historic map of the Hill District to orient the streets to each other.

29. "Robin to Speak at Hill District Forum at IKS," *Pittsburgh Courier*, April 25, 1953.

30. "Redevelopment to Erase Blight in Hill District," *Pittsburgh Courier*, September 23, 1950.

31. Jones, "Facts and Figures on - City of Pittsburgh's Housing for Negroes."

32. Gaines T. Bradford, "Problems of Relocation of Negro Families; a Statement by Gaines T. Bradford, Director of Community Services, Urban League of Pittsburgh, before the United States Senate Subcommittee on Housing, in the New Post Office Building, Pittsburgh Pennsylvania, December 13, 1957," in *Urban League of Pittsburgh: Administration Department, Affiliates File, National Urban League* (Washington, D.C.: Library of Congress, 1957), p. 4.

33. "The Pittsburgh Press and Low-Cost Housing," *Pittsburgh Courier*, September 2, 1950.

34. "The Pittsburgh Press and Low-Cost Housing."

35. R. Maurice Moss, "Letter: March 9, 1950 to Alexander J. Allen, Executive Secretary, Urban League of Pittsburgh," in *Urban League of Pittsburgh: Administration Department, Affiliates File National Urban League* (Washington, D.C.: Library of Congress, 1950). Percival Prattis was active in the Urban League of Pittsburgh and was on staff at the *Pittsburgh Courier*.

36. Marion B. Jordan, "Letter to the Editor," *Pittsburgh Post-Gazette*, n.d., included in September 3, 1957 letter to Mr. Madison S. Jones, Housing Specialist, NAACP National Office, in *National Association for the Advancement of Colored People* (Washington, D.C.: Library of Congress, 1957).

37. Bradford, "Problems of Relocation of Negro Families."

38. Bradford, "Problems of Relocation of Negro Families."

39. "Loendi Members Must Plan for New Location," *Pittsburgh Courier*, November 16, 1957.

40. "Redevelopment to Be Topic of Forum Meetings," *Pittsburgh Courier*, March 28, 1953.

41. "Redevelopment to Be Topic of Forum Meetings."

42. Donnell, oral history interview.

43. "Robin Explains Relocation to Hill District Businessmen," *Pittsburgh Courier*, January 31, 1953.

44. Jason Klanderud, "Transformation of Lower Hill District from Construction of Civic Arena and Crosstown Parkway." This is map 4.2, created for this chapter to show the location of the Civic Arena in relation to the streets of the Lower Hill District.

45. "Test Borings Start on 'Deep Wylie,'" *Pittsburgh Courier*, September 25, 1954.

46. John L. Clark, "Wylie Ave.," *Pittsburgh Courier*, January 23, 1954.

47. "A Statement from the Commission on Human Relations before the Senate Sub-Committee on Housing," 1.

48. "A Statement from the Commission on Human Relations before the Senate Sub-Committee on Housing," 12.

49. "Hill District Community Council Should Reflect Area's Redevelopment Views," *Pittsburgh Courier*, September 20, 1952.

50. R. Maurice Moss, "Testimony before the Joint Congressional Committee to Investigate Housing, Statement of the Urban League of Pittsburgh, Presented in Pittsburgh, PA—October 10, 1957," in *Urban League of Pittsburgh: Administration Department, Affiliates File, National Urban League* (Washington, D.C.: Library of Congress, 1957).

51. Alexander, "The Great Migration in Comparative Perspective."

52. George Barbour, "Word on Lower Hill: 'Say Goodbye Next Spring,'" *Pittsburgh Courier*, August 27, 1955.

53. Barbour, "Word on Lower Hill: 'Say Goodbye Next Spring.'"

54. Ralph E. Koger, "Councilman Jones Homer Green Clash!," *Pittsburgh Courier*, April 13, 1957.

55. Koger, "Councilman Jones Homer Green Clash!"

56. "600 Block, Wylie Ave., to Be Razed May 1," *Pittsburgh Courier*, April 14, 1951.

57. John L. Clark, "Wylie Ave.," *Pittsburgh Courier*, February 14, 1953.

58. Clark, "Wylie Ave.," February 14, 1953.

59. Clark, "Wylie Ave.," February 14, 1953.

60. "Hill Office Open to Give Answers," *Pittsburgh Courier*, April 14, 1956.

61. Jones, "Facts and Figures on - City of Pittsburgh's Housing for Negroes," *Pittsburgh Courier*, April 29, 1950.

62. "Hill Office Open to Give Answers"; "Hill Residents Can Purchase New Homes," *Pittsburgh Courier*, July 14, 1956.

63. Marion B. Jordon, "A Statement by Mrs. Marion B Jordon, Executive Secretary, Pittsburgh Branch of the National Association for the Advancement of Colored People, (NAACP) before the Senate Sub-Committee on Housing, Friday, December 13, 1957, 2 P.M., New Post Office Building, Grant Street, Court Room #3,

8th Floor," in NAACP Branch Geographical File: Pittsburgh Pa., *National Association for the Advancement of Colored People* (Washington, D.C.: Library of Congress, 1957).

64. "A Statement by Mrs. Marion B. Jordon."

65. "HCIA Prexy Says Neighborhood Burdened with Taverns, No Police and Youth Mobs," *Pittsburgh Courier*, October 19, 1957.

66. "Homewood-Frankstown Businesses for Sale," *Pittsburgh Courier*, September 11, 1954; George E. Barbour, "Whites Fight Exodus, Negroes Decry Homes Prices in Homewood," *Pittsburgh Courier*, July 16, 1955; George Barbour, "Shopping Center May Get 'Green Light,'" *Pittsburgh Courier*, March 24, 1956.

67. "A Statement from the Commission on Human Relations before the Senate Sub-Committee on Housing."

68. "A Statement by Mrs. Marion B. Jordon."

69. Barbour, "Shopping Center May Get 'Green Light.'"

70. Barbour, "Whites Fight Exodus, Negroes Decry Homes Prices in Homewood."

71. "New Home Building Here Declines for 2nd Month," *Pittsburgh Courier*, November 4, 1950.

72. "Want to Live in Upper Hill," *Pittsburgh Courier*, October 27, 1956.

73. "Plan Three Housing Projects," *Pittsburgh Courier*, December 14, 1957.

74. "Plan Three Housing Projects."

75. "Council Delays Action on Herron Hill Tower," *Pittsburgh Courier*, February 26, 1955.

76. "Upper 5th Ward Area to Be Redeveloped," *Pittsburgh Courier*, May 2, 1953.

77. "Council Delays Action on Herron Hill Tower," *Pittsburgh Courier*, February 26, 1955.

78. Hazel Garland, "Things to Talk About," *Pittsburgh Courier*, December 12, 1953.

79. Harold L. Keith, "Young's Backers Blast Condition of Houses. Streets in Hill District," *Pittsburgh Courier*, October 3, 1953.

80. John L. Clark, "Wylie Ave.," *Pittsburgh Courier*, February 14, 1953.

81. John L. Clark, "Wylie Ave.," *Pittsburgh Courier*, March 18, 1961.

82. "Challenge," *Pittsburgh Courier*, October 21, 1950.

83. "New Home Building Here Declines for 2nd Month."

84. "Court Battle Blocks Housing; Aids Slums," *Pittsburgh Courier*, August 29, 1953.

85. "Redevelopment Authority Hears Need for Homes," *Pittsburgh Courier*, November 19, 1955.

Chapter Five

1. "Heart Attack Causes Death of Leon Clark," *Pittsburgh Courier*, April 22, 1950.

2. Otto A. Davis and Norman J. Johnson, "The Jitneys: A Study of Grassroots Capitalism," *Journal of Contemporary Studies* 7, no. 1 (Winter 1984): 81–102. Davis and Johnson identified at least three distinct types of jitney services: line-haul jitneys competed with public transportation such as streetcars or buses, the second type of jitney served entry points into the city, and the third type assisted shoppers home from grocery stores.

3. John L. Clark, "Wylie Ave.," *Pittsburgh Courier*, May 16, 1953.

4. "Jitney Drivers Sing the 'Blues' as Cops Arrest Them in Big Slues," *Pittsburgh Courier*, May 1, 1954.

5. "Jitney Drivers Sing the 'Blues.'"

6. John L. Clark, "Wylie Ave.," *Pittsburgh Courier*, December 14, 1957.

7. Clark, "Wylie Ave.," December 14, 1957.

8. Marcia Joyce Donnell, oral history interview by Jessica D. Klanderud, December 12, 2012, Personal Collection, Hill House Senior Services Center, 2038 Bedford Avenue, Pittsburgh, Pa.

9. Donnell, oral history interview.

10. "Leroy Jones" (alias chosen by interviewee), oral history interview by Jessica D. Klanderud, January 18, 2013, Personal Collection, Hill House Senior Services Center, 2038 Bedford Avenue, Pittsburgh, Pa.

11. Donnell, oral history interview; Sarah Tomlin, oral history interview by Jessica D. Klanderud, December 12, 2012, Personal Collection, Hill House Senior Services Center, 2038 Bedford Avenue, Pittsburgh, Pa.

12. Jeanne S. Scott, "Branch Report, December 11, 1947," in *NAACP Branch Geographical File: Pittsburgh PA, National Association for the Advancement of Colored People* (Washington, D.C.: Library of Congress, 1947).

13. "Cop 'Blackjacks' Owl Cab Driver," *Pittsburgh Courier*, October 20, 1956.

14. "Cop 'Blackjacks' Owl Cab Driver."

15. "Cop 'Blackjacks' Owl Cab Driver."

16. John L. Clark, "Wylie Ave.," *Pittsburgh Courier*, December 14, 1957.

17. Clark, "Wylie Ave.," December 14, 1957.

18. Donnell, oral history interview.

19. John L. Clark, "Wylie Ave.," December 14, 1957.

20. John L. Clark, "Wylie Ave.," *Pittsburgh Courier*, April 11, 1953.

21. John L. Clark, "Wylie Ave.," *Pittsburgh Courier*, March 7, 1953.

22. John L. Clark, "Wylie Ave.," *Pittsburgh Courier*, February 7, 1953.

23. Editorials, *Pittsburgh Courier*, June 27, 1959.

24. "Police Department Must Clean House," *Pittsburgh Courier*, February 20, 1954.

25. John L. Clark, "Wylie Ave.," *Pittsburgh Courier*, April 17, 1954.

26. George S. Schuyler, "'Revolt' Blamed for Loss of Police Respect," *Pittsburgh Courier*, February 19, 1966.

27. Marion B. Jordon, "Report of the Executive Secretary - June 7, 1956 NAACP Branch Geographical File: Pittsburgh Pa.," in *National Association for the Advancement of Colored People* (Washington, D.C.: Library of Congress, 1956).

28. John L. Clark, "Wylie Ave.," *Pittsburgh Courier*, March 25, 1950.

29. John L. Clark, "Wylie Ave.," *Pittsburgh Courier*, May 24, 1958.

30. "LeRoy Jones," oral history interview; Donnell, oral history interview; Tomlin, oral history interview.

31. "'Con' Games Flourishing in District," *Pittsburgh Courier*, September 22, 1951.

32. Frank E. Bolden, "Heroes in Blue," *Pittsburgh Courier*, July 23, 1955.

33. Bolden, "Heroes in Blue," *Pittsburgh Courier*, September 19, 1955; Bolden, "Heroes in Blue," *Pittsburgh Courier*, October 1, 1955; Bolden, "Heroes in Blue," *Pittsburgh Courier*, October 15, 1955.

34. Ralph E. Koger, "Director Rosenberg Has Chance to Name More Negroes as Detectives . . . Will He?," *Pittsburgh Courier*, November 7, 1959.

35. Koger, "Director Rosenberg Has Chance to Name More Negroes."

36. "Jaundiced Justice," *Pittsburgh Courier*, September 20, 1952.

37. John L. Clark, "Political Picture," *Pittsburgh Courier*, October 6, 1945.

38. "Destout Gets to Know Vicemongers," *Pittsburgh Courier*, July 14, 1956.

39. "Destout Gets to Know Vicemongers."

40. "Dope Suspect Has Marihuana Fields near Pitt Stadium," *Pittsburgh Courier*, July 7, 1951.

41. "Dope for 'Teen Angers' Subject of Hill Forum," *Pittsburgh Courier*, April 7, 1951.

42. "Dope for 'Teen Angers' Subject of Hill Forum."

43. "Police Raid Teen-Age Den," *Pittsburgh Courier*, December 8, 1951.

44. "Police Raid Teen-Age Den."

45. Frank E. Bolden, "My Fight with the Devil," *Pittsburgh Courier*, December 1, 1951; "LeRoy Jones," oral history interview.

46. "Blames Thefts on Dope Habit," *Pittsburgh Courier*, September 15, 1951.

47. "Blames Thefts on Dope Habit."

48. Bolden, "My Fight with the Devil."

49. Bolden, "My Fight with the Devil."

50. Bolden, "My Fight with the Devil."

51. Frank E. Bolden, "King Count Frank Tells How a Woman Ruined Him," *Pittsburgh Courier*, November 10, 1951.

52. Bolden, "King Count Frank Tells How a Woman Ruined Him."

53. Bolden, "King Count Frank Tells How a Woman Ruined Him."

54. Bolden, "King Count Frank Tells How a Woman Ruined Him."

55. Bolden, "King Count Frank Tells How a Woman Ruined Him."

56. Donnell, oral history interview.

57. Frank E. Bolden, "King Count Frank," *Pittsburgh Courier*, November 24, 1951.

58. "LeRoy Jones," oral history interview.

59. Charles "Teenie" Harris, *Funeral procession for Leon "Pigmeat" Clark, with women holding floral arrangement, including Ruby Wheeler Woods front right, on Webster Avenue, Hill District, April 19, 1950*, black-and-white, Kodak safety film, Carnegie Museum of Art, Pittsburgh. Heinz Family Fund, 2001.35.3241, Charles "Teenie" Harris Archive; Charles A. Harris, oral history interview by Benjamin Houston, January 1, 2009, Center for Africanamerican Urban Studies and the Economy: Remembering Africanamerican Pittsburgh, Carnegie Mellon University, Pittsburgh, Pa.

60. "Police Douse Lights on 'Nocturnal Sisterhood,'" *Pittsburgh Courier*, August 29, 1953.

61. John L. Clark, "Wylie Ave.," *Pittsburgh Courier*, December 14, 1957.

62. Clark, "Wylie Ave.," December 14, 1957.

63. Jason Klanderud, Prostitution Shift as Noted by John L. Clark's "Wylie Ave." column from July 17, 1957. This is map 5.1 created for this project using data from Wylie Ave.

64. John L. Clark, "Wylie Ave.," *Pittsburgh Courier*, August 4, 1956.

65. "Four Arrested on Morals Charges," *Pittsburgh Courier*, June 2, 1951.

66. John L. Clark, "Wylie Ave.," *Pittsburgh Courier*, April 14, 1956.

67. John L. Clark, "Wylie Ave.," *Pittsburgh Courier*, May 23, 1953.

68. "Woman Shoots after He 'Tried to Put Me on Dope,'" *Pittsburgh Courier*, June 15, 1957.

69. "LeRoy Jones," oral history interview.

70. Jason Klanderud, Dinwiddie Street and Fifth Avenue High School. This is map 5.2 created to show the location of Dinwiddie Street and Fith Ave High School from LeRoy Jones interview.

71. "LeRoy Jones," oral history interview.

72. John L. Clark, "Wylie Ave.," *Pittsburgh Courier*, January 26, 1957.

73. John L. Clark, "Wylie Ave.," *Pittsburgh Courier*, December 14, 1957.

74. John L. Clark, "Wylie Ave.," *Pittsburgh Courier*, February 24, 1962.

Chapter Six

1. "New NAACP Secretary," *New Pittsburgh Courier*, April 15, 1967, 5.

2. Quoted in Laurence Glasco, "The Civil Rights Movement in Pittsburgh: To Make This City 'Some Place Special,'" unpublished scholarly article, University of Pittsburgh.

3. Alma S. Fox, oral history interview by Johanna Hernandez, July 26, 2007, Center for Africanamerican Urban Studies and the Economy: Remembering Africanamerican Pittsburgh, Carnegie Mellon University, Pittsburgh, Pa.

4. Quoted in Ralph Proctor Jr., *Voices from the Firing Line: A Personal Account of the Pittsburgh Civil Rights Movement* (Pittsburgh, Pa.: Introspec Press, 2014), 208.

5. Proctor, *Voices from the Firing Line*, 209.

6. Civic Unity Council, "Highland Park Swimming Pool: Season of 1950," in *National Association for the Advancement of Colored People*, Archives Services Center, University of Pittsburgh, Pittsburgh, Pa., 1950, 2.

7. Civic Unity Council, "Highland Park Swimming Pool: Season of 1950."

8. "Officer Stabbed, Bathers Hurt in Riot at City Pool," *Pittsburgh Post-Gazette*, August 21, 1931.

9. "Officer Stabbed, Bathers Hurt in Riot at City Pool."

10. "Pittsburgh NAACP to End Pool Bias in County by July," *Pittsburgh Courier*, November 10, 1951.

11. "Atty. Richard Jones, NAACP Prexy, Tells Negro Citizens to Use Highland Park Pool," *Pittsburgh Courier*, July 28, 1951.

12. "Atty. Richard Jones, NAACP Prexy, Tells Negro Citizens to Use Highland Park Pool."

13. "Release 3 Youths as Probe Goes On," *Pittsburgh Courier*, August 25, 1951.

14. Civic Unity Council, "Highland Park Swimming Pool: Season of 1948," in *National Association for the Advancement of Colored People*, Archives Services Center, University of Pittsburgh, Pittsburgh, Pa., 1948.

15. "Highland Park Swimming Pool: Season of 1949," in *National Association for the Advancement of Colored People*, Archives Services Center, University of Pittsburgh, Pittsburgh, Pa., 1949.

16. Copy of Letter No. 1, Office of the Mayor, David L. Lawrence to Youth for Wallace, July 29, 1948, in *National Association for the Advancement of Colored People*, Archives Services Center, University of Pittsburgh, Pittsburgh, Pa., 1948, 5.

17. Letter No. 3, Ms. Esther Bliss to Mr. Howard B. Stewart, August 3, 1948, in *National Association for the Advancement of Colored People*, Archives Services Center, University of Pittsburgh, Pittsburgh, Pa., 1948.

18. "Highland Park Pool Scene of More Disorder," *Pittsburgh Post-Gazette*, August 23, 1948.

19. "Albert Guilty of Riot Plot at Highland Pool," *Pittsburgh Post-Gazette*, April 25, 1950.

20. "Albert Guilty of Riot Plot at Highland Pool."

21. "Retrial Denied in Highland Pool Riot Case," *Pittsburgh Post-Gazette*, July 21, 1951.

22. "Release 3 Youths as Probe Goes On."

23. "Rights Leaders Pledge Closer Cooperation at Civil Rights Picnic," *Pittsburgh Courier*, August 28, 1965.

24. Marcia Joyce Donnell, oral history interview by Jessica D. Klanderud, December 12, 2012, Personal Collection, Hill House Senior Services Center, 2038 Bedford Avenue, Pittsburgh, Pa.

25. Donnell, oral history interview.

26. Sala Udin, oral history interview by Johanna Hernandez and Benjamin Houston, July 23, 2007, Center for Africanamerican Urban Studies and the Economy: Remembering Africanamerican Pittsburgh Oral History Project, Carnegie Mellon University, Pittsburgh, Pa.

27. "Arena Improves Hiring Policy," *Pittsburgh Courier*, October 28, 1961.

28. "Braun's Tells NAACP 'We'll Hire Negroes,'" *Pittsburgh Courier*, June 23, 1962.

29. Charles "Teenie" Harris, *Protest March with Women and Men Holding Signs for Equal Rights and CORE, Heading Toward Downtown on Centre Avenue with Epiphany Church in background*, c. 1960–1968, black-and-white, Kodak safety film, Carnegie Museum of Art, Pittsburgh. Charles "Teenie" Harris Archive.

30. Arthur J. Edmunds, *Daybreakers: The Story of the Urban League of Pittsburgh, the First Sixty-Five Years* (Pittsburgh, Pa.: Urban League of Pittsburgh, 1983), 113–15.

31. "UNPC to Prod City on 'No-Negro' Bureaus and Visit U.S. Coordinators," *Pittsburgh Courier*, September 25, 1965.

32. "UNPC to Sit Down with A & P Heads," *Pittsburgh Courier*, January 8, 1966.

33. "BPA Protests CTS's New Move," *Pittsburgh Courier*, July 2, 1966.

34. "UNPC, A&P Now Talking Same Language," *Pittsburgh Courier*, February 26, 1966.

35. "King, Powell Unit May Both Visit Pittsburgh," *Pittsburgh Courier*, August 28, 1965.

36. The terms *skilled* and *unskilled* labor are complicated. Manual laborers that do not have union membership or affiliation are not *unskilled*. All laborers exhibit skill in their work. Extra education and training do not inherently make one worker more skilled than another. Union membership, likewise, does not inherently make one worker more skilled than another but the terms do delineate between workers with a greater degree of training and therefore access to positions with higher pay.

37. "Kaufmann's to Integrate Work Force," *Pittsburgh Courier*, March 19, 1966.

38. "Store Was Given an Ultimatum," *Pittsburgh Courier*, February 26, 1966.

39. "Met with 105 Businessmen," *Pittsburgh Courier*, July 16, 1966.

40. "Warn PAT on Hiring Policies," *Pittsburgh Courier*, March 12, 1966.

41. "CORE Becomes Non-Violently Active Here," *Pittsburgh Courier*, June 28, 1952.

42. "CORE Becomes Non-Violently Active Here."

43. "Pastors Hold Civil Rights Series," *Pittsburgh Courier*, November 18, 1961.

44. "NAACP, NALC to Picket New Arena!," *Pittsburgh Courier*, October 21, 1961.

45. "Arena Improves Hiring Policy," *Pittsburgh Courier*, October 28, 1961.

46. Ralph E. Koger, "UNPC Tests Union Bias Many Ways," *Pittsburgh Courier*, August 21, 1965.

47. David Lawrence, "Economic Basis behind Civil Rights Struggle," *Rome News-Tribune* (Rome, GA), June 9, 1963.

48. "Hill District Street-Sweeping Plan Adopted in City Clean-up Effort," *Pittsburgh Courier*, July 31, 1965.

49. Ralph E. Koger, "Inspector Kelly Tells Hill Leader," *Pittsburgh Courier*, June 4, 1966.

50. Koger, "Inspector Kelly Tells Hill Leader."

51. "Leroy Jones" (alias chosen by interviewee), oral history interview by Jessica D. Klanderud, January 18, 2013, Personal Collection, Hill House Senior Services Center, 2038 Bedford Avenue, Pittsburgh, Pa.

52. Donnell, oral history interview.

53. "Expands 'Filth' Drive," *Pittsburgh Courier*, June 12, 1965.

54. "Expands 'Filth' Drive."

55. "Pittsburgh This Week," *Pittsburgh Courier*, December 15, 1962.

56. "New Transit Ideas Presented at PAT-UNPC Summit Meeting," *Pittsburgh Courier*, March 19, 1966.

57. New Transit Ideas Presented at PAT-UNPC Summit Meeting."

58. New Transit Ideas Presented at PAT-UNPC Summit Meeting."

59. "Courier Drive Bears Fruit—Trolleys Going," *Pittsburgh Courier*, February 26, 1966.

60. "BPA Protests CTS's New Move," *Pittsburgh Courier*, July 2, 1966.

61. Charles "Teenie" Harris, *Men and women boarding the 85 Bedford trolley with billboard in background advertising Heinz green pea soup, Hill District, October 1946*, black-and-white, Ansco safety film, Carnegie Museum of Art, Pittsburgh. Heinz Family Fund, 2001.35.6700, Charles "Teenie" Harris Archive.

62. "On the Hill," *New Pittsburgh Courier*, June 24, 1967.

63. "On the Hill."

64. "On the Hill."

65. "UNPC Will Hold Supper and Evening of Music," *Pittsburgh Courier*, February 20, 1965.

66. "Courier Drive Bears Fruit—Trolleys Going," *New Pittsburgh Courier*, February 26, 1966.

67. "Harrisburg 'March' on Rights Scheduled," *Pittsburgh Press*, December 2, 1965.

68. "Scranton Gets Bill to Make Poverty Centers Slumlord Repositories," *Pittsburgh Courier*, December 25, 1965.

69. Carl Morris, comment, *New Pittsburgh Courier*, November 11, 1967.

70. Morris, comment.

71. Morris, comment.

72. Langston Hughes, *Pittsburgh Courier*, August 21, 1965.

73. "Out of the Ashes Someone Better Learn New Negro," *Pittsburgh Courier*, August 28, 1965.

74. "Bond Issue Puts in Focus Civil Rights Vs. Viet Nam," *New Pittsburgh Courier*, February 5, 1966.

75. J. A. Rogers, "History Shows," *New Pittsburgh Courier*, January 1, 1966.

76. Ethel Payne, "The 'Inhuman' War in Viet Is SCLC's Battleground," *New Pittsburgh Courier*, August 26, 1967.

77. Payne, "The 'Inhuman' War in Viet Is SCLC's Battleground."

Chapter Seven

1. Mark Whitaker, *Smoketown: The Untold Story of the Other Great Black Renaissance* (New York: Simon and Schuster, 2018), 310–11, 323.

2. Whitaker, *Smoketown: The Untold Story*, 336, quoted from Bonnie Lyons, "An Interview with August Wilson," in Jackson R. Bryer and Mary C. Hartig, eds., *Conversations with August Wilson* (Jackson, Miss.: University Press of Mississippi, 2006), 206.

3. "Crisis Worsens as 'White Backlash' Gains Support," *New Pittsburgh Courier*, November 5, 1966.

4. "Crisis Worsens as 'White Backlash' Gains Support."

5. "Order Will Return When Poverty Goes," *New Pittsburgh Courier*, November 19, 1966.

6. "Order Will Return When Poverty Goes."

7. Tom Williams, "Letters to the Editor," *New Pittsburgh Courier*, August 19, 1967.

8. Alfred Duckett, "Big Mouth," *New Pittsburgh Courier*, July 29, 1967.

9. Ralph E. Koger, "250 Militants Storm City Hall," *New Pittsburgh Courier*, September 2, 1967.

10. Koger, "250 Militants Storm City Hall."

11. "Informer Tells Cops of Plan," *New Pittsburgh Courier*, August 12, 1967.

12. "Informer Tells Cops of Plan."

13. "Mayor Barr Hit by Protests and Militants," *New Pittsburgh Courier*, August 19, 1967.

14. Ralph Proctor Jr., *Voices from the Firing Line: A Personal Account of the Pittsburgh Civil Rights Movement* (Pittsburgh, Pa.: Introspec Press, 2014), 303.

15. Proctor, *Voices from the Firing Line*, 301–2.

16. "CAIR Holds D.C. 'Senate' Meet on North Side," *New Pittsburgh Courier*, October 14, 1967.

17. "CAIR Holds D.C. 'Senate' Meet on North Side."

18. "CAIR Holds D.C. 'Senate' Meet on North Side."

19. "CAIR Holds D.C. 'Senate' Meet on North Side." Poverty provisions often focused on mothers, illegitimacy, and the ideal of a male breadwinner. Birth control,

the threat of state mandated foster care, and the "pushing out of fathers" were all common requirements to receive state aid.

20. Ralph E. Koger, "Civil Rights Leaders Jolt NAACP Confab," *New Pittsburgh Courier*, November 4, 1967.

21. Koger, "Civil Rights Leaders Jolt NAACP Confab."

22. Koger, "Civil Rights Leaders Jolt NAACP Confab."

23. "Peace Units, Black Power May Unite," *New Pittsburgh Courier*, April 6, 1968.

24. Benjamin Mays, "My View," *New Pittsburgh Courier*, December 23, 1967.

25. Sala Udin, oral history interview by Johanna Hernandez and Benjamin Houston, June 7, 2007, Center for Africanamerican Urban Studies and the Economy: Remembering Africanamerican Pittsburgh Oral History Project, Carnegie Mellon University, Pittsburgh, Pa.

26. Udin, oral history interview.

27. Rhonda Y. Williams, *Concrete Demands: The Search for Black Power in the 20th Century* (New York: Routledge, 2014), 5.

28. Udin, oral history interview.

29. The number of stakeholders in street violence complicates definitions of street violence. While many participants describe their actions as retaliatory or as a rebellion, those in the city government often refer to riots, or in the case of Pittsburgh, as disorders or turmoil. These definitions undermine the agency of the participants and limit the appearance that city structures lost control of the street violence. Many historians of the African American urban experience have wrestled with this definitional problem and a variety of conventions exist. While I feel that it is important to use the terms that people at the time used, I also feel it is important to reveal the struggle between stakeholders over the definition of street violence. It appears clear that many of the participants in the eight days of street violence in Pittsburgh did so with knowledge of their actions and an intentionality that disproves the idea of a "mob" mentality and supports the idea of retaliatory working-class street violence. For a detailed description of the Pittsburgh "riots," see also, Alyssa Ribeiro, "'A Period of Turmoil': Pittsburgh's April 1968 Riots and Their Aftermath," *Journal of Urban History* 39, no. 2 (2013).

30. Thomas Picou, "Did Dr. King's Assassination Cause Riots?," *New Pittsburgh Courier*, April 20, 1968.

31. While many reporters, government officials, and other citizens used the term "riot" for the violent street demonstrations following King's assassination on April 4th, 1968, I have focused instead on the rising tide of street violence as a whole, including police-sponsored violence against African Americans and increased perceptions of the street as a field of violence. This violence was not isolated to the incidents from April 5th–9th but instead was a result of increased tensions within African American working classes and their dissatisfaction with the response of the government to those concerns. This was a street protest or rebellion. The methods differed from those of the middle classes, but the intent was to facilitate change. The term "riot" connotes disorderly conduct and a lack of internal organization as well as a derision of the act itself. These assumptions are unclear at best. Those participating in street violence

understood the political connotations of their actions and participated in the rebellion willingly and with stated goals in some cases. The problem with the language occurs because of the differences in how observers and participants described the actions of the agitators. I will attempt to clarify who is speaking in each case but overall, I will focus on the use of street violence as a political tool of the working classes.

32. Alvin Rosensweet, "Six Days Shattered City's Image of Racial Harmony," *Pittsburgh Post-Gazette*, April 13, 1968.

33. Rosensweet, "Six Days Shattered City's Image of Racial Harmony."

34. "Carmichael Calls for 'Retaliation' of Killing," *New Pittsburgh Courier*, April 13, 1968.

35. "Carmichael Calls for 'Retaliation' of Killing."

36. Proctor, *Voices from the Firing Line*, 374.

37. Proctor, *Voices from the Firing Line*, 375–76, quoted from Proctor.

38. Proctor, *Voices from the Firing Line*, 377–78.

39. Proctor, *Voices from the Firing Line*, 378.

40. Proctor, *Voices from the Firing Line*, 378.

41. Rosensweet, "Six Days Shattered City's Image of Racial Harmony."

42. Robert Johnson, "Fires, Looting Most Obvious," *Pittsburgh Press*, April 10, 1968.

43. Proctor, *Voices from the Firing Line*, 377.

44. Proctor, *Voices from the Firing Line*, 377.

45. "Guard, State Troopers Sent in to Quell Hill District Disorder," *Pittsburgh Post-Gazette*, April 8, 1968; Jack Ryan, "Hill Takes on Appearance of Battlefield," *Pittsburgh Post-Gazette*, April 8, 1968.

46. Art Glickman and Edward Blank, "'Longest Day' Staged in City Riots," *Pittsburgh Press*, April 8, 1968.

47. Odessa Wilson, oral history interview by Jessica D. Klanderud, January 11, 2013, Personal Collection, Hill House Senior Services Center, 2038 Bedford Avenue, Pittsburgh, Pa.

48. "Leroy Jones" (alias chosen by interviewee), oral history interview by Jessica D. Klanderud, January 18, 2013, Personal Collection, Hill House Senior Services Center, 2038 Bedford Avenue, Pittsburgh, Pa.

49. Proctor, *Voices from the Firing Line*, 383–84.

50. "Arthur" (name omitted at interviewee's request, alias chosen by interviewee), oral history interview by Jessica D. Klanderud, January 18, 2013, Personal Collection, Hill House Senior Services Center, 2038 Bedford Avenue, Pittsburgh, Pa.

51. Proctor, *Voices from the Firing Line*, 381.

52. Proctor, *Voices from the Firing Line*, 382.

53. Alyssa Ribeiro, "'A Period of Turmoil' - Pittsburgh's April 1968 Riots and Their Aftermath" (master's thesis, University of Pittsburgh, 2005).

54. Proctor, *Voices from the Firing Line*, 382–82.

55. Jay R. Roszman, "The Curious History of Irish 'Outrages': Irish Agrarian Violence and Collective Insecurity, 1761-1852," *Historical Research* 91, no. 253 (2018): 481–504.

"From the state's perspective, outrages were dangerous because Irish peasants used violence to enforce their own notions of law and order that clashed with expanding

British legal institutions and undermined the state's claim to a monopoly on the use of force."

56. "Riots as Social Protest," *New Pittsburgh Courier*, August 17 1968.

57. "Riots as Social Protest."

58. Proctor, *Voices from the Firing Line*, 386.

59. Proctor, *Voices from the Firing Line*, 388–89. Emphasis in the original.

60. Proctor, *Voices from the Firing Line*, 391.

61. Helen Mendoza, oral history interview by Jessica D. Klanderud, January 11, 2013, Personal Collection, Hill House Senior Services Center, 2038 Bedford Avenue, Pittsburgh, Pa.

62. "Arthur," oral history interview.

63. Rosensweet, "Six Days Shattered City's Image of Racial Harmony."

64. Robert M. Vickers, oral history interview by Jessica D. Klanderud, January 11, 2013, Personal Collection, Hill House Senior Services Center, 2038 Bedford Avenue, Pittsburgh, Pa.

65. "Arthur," oral history interview.

66. Marcia Joyce Donnell, oral history interview by Jessica D. Klanderud, December 12, 2012, Personal Collection, Hill House Senior Services Center, 2038 Bedford Avenue, Pittsburgh, Pa.

67. Jack Ryan, "Big Daddies Keep Their Section Quiet," *Pittsburgh Post-Gazette*, April 12, 1968; Jack Ryan, "'Cool It' Brigade Marches," *Pittsburgh Post-Gazette*, April 11, 1968.

68. "Arthur," oral history interview.

69. "LeRoy Jones," oral history interview.

70. "Pittsburgh Hit by Gangs in the Hill District," *Pittsburgh Post-Gazette*, April 6, 1968.

71. Rosensweet, "Six Days Shattered City's Image of Racial Harmony."

72. "Pittsburgh Hit by Gangs in the Hill District," *Pittsburgh Post-Gazette*, April 6, 1968.

73. Roger Stuart and William Mausteller, "Uneasy Calm in Hill after Looting Spree," *Pittsburgh Press*, April 6, 1968.

74. "County Facing Big Payoffs for Disorders," *Pittsburgh Post-Gazette*, April 13, 1968.

75. "Gov. Shafer Calls Hill a Disaster," *Pittsburgh Post-Gazette*, April 13, 1968.

76. "Gov. Shafer Calls Hill a Disaster."

77. "Gov. Shafer Calls Hill a Disaster."

78. Alvin Rosensweet, "Ministers Call for Negro Aid," *Pittsburgh Post-Gazette*, April 9, 1968; Thomas M. Hritz, "'It's Not a Riot,' Slusser Insists," *Pittsburgh Post-Gazette*, April 9, 1968.

79. "'It's Not a Riot,' Slusser Insists."

80. "Gov. Shafer Calls Hill a Disaster."

81. Jack Ryan, "Big Daddies Keep Their Section Quiet," *Pittsburgh Post-Gazette*, April 12, 1968.

82. Thomas Picou, "Did Dr. King's Assassination Cause Riots?," *New Pittsburgh Courier*, April 20, 1968.

83. "County Facing Big Payoffs for Disorders," *Pittsburgh Post-Gazette*, April 13, 1968.

84. Rosensweet, "Six Days Shattered City's Image of Racial Harmony."

85. "Black Power, What Chance?," *New Pittsburgh Courier*, April 6, 1968.

86. "Black Power, What Chance?"

87. Jerry Dorsch, "Letter to the Editor," *New Pittsburgh Courier*, April 6, 1968.

88. Alfred Duckett, "Big Mouth," *New Pittsburgh Courier*, April 13, 1968.

89. "To Be Equal a Matter of Priorities," *New Pittsburgh Courier*, April 13, 1968.

90. "Haden's Office, Herron Hill Jr. High Hit by Fires," *New Pittsburgh Courier*, March 1, 1969.

91. William Robinson, "Huff Boxes Way to Head Pgh. 'Negro,'" *New Pittsburgh Courier*, March 15, 1969.

Epilogue

1. Barbara Ransby, "The Ferguson Uprising and Its Reverberations," in *Making All Black Lives Matter: Reimagining Freedom in the Twenty-First Century* (Oakland: University of California Press, 2018), 47–80, 49.

2. A. J. Willingham, "How the Iconic 'Whose Streets? Our Streets!' Chant Has Been Co-Opted," CNN, September 19, 2017, https://www.cnn.com/2017/09/19/us/whose-streets-our-streets-chant-trnd/index.html.

3. Barbara Ransby, *Making All Black Lives Matter*, 4.

4. Ransby, *Making All Black Lives Matter*, 3.

5. Ransby, "The Ferguson Uprising and Its Reverberations," 67.

6. Ransby, *Making All Black Lives Matter*, 6.

7. Ransby, "The Ferguson Uprising and Its Reverberations," 70.

8. Kimberly McNair, "Beyond Hashtags: Black Twitter and Building Solidarity across Borders," in *#Identity: Hashtagging Race, Gender, Sexuality, and Nation*, ed. Abigail De Kosnik and Keith P. Feldman (Ann Arbor: University of Michigan Press, 2019), 283–98, 284

9. Jelani Cobb, "Ferguson October: A Movement Goes on Offense," *New Yorker*, October 15, 2014, http://www.newyorker.com/news/news-desk/ferguson-october.

10. "Pittsburgh Man Wins $119K in Civil Rights Suit against Police," CBS News, March 31, 2014, https://www.cbsnews.com/news/pittsburgh-man-wins-119-thousand-in-civil-rights-suit-against-police/.

11. Alex Zimmerman, "99 Problems: Run-in with Jordan Miles Wasn't First Controversial Incident for Three 99-Car Cops," *Pittsburgh City Paper*, December 17, 2014, https://www.pghcitypaper.com/pittsburgh/99-problems-run-in-with-jordan-miles-wasnt-first-controversial-incident-for-three-99-car-cops/Content?oid=1797137.

12. Rebecca Nuttall, "Neighborhood Watched: Residents Say Negative Picture of Homewood Painted at Miles' Trial Is a 'Shame,'" *Pittsburgh City Paper*, accessed June 15, 2022, https://www.pghcitypaper.com/pittsburgh/neighborhood-watched-residents-say-negative-picture-of-homewood-painted-at-miles-trial-is-a-shame/Content?oid=1742870.

13. John Bowden, "Pittsburgh-Area Cops Called Black Lives Matter Protesters 'Thugs,' 'Terrorists' in Facebook Group: Report," Text, *The Hill* (blog), March 22, 2021, https://thehill.com/homenews/state-watch/544394-pittsburgh-area-cops-called -black-lives-matter-protesters-thugs/.

14. "'A City Divided'—an Examination of the Jordan Miles Case—Should Be Required Reading for Police, Public Officials," *Pittsburgh Post-Gazette*, March 4, 2020, https://www.post-gazette.com/ae/books/2020/03/03/A-City-Divided-David-Harris -Jordan-Miles-Race-Fear-Law-Police-Confrontations/stories/202003080008; David A. Harris, *A City Divided: Race, Fear and the Law in Police Confrontations* (New York: Anthem Press, 2020).

15. "Antwon Rose II Murder," *Clio*, December 12, 2019, https://theclio.com/entry /90070; "What We Know about the Police Shooting Death of Antwon Rose Jr.," PBS NewsHour, June 22, 2018, https://www.pbs.org/newshour/nation/what-we-know -about-the-police-shooting-death-of-antwon-rose-jr.

16. Sabaah Folayan and Damon Davis, *Whose Streets?*, documentary (Magnolia Pictures, 2017).

17. Reid J. Epstein and Patricia Mazzei, "G.O.P. Bills Target Protesters (and Absolve Motorists Who Hit Them)," *New York Times*, April 21, 2021, https://www .nytimes.com/2021/04/21/us/politics/republican-anti-protest-laws.html.

18. "Transphobia, Hostility about Protesters in Private Cop Group," AP News, March 22, 2021, https://apnews.com/article/police-private-facebook-groups-hate-22 355db9b0b7561ce91fa2ddfbcd2fc1.

19. Folayan and Davis, *Whose Streets?*.

Index

Page numbers in italics refer to illustrations.

A&P, 138

African American, women: beauty contests and, 28–29; as civil rights activists, 128–29, *130*, *137*; domestic service and, 21; motherhood and, 17, 32–33, 38–39, 42–43, 49–51, 55–56; as police officers, 113, 115; respectability politics and, 36, 49–51, 68, 70–71; as sex workers, 59–60, 64, 68–71, 73, 108, 119–23, 125, 141; social networks and, 17, 25–26, 28–30, 36–38, 49–50; as social workers, 49, 74; as waitresses, 69–70

African American, youth; education and 21, 34, 46, 50–54, 63, 74, 194n18; gangs and, 53–54, 119, 156, 166–67; gender and, 45; juvenile delinquency and, 39, 42–55 passim, 65–66, 85, 99, 113; play and 17, 37–38, 42–49, 52, 54–55, 193–94n15; respectability politics and, 57, 75, 106–7

African Americans: car ownership and, 110, 112; education and, 9–10, 23, 74, 139, 194n18; family life and, 27, 36–38, 42, 45–46, 52, 55, 175; fashion and, 27, 29, 36, 64; industrial labor and, 3–4, 8–10, 12, 21, 40, 84; as migrants from the South, 3–4, 7–16, 20–23, 40–41, 45, 59, 66, 77, 79; racial discrimination and, 10–12, 16, 34, 37, 40, 43, 67, 77–78, 83, 88, 91, 94–95, 103, 114, 116, 130–31, 133–34, 136, 138–40, 192n51; racial pride and, 22, 57–58, 80–82, 104; racial uplift and, 11, 15–16, 22, 32–34, 42, 44–45, 55–57, 74, 95, 106; respectability and, 6–8, 15, 17, 32, 36, 39, 43, 49, 51, 57–58, 70–71, 73–75, 91, 106, 109, 115, 125–26, 168, 177, 179; unions and 3, 30–31, 84, 111, 138–40, 170–71, 206n36; veterans, 75, 79–80, 83

Allegheny Conference on Community Development, 85

Allegheny County Committee on Community Development, 90

Allen, Alexander J., 90

American Services Institute, 95

Association for the Study of Negro Life and History, 66

Baltimore, Md., 5, 26

barbershops, 25, 57, 61, 76

Barbour, George, 96, 100

Barr, Joseph, 152, 167, 169

bars and night clubs, 34–35, 70, 131–32, 37, 61, 23, 51. *See also* Crawford Grille

Bates, John "Kid," 53

beauty contests, 28–29, 81

Bedford Avenue, 47, 92, 94, 142

Beechview, Pa., 92

Bell, Lloyd, 164

Beltzhoover, Pa., 92, 104–5, 169–70

Bidwell Presbyterian Church, 52, 152

Bigelow Boulevard, 90

Black Freedom Movement, 12, 58, 86, 104, 147, 149–50, 154, 178. *See also* Carmichael, Stokley; Congress of Racial Equality (CORE); Fox, Alma; National Association of Colored People (NAACP); United Movement for Progress (UMP); United Negro Protest Committee (UNPC); Young Progressives

Black Lives Matter Movement, 176–84
Black militancy, 13–14, 145–46, 149, 151–55, 157, 167, 170–75
Black Power, 86, 150–52, 155, 171–72
Black resistance, 6, 85, 88, 178
Black Twitter, 180
Bloomfield, Pa., 3
Bolden, Frank E., 115–16, 118–19
Boxley, Charlotte, 50–51
Braddock, Pa., 151
Brown, Byrd, 128, 158, 171
Brown, Michael, 176–78
Business and Professional Association (BPA), 80, 96, 139, 142–43

cab companies, 102, 109–12. See also jitneys
Carmichael, Stokley, 157
Centre Avenue, 24, 63, 73, 128, 136, 137, 162, 165–67. See also Freedom Corner
Chicago Defender, 5, 9, 20
Chicago, Ill., 13–15, 26, 180
churches. See houses of worship
Citizens Committee for Hill District Renewal (CCHDR), 140–41
city government: City Planning Commission, 86; Department of Lands and Buildings, 96; Port Authority Transit (PAT), 139, 142–45; Urban Redevelopment Authority (URA), 76, 85, 88–89, 92, 95–97, 101–4, 121
city government. See also Barr, Joseph; Lawrence David L.
Civic Arena, 76, 86–87, 93–99, 126, 136–37
Civic Unity Council, 133
Clark, John L. 20, 23; on class conflict, 59–60, 65, 68–70, 74; on crime and the police, 113–15, 117; on the Depression's effects, 67; on female gamblers, 71–72; on juvenile delinquency, 51, 111–12; on prostitution, 121, 123, 125; on public transportation, 109–12; on redevelopment, 94, 96–97, 103–4. See also Pittsburgh Courier

Clark, Leon "Pigmeat," 106–7, 121
class: alliances and cross-class interaction, 1, 12, 18, 37, 57–58, 75, 81–82, 129–31, 135–40; conflicts and divisions, 7–10, 13–19, 21–23, 27–30, 35–36, 41–43, 49–52, 55–56, 59, 63–66, 68–69, 77–78, 85–86, 105–8, 112–13, 117, 120, 126–27, 141–42, 146–54, 168, 172–73; elites, 4–5, 9–10, 15–19, 26–31, 35–37, 60, 63–66, 77, 91–92, 95–97, 103, 108–9, 112, 116, 126, 135, 141–42, 145, 148–49, 163, 169–71, 173–75; middle, 6, 9–12, 16–19, 26, 29–37, 39–56 passim, 59–60, 63–66, 71–72, 74, 76–78, 86–87, 91, 94–100, 102–8, 111–20, 125–27, 129–30, 136, 139–42, 145–47, 149–54, 156–58, 160–61, 163, 165, 167–68, 170–71, 173–75, 194n18; street capitalists and, 57–63, 106–8, 110; working, 6–9, 27, 31, 33–34, 38–39, 44–46, 49–50, 52–53, 59, 67, 72, 88–89, 94, 96, 103–4, 125, 145–46, 166, 177; working poor, 7, 33, 39, 67, 96, 103–4, 125, 177
Clemente, Roberto, 5
Cleveland, OH, 13, 26, 180
Colwell Street, 121–23
Committee Against Inadequate Relief (CAIR), 152
Committee of Racial Equality (CORE), 137, 139–40
communism, 66, 80, 134–35, 172
Craig, David, 168
Crawford Grille, 23, 34, 76, 106, 109, 121
Crawford Street, 73, 87, 148. See also Freedom Corner
Crosstown Boulevard, 86, 92
Crystal Palace Barbershop, 57, 76

Dameron, John W., 144–45
"Deep Wylie." See Washington, Chester L.
deindustrialization, 8, 177–78
Devilliers Street, 101

Dinwiddie Street, 118, 124, *124*
domestic employment, 9, 21, 34, 38, 195n42
Donnell, Marcia, 34, 36, 42, 52, 54, 61, 80, 92, 110–12, 120, 136
Dorsch, Jerry, 172
"Double V" campaign, 76–78, 83
downtown Pittsburgh, 79; protests and, 128–30, *130*, 137, 151, 156, 158–60, 164, 166–68; public transportation and, 139
drugs, 68, 113, 115, 117–19, 123, 141, 181
Duckett, Alfred, 151, 173

East Liberty, Pa., 76, 88, 101–2, 105, 127, 131–35, 140, 164
East Pittsburgh Police Department, 182–83
Eldridge, Roy, 5
entertainment and leisure, 5, 16, 23, 30–37, 42–47, 121, 109. *See also* Friendly Rivalry Often Generates Success (FROGS); fraternal organizations; gambling; parades; sex work; social clubs
Epiphany Street, 72, 73, 87, 121, 123, *137*
Evers, Charles, 153–54

Fair Employment Practices Commission (FEPC), 12, 83
Ferguson, MO, 176–80, 183–84
Fifth Avenue, 24, 73, 79–80, *79*, 90, 165
Fifth Avenue High School, 124, *124*
Fischer, Jeff, 68
Forbes Avenue, *87*
Forbes, James, 72
Fox, Alma, 128–29, 158–59
Frank, King Count, 118–20
Frank, Lee K., 35–36
Frankstown Avenue, 63, 98–100
fraternal organizations, 22, 27, 30–31, 34–35, 64, 80. *See also* social clubs
Freedom Corner, 128, 136, 151, 158, 168
Friendly Rivalry Often Generates Success (FROGS), 25–31, *28*, 64

Fullerton Avenue, 22, 24, 34, 67, 72, 73, 76, *87*, 112, 123, 190n13
Fullerton Street Gang, 119

gambling, 57, 71–72, 107, 110–11, 113, 117, 123, 125, 141. *See also* numbers business
gangs: African American, 53–54, 119, 156, 165–67, 169; white, 53–54, 132–35
Garland, Hazel, 102–3
Gaston, Barbara, 25, 45–46, 50, 81
gender, 27, 30, 39, 45, 64, 70–71, 118–19, 128
ghettoization, 1, 6, 13, 22, 25, 95–100, 141, 154, 163, 170. *See also* housing
Goode, James T., 92
Great Depression, 52, 63–68, 74
Great Migration, 3–4, 8, 10, 13, 20, 41, 66, 79. *See also* African Americans
Greater Pittsburgh Citizens' Coordinating Committee (GPCCC), 83–84
Green, Homer, 96
Greenlee, Gus, 57, 61, 63, 106, 109, 121. *See also* Crawford Grille
Grey, Elbert R. Sr., 52–54
Griffin, Eleanor Hughes, 62

Harris, Charles Jr., 60–61
Harris, Charles "Teenie," 5, 27, 60–61, 72, 79–80, 106, 129, 137–38, 143, 158
Harris, George, 60–61, 63, 76, 82, 109
Harris, William A. "Woogie," 57–58, 61, 63, 106
Harris's Confectionary, 60–61, 62, 76, 82, 109. *See also* Harris, George
Hartman, Stella E., 51
Hayden, Charles "Bouie," 151, 174
Hazel Street, 73, *87*
Hazlett, Theodore L. Jr., 154
Highland Park, 64, 131–35
Hill District: formation of, 1–3, 2; as separate city within a city, 1, 4, 6, 12, 18–19, 22, 24, 37. *See also* Lower Hill District; Middle Hill District; Upper Hill District

Hill District Board of Trade, 139
Hill District Community Council, 90,
    96–97, 132
Hill House Association, 145
Homewood Avenue, 100
Homewood Community Improvement
    Association (HCIA), 98
Homewood, Pa., as emerging African
    American neighborhood, 63, 76, 82,
    88, 89, 92, 97–102, 105, 131; police
    brutality and, 166, 170, 181; public
    transportation and, 142; social protest
    and, 140; street violence and, 151–52,
    159–61, 173–75
Homewood-Brushton, Pa., 104, 156,
    169–70, 174–75
Horne, Lena, 5, 22
houses of worship, 11, 23; Bidwell
    Presbyeterian Church, 152; Ebenezer
    Baptist Church, 157–58; Epiphany
    Church, 137. See also religion
housing: displacement and, 76–77, 79,
    88–89, 91–92, 97–104; migrants and,
    2, 10–11, 22; poor conditions of, 16,
    37–38, 49, 77, 85–87, 153, 163, 173
Howell, William S., 98
Huff, Larry, 174
Hughes, Langston, 146

immigrants, European, 2–5, 40–41,
    86, 91
infant mortality, 32, 42, 44
Irene Kauffman Settlement House
    (IKS), 46, 48–49, 92, 118, 139
Irvis, K. Leroy, 138, 157–58, 162
Italians, 40, 72, 90, 115

Jackson, Algernon B., 67
jazz, 5, 121
Jews, 40, 90, 195n42
jitneys, 59–60, 64, 73, 108–12, 139,
    141–42, 148, 202n2
Jones, Julia Bumry, 25
"Jones, Leroy," 63
Jones, Paul F., 86, 96, 111

Jones, Paul L., 97
Jones, Richard L., 88, 132
Jordan, Marion, 98

Kaufmann's Department Store, 128, 139
Kay Boys' Club, 46–47
Kelly, John, 141
Kerner Commission, 163
Ketchum, Dewayne, 59, 82
Ketchum, Theodore, 59, 76
Ketchum's Tailor Shop, 59, 76
kin networks, 25, 59, 108
King, Martin Luther, Jr.: antipoverty
    movement and, 154; responses to
    assassination of, 19, 149–50, 155–79
    passim; SCLC and, 147
Kittel, Frederick August Jr. See Wilson,
    August
Knoxville, Pa., 170
Koger, Ralph E., 116, 141, 153
Kreisberg, Olga Verin, 41

labor, illegal, 7, 57–61, 63, 66–69, 71–75,
    106–10, 117, 121, 125, 141, 175.
    See also drugs; jitneys; numbers
    businesses; sex work
labor, legal, 7, 17, 59–60, 108, 110, 175
Lawrence, David L., 101, 104, 133, 140
Lawrenceville, Pa., 3, 131–33, 167
Lewis, Carrie, 181
Loendi Club, 26–27, 30, 64, 92, 96
Logan, B. H., 20
Logan, Rayford W., 66
Logan Street, 67, 93–94, 120
Lovuola's Farm, 27, 28
Lower Hill District: businesses and, 59;
    housing and, 138; location of, 24, 87,
    93; policing and, 113, 164; sex work
    and, 72, 73, 120–25, 122; social
    networks and, 60, 108, 117; social
    protest and, 140, 168; street violence
    and, 165–68; systems of reciprocity
    and, 57, 73; as target for reform, 33;
    urban redevelopment and, 77, 88–105
    passim, 126–27; urban renewal and,

76, 85–87, 95–96. *See also* Epiphany Street; Fullerton Avenue; Wylie Avenue

McCoy, James Jr., 142, 144–45
McKeesport, Pa., 151
Madden, J. Warren, 51
Manchester, PA, 102, 145, 147
Mays, Benjamin, 154
Mellon Bank, 85, 90
Mendoza, Helen, 36–37, 54–55, 161, 164
Middle Hill District, 76. *See also* Centre Avenue; Crawford Avenue; Freedom Corner
Miles, Jordan, 180–82
Morris, Carl, 145–46, 174
Moss, R. Maurice, 90–91, 138

National Advisory Commission on Civil Disorder. *See* Kerner Commission
National Association for the Advancement of Colored People (NAACP): integration of Highland Park Pool and, 132–33, 135; outreach and, 10, 12, 35–36, 44, 51, 91, 94–95, 192n51; Owl Taxi Cab Company and, 111; police brutality and, 114; protests and, 128–29, 137, 140, 147, 158, 168; redevelopment and, 98–100, 104; strategies and, 22, 40–41, 66, 137–38, 174
National Guard, 156, 160, 162, 164, 167–68
"New Negro," 14–15, 22, 146
New Pittsburgh Courier, 150–51, 156. See also *Pittsburgh Courier*
New York City, 14, 26, 57, 63, 148, 180
Nixon, Alice, 152
Northside, 53–54, 102–5, 112, 127, 145, 151–52, 156, 160, 169
numbers business: organized crime and, 113–15; origins of, 57; police complicity and, 117; social networks and, 61, 63–64, 72–73, 110–11, 125, 141; as vice, 11, 51, 141; Wylie Avenue and, 59.

See also Clark, Leon "Pigmeat"; Crawford Grille; Greenlee, Gus; Harris, William "Woogie"

Oakland, PA, 2, 85, 92, 160, 166–67
old Pittsburghers (OPs), 8–12, 20, 23, 41
Oliver High School, 145–46
Owl Taxi Cab Company, 111

parades: formal, 79–82, 79; informal, 82; public health and, 33–34; social networks and, 32, 37, 75, 77; social protest and, 76–77, 83, 104, 136–37, 137
Pennsylvania Drilling Company, 93
Perry High School, 159
Philadelphia, PA, 13, 26, 145
Pittsburgh City Paper, 181
Pittsburgh Courier: civil rights and, 78, 141–42, 156–57, 170; on drugs and vice, 117, 125; FROG Week and, 25–31, 64; migrants and, 9, 20–21; redevelopment and, 126; significance of, 5; society page and, 35; street fairs and, 32, 36; youth and, 43–45, 47–48, 52–54. *See also* Bolden, Frank E.; Clark, John L.; Jones, Julia Bumry; Washington, Chester L.
Pittsburgh Housing Authority, 88, 90
Pittsburgh Newsboys' Home, 47
Pittsburgh Post, 70, 91
Pittsburgh Post-Gazette, 132, 134, 156, 167–68, 182
Pittsburgh Press, 145, 160
Pittsburgh Railways Company, 83–84, 110
Pittsburgh Redevelopment Authority, 92
Point State Park, 168
police: Black officers and, 18, 107, 113–16, 158; brutality and, 18, 57–58, 60, 107–8, 113–14, 119–20, 135, 149–50, 154–55, 163, 166, 170, 176–84; Center Avenue Police Station, 119–20, 158; ineffectiveness and corruption of, 113, 115–17, 125, 133–34;

police (cont.)
  surveillance and state suppression,
    18–19, 57, 80–82, 106, 108–9, 111,
    118, 121, 150, 156–70 passim, 159.
    See also drugs; gambling; gangs;
    National Guard; numbers business;
    sex work
Posey, Cum, 53
Posvar, Wesley, 164
Proctor, Ralph, 152, 157, 160–62, 164
prostitution. See sex work
public transportation, 4, 83–85, 105,
    110, 112, 139, 142–45, 144

racial discrimination: employment and,
    83–84, 116, 138–40; Great Depression
    and, 66–67; housing and, 11, 88, 91,
    94–95, 103; police and, 114; preva-
    lence of, 37, 40, 78; public accommo-
    dations and, 34, 77–78, 132, 192n51,
    103, 131, 133–35
Reed, Kayla, 184
reform: children and, 42–52 passim;
    class tensions and, 12, 41, 43, 105; fair
    employment, 10, 12, 83–85, 129–31,
    138, 140, 142; fair housing, 12, 18,
    75–77, 79, 91–92, 94–95, 129, 145;
    integration of public accommoda-
    tions and, 131; migrants and, 11–12,
    41; public health campaigns, 32–34,
    36, 39, 42–44, 51, 87, 141. See also
    Black Freedom Movement; National
    Association for the Advancement of
    Colored People (NAACP); United
    Negro Protest Committee (UNPC);
    Urban League of Pittsburgh (ULP);
    United Negro Protest Committee
    (UNPC)
Reid, Ira De A., 39–41, 47, 49, 54,
    71–72, 86
religion: class and, 6, 10–11, 35–36, 52,
    70–71; social networks and, 7, 9–10,
    52, 82; social protest and, 140,
    152–53, 157–58; toleration of vice
    and, 70, 72. See also houses of worship

Renaissance I, 85–86
respectability politics: as challenge to
    housing discrimination, 91; children
    and, 32, 43, 51; critique of, 177, 179;
    disavowal of street violence and, 168;
    jitneys and, 108–9; performance of,
    6–8, 15; street capitalists and, 57, 75,
    106–7; systems of reciprocity vs., 17,
    38–39, 58, 63–64, 68–69, 73–74, 77,
    125–26; women and, 36, 49–51, 68,
    70–71
restaurants, 61, 67, 69–70, 96
Rice, Tamir, 180
riots. See street violence
Robin, Jack P., 86, 92, 96
Robinson, William, 174
Robinson, Jackie, 5, 146
Roosevelt, Franklin D., 66
Rose II, Antwon, 182–83
Rose Street School, 38
Rosenberg, Louis, 116
Rosensweet, Alvin, 160
Rosfeld, Michael, 182–83
Ryan, Jack, 166, 170

Seabrook, Alex, 153
Second Great Migration, 85
sex work: conditions of, 59–60, 68, 108;
    informal economy and, 64, 69–71, 73,
    121, 125, 141; pimps and, 119, 124;
    sites of, 71–72, 73, 120–21, 124,
    197n33; urban renewal and, 121–23,
    122
Shafer, Raymond, 164, 166, 168
Sixth Avenue, 90, 130
Slusser, James W., 168–69
social clubs: Black-controlled spaces
    and, 26–27; girls and, 11; social
    networks and, 30, 35–36; The Ducks,
    64. See also Friendly Rivalry Often
    Generates Success (FROGS)
social networks: across class lines, 12,
    18, 31–32, 37, 63, 74–75, 81; Black
    Lives Matter and, 176–80, 184;
    Black-controlled public spaces and,

20, 22–23; children and, 44, 46, 53–55; civil rights and, 83, 128–47 passim, 149, 155; development of, 3–4; elites and, 36–37; employment and, 83–85; entertainment and, 34–35; jitneys and, 110; medical services and, 33–34; middle class and, 12–13, 36–37, 60, 63–64, 85–86, 142, 147; migrants and, 8–9, 11–12, 21–23; numbers business and, 61, 63–64, 72–73, 110–11, 125, 141; Old Pittsburghers and, 8, 12, 23; parades and, 32, 37, 75, 77, 80–81; religion and, 7, 9–10, 52, 82; rioting and, 162–63, 170; significance of Wylie Avenue and, 20–25; social clubs and, 27, 30, 35–36; street capitalists and, 60–63, 74–75, 106–7; strikes and, 112; as survival tool, 7; systems of reciprocity and, 38–39, 55–57; urban renewal and, 76–77, 85–88, 94, 97, 105, 126, 131; women and, 25–26, 28–30, 36–38, 49–50; working class and, 37, 53, 60–61, 108, 117, 141, 148–49, 152

social workers, 9, 16, 38–39, 41–56 passim, 74, 97, 194n18

sociologists, 13, 39–40, 42, 44–45, 52, 194n18

Southern Christian Leadership Conference (SCLC), 147

Southside, 2, 92, 104

Spivey, Charles S., 104

Stanton, Dolores, 62

steel industry, 3–4, 8–10, 20–21, 34, 46, 77

street capitalists: class and, 57–63; policing and, 18, 106, 108–9, 113, 125; respectability politics and, 57, 75, 106–7; shift away from, 110, 118, 126–27; systems of reciprocity and, 17, 57–60, 63, 74, 106–8

street democracy, 18, 149, 175

street violence: definitions of, 209n29; depictions of African American men and, 169–70; desegregation of

Highland Park Pool and, 131–35; as disorders, 132, 134–35, 155–56, 166–71, 209n29; gangs and, 53–54, 119, 132–35, 156, 165–67, 169; Homewood and, 151–52, 159–61, 173–75; Lower Hill and, 165–68; as outrages, 163–64, 176, 179, 210–11n55; police brutality and, 18, 57–58, 60, 107–8, 113–14, 119–20, 135, 149–50, 154–55, 163, 166, 170, 176–84; policing and, 158–60, 159, 163–64, 166–67; reactions to, 156–57, 160, 165–70; as response to Martin Luther King Jr.'s assassination, 149–75 passim; as riots, 132, 134–35, 146, 150–53, 155–56, 158, 160–68, 179, 209n31; systems of reciprocity and, 161–63; unlikelihood of Pittsburgh and, 154–57; women and, 169; Wylie Avenue and, 160, 164–65

streetcars, 82–85, 94, 110, 112, 142–43, 144. See also public transportation

Student Nonviolent Coordinating Committee (SNCC), 155

Suber, Mary Lee, 118–19

systems of reciprocity: development of, 25; Lower Hill and, 57, 73; redevelopment and, 103, 105, 149; respectability politics vs., 17, 38–39, 58, 63–64, 68–69, 73–74, 77, 125–26; rioting and, 161–63, 178–79; social networks and, 38–39, 55–57; street capitalists and, 17, 57–60, 63, 74, 106–8

theater of the street, 4, 19, 58, 129, 157, 174–75

372nd Infantry, 79

Tomlin, Sarah, 34–35, 111

Townsend Street, 67, 121

Triangle Theater, 31

trolleys. See streetcars

Udin, Sala, 27, 136, 154–55

unions, 3, 30, 84, 138–40, 171–72, 206n36

United Movement for Progress (UMP), 152

United Negro Protest Committee (UNPC), 135, 138–45

University of Pittsburgh, 9, 23, 44, 74, 85, 128, 164, 182

Upper Hill district: location of, 2, 24; middle class and elites, 86, 97; redevelopment and, 99, 101–3, 136; sex work and, 122–23. *See also* Bedford Avenue; Bigelow Boulevard

urban: blight, 17–18, 38, 55, 57, 76–77, 85–86, 95–96, 98, 101–4, 112, 117, 120–21, 123, 141; redevelopment, 76–77, 88–105 passim, 126–27, 136, 145, 149; renewal, 76–77, 85–88, 94–97, 105, 121–23, 122, 126, 131

Urban League of Pittsburgh (ULP), 9–12, 15–16, 32–33, 35–36, 40–45, 47, 88, 152, 158. *See also* Moss, R. Maurice

U.S. Commission on Human Relations, 94–95, 98–99

U.S. Senate Subcommittee on Housing, 94, 101

Vann, Robert L., 5, 20. See also *Pittsburgh Courier*

Vickers, Robert, 34, 36, 46, 165

Vietnam War, 146–47, 151, 154, 172–73

Waring, J. H. N. Jr., 65

Washington, Chester L., 31, 71

Webster Avenue, 92, *107*, 139, 143

Welch, John, 82, 161

Weldon, Sally, 68

Whitcomb Street, 121, 123

whiteness, 2–5, 41

whites: gangs and, 53–54, 132–35; reactions to street violence, 156–57, 160, 165–70; redevelopment and, 99–100, 145; as residents of the Hill District, 22, 87, 91, 94; resistance to civil rights activism, 78, 131–35, 138, 150

Wilkinsburg, Pa., 92

Williams, Tom, 150–51

Wilson, August, 1, 5, 148–49

Wilson, Darren, 176

Wilson, Odessa, 36, 38, 50, 54, 81, 161

Woods, Ruby Wheeler, *107*

Woolworth's, 129, *130*

World War I, 3, 16, 22, 24, 37, 40, 79

World War II, 12, 14, 54, 75, 77, 79–80, 104, 129

"Wylie Ave." *See* Clark, John L.

Wylie Avenue: August Wilson and, 148; business district, 31, 58–60; children and, 53–54; as "Crossroads of the World," 20, 23, 190n13; Ebenezer Baptist Church and, 157–58; parades and, 79, 80–82; policing and, 114, 116–17; redevelopment and, 76, 92–94, 100, 126–27; regulars and, 17, 57, 59, 74, 126; renewal and, 77, 85; sex work and, 72, 120–21; significance of, 16, 20, 22–25; street violence and, 160, 164–65. *See also* Clark, John L.; Harris, George; Harris, William A. "Woogie"; Washington, Chester L.

Yellow Cab Company, 110–11

Young Men's Christian Association (YMCA), 40–41, 46–49, 54

Young Progressives, 133–35

Young Women's Christian Association (YWCA), 40–41, 47–49, 80

9 781469 673721